gandhi

Arvind Sharma

gandhi

A Spiritual Biography

Yale UNIVERSITY PRESS

New Haven & London

Published with assistance from the foundation established
in memory of James Wesley Cooper of the Class of 1865,
Yale College.

Portions of *I Found No Peace* by Webb Miller are reproduced
by permission of the family of Webb Miller.

Yale University Press books may be purchased in quantity for
educational, business, or promotional use. For information, please
e-mail sales.press@yale.edu (U.S. office) or sales@yaleup.co.uk
(U.K. office).

Designed by Lindsey Voskowsky.
Set in Sabon, Century Gothic, and Bondoluo Peek types
by Integrated Publishing Solutions.
Printed in the United States of America.

ISBN 978-0-300-18596-6

A catalogue record for this book is available from the Library of
Congress and the British Library.

Library of Congress Control Number 2013933796.

This paper meets the requirements of ANSI/NISO Z39.48–1992
(Permanence of Paper).

10 9 8 7 6 5 4 3 2 1

contents

Introduction

1

part one

1. Birth and Adolescence

9

2. Child Marriage

16

3. God Enters Gandhi's Life

22

4. Gandhi in London

29

5. Gandhi and Raychand

42

6. Gandhi's Conversion Experience

54

7. Out of Africa

60

8. Spiritual Warfare

72

9. Touching the Untouchable

84

10. Fighting Fire with Light

92

••••
part two
▲▲▲▲

11. Mahatma Gandhi and Ramana Maharshi

101

12. Spiritual Temptations

112

13. Spiritual Serendipity

119

Contents

14. Beefing Up Vegetarianism
125

15. The Sex Life of a Celibate
133

16. The Bhagavad Gita, Gandhi's Other Mother
145

17. Gandhi, God, and Goodness
155

18. Demythologizing and Analyzing Gandhi
171

19. Gandhi's Spiritual Biography and Contemporary History
189

Notes
207

Index
241

Contents   vii

gandhi

introduction

I

History is more than the biography of those who make it. Nevertheless, some people leave their mark on history in such an elusive way that historiography perpetually fails to capture it. Gandhi is surely one such figure. His life possesses a quality that exceeds all accounts of it, although more than four hundred published biographies exist. Hence one more book on Gandhi; and there is room for many more, without superfluity.

To be specific, this book is a spiritual biography of Gandhi (1869–1948), known as Mahatma Gandhi. The first part of the name Mahatma Gandhi, that is to say, the term Mahatma, is not a name but a title. Gandhi's proper name was

Mohandas Karamchand and not Mahatma. Although biographies and histories use the term Mahatma, most are really accounts of Mohandas Karamchand Gandhi, not Mahatma Gandhi, because most of them focus on the familial, religious, social, and political dimensions of his life. They do not overlook the spiritual dimension of his life, to be sure, but rather take account of it as impinging on these other dimensions; they do not focus on the spiritual dimension as such. Gandhi himself, however, considered this dimension primary and the other dimensions secondary. He wrote: "What I want to achieve,—what I have been striving and pining to achieve these thirty years—is self-realization, to see God face to face, to attain *Moksha*. I live and move and have my being in the pursuit of this goal. All that I do by way of speaking and writing, and all my ventures in the political field, are directed to this same end."[1]

Gandhi uses an evocative Sanskrit word in this passage, *moksha,* which literally means "freedom." In the Hindu context it possesses a more concrete connotation, that of freedom from being reincarnated repeatedly in the mundane world where one is under the grip of one's passions. Gandhi's biography gradually turns into history as he leads a nation to political freedom, or political moksha, as he marches toward his own spiritual moksha.

That Mahatma Gandhi's name contains a title, namely Mahatma ("great soul," a name given to saints in India), and that it doubles as his name, is not unique to him. The same is the case with two other famous names in history: Jesus Christ and Gautama Buddha. The word Christ means "anointed one" and is a messianic title, while the word Buddha is a title meaning "enlightened one." These nominal facts lead to a substantial point and provide a clue to a very important dimension of the lives of these figures—that they combined in themselves two dimensions: an ordinary one, which they might share with any human being, and an extraordinary one, which set them apart from other human beings. Jesus as Jesus was an ordinary Jew of Palestine, but in his role as Christ he stood apart from others as their redeemer. Gautama as Gautama was an ordinary prince, like many others in North India in the sixth century BCE, but as Buddha, he stood apart as the "man who woke up" while others slept. Similarly, Gandhi as Gandhi was a lawyer like so many others, but as Mahatma, his person became a vehicle through which he established new norms of human conduct.

This book addresses the Mahatma side of Gandhi's personality. As we begin to do so, two points immediately catch our attention. The first is that although Jesus Christ and Gautama Buddha also emphasized morality, there was also a further claim of being the Messiah and the Son of God in the case of Jesus and of being an Enlightened person in the case of the Buddha. For Gandhi, however, morality and religion were synonymous, so a spiritual biography of Gandhi contains a remarkably strong moral component, strongly colored by theism, but still moral. The fact that his experiments with truth were carried out in public did not, for Gandhi, detract from their spiritual value. He wrote: "There are some things which are known only to oneself and one's Maker. These are clearly incommunicable. The experiments I am about to relate are not such. But they are spiritual, or rather moral; for the essence of religion is morality."[2] The second point is that Gandhi, as a Hindu, believed in rebirth. If we lead a religious or spiritual life and we regard our existence as commencing at our birth and ending at our death, then we will look upon ourselves as *human beings having a spiritual experience*. If, however, we believe in reincarnation, then we admit to being spiritual beings right away and may then look upon ourselves as *spiritual beings having a human experience*. Some aspects of Gandhi's life may appear less puzzling when viewed in this light.

II

Anyone familiar with the life and work of Gandhi feels compelled to ask the following question at some point: What was the source of his strength, even power? In a way, this book is another attempt to answer this question. How is it that he could ask people to face blows from the police without retaliating, and they would be ready to do so? That he would ask women to court arrest—and face the vicious uncertainty of finding themselves in the hands of an imperial police notorious for kicking people in the crotch—and they would do so? That he would hint to Muslim women that they need not observe purdah in his presence, because he was like their father or brother, and they would comply? It is not that everyone acted as he asked, or as he wanted them to. Even his trusted colleagues let him down at critical times. To that extent, he was fallible and like the rest of us. What calls for an explanation is not that he failed at times; what requires an explanation is how he could succeed to the extent that he did. What was the source of his "power of making heroes out of clay," as his political mentor, G. K. Gokhale, put it?[3]

Some have traced the source of this power to *personal* attributes, to the fact that he practiced what he preached. This may be why some claim that what Alcibiades said of Socrates can be said of Gandhi: "He is the only man who can truly make me feel ashamed."[4]

Others have traced the source of this power to *national* factors and found its roots in his Indian background. One such person is Pandit Jawaharlal Nehru, India's first prime minister, who wrote many years ago: "He seems to be the vehicle and embodiment of some greater force of which even he is perhaps only dimly conscious. Is that the spirit of India, the accumulated spirit of the millennia that lie behind our race, the memory of a thousand tortured lives? . . . Has he drunk somewhere from the sacred spring of life that has given strength to India through the ages?"[5]

There have, however, been many national leaders before and after Gandhi, but there has been only one Gandhi. Most observers therefore have traced the source of his power to his *spiritual* beliefs, to what some consider the power of spirit over the material world. When Louis Fischer spent a week with Gandhi in 1942 and had a journalist's gall to ask Gandhi himself for the secret of his success, Gandhi responded: "I think my influence is due to the fact that I pursue the truth. That is my goal. . . . Truth . . . is not merely a matter of words. It is really a matter of living the truth."[6]

Gandhi believed so fervently in the life of the spirit that he had only a handful of material possessions when he died—a watch, sandals, spectacles, and a few similar items.[7] Not only did he possess few material assets when he died, but while he lived he was not a great politician, a formidable legislator, a smooth diplomat, a profound philosopher, a distinguished author, an illustrious artist, or a respected scholar—like the usual people who make their mark. Though saintly, he was not a saint in the traditional sense of the term, for he did not perform miracles, lay claim to visual encounters with divinity, or voluntarily stay in seclusion for long periods of time. Gandhi's claim was made upon our conscience; he demonstrated that spirituality is to be found at the core of our humanity. As a scholar of modern Indian thought, V. S. Naravane, writes: "Gandhi himself, it may be added, was fully aware of the nature of his power; and his entire plan of action was based upon this awareness." He quoted Gandhi himself to make the point: "It is a fundamental principle of *Satyagraha* . . . that the tyrant whom the *satyagrahi* seeks to resist has power over his body and his material possessions, but he cannot have any power over his soul. The soul can remain unconquered and unconquerable even when the body is imprisoned. The whole science of Satyagraha was born from a knowledge of this fundamental truth."[8]

Thus a ruler can imprison a person's *body*, but the *spirit* is incapable of being imprisoned (or, for Gandhi, of being killed). It was this spiritual leverage that Gandhi fastened on to, and we fasten on to in Gandhi. It was with this power that Gandhi faced the might of an empire. Gandhi used his confidence in the power of the soul to help liberate the colonially imprisoned bodies of millions of his countrymen and women. His "science of Satyagraha" was his way to protest in the name of truth or justice, or uphold truth or justice.

III

Biographies are usually chronological in nature, although it is also possible to probe certain dimensions or aspects of a person's life thematically. This account of Gandhi's spiritual life is an attempt to blend these two approaches. The first part of the book relates the story of Gandhi's life, focusing on the points at which it strikes a spiritual note; the ensemble these notes are part of emerges in the second part, where the melodies and harmonies are teased out. Roughly the first half of the book, up to chapter 10, is essentially narrative in character, then, with occasional thematic forays; the second half is essentially thematic, though containing some narrative elements. The two approaches have been blended in the hope that the ensuing binocular vision provides a satisfying view of the range and depth of Gandhi's spiritual life.

part one

....

1

....

Birth and

Adolescence

I

Traditionally, the Chinese have counted age from the moment
of conception; a baby is considered a year old at birth. The
Hindus go back further, to a former life; a baby is several
centuries old by the time it is born. This method of counting
birthdays renders problematic the custom of commencing a
biography by stating that its subject was *born* on a particular
day. Perhaps in the case of a person like Gandhi, we should
say that he was *reborn*. For Gandhi was a Hindu, and Hindus
by and large believe in reincarnation. Gandhi certainly did.[1]

However we might characterize his birth, the one we are
concerned with occurred on October 2, 1869, in the city of
Porbandar, on the western coast of India. The time and place

of his birth were destined to have a crucial bearing on the trajectory of his life. For Gandhi was born when India was part of the British Empire—an empire then at its meridian. An Indian effort to dislodge the British had ended in a British victory in 1858, and it was not until after 1905 that British rule over India came under serious challenge again.

As Louis Fischer points out, the year in which Gandhi was born, 1869, was also the year in which the "Suez Canal was opened, Thomas A. Edison patented his first invention, France celebrated the hundredth anniversary of the birth of Napoleon Bonaparte, and Charles W. Eliot became president of Harvard University. Karl Marx had just published *Capital*, Bismarck was about to launch the Franco-Prussia war," and "Victoria ruled over England and India."[2]

Gandhi's birthplace is a port city washed by the Sea of Oman. Porbandar looks like a flash of light to an approaching traveler on account of the color of the stone and limestone of which most of it was built, which gives it a marble-like appearance. It was in fact known as the White City. It was also known as the City of Sudama, an indication of its mythic origins: Sudama was a childhood friend of the Hindu divinity Krishna.

The city passed into British hands in the early nineteenth century but did not come under direct British control. It was indirectly governed through local rulers, who were overseen by British political agents. Gandhi's ancestors were the Diwans, or chief executive officers, of the state of Porbandar, its capital being the coastal harbor city itself. Gandhi's father, Karamchand Gandhi, had inherited the position. He was thrice widowed by the time he was forty, when he married Putlibai, who was eleven at the time. Karamchand had two daughters from his earlier marriages, and Putlibai bore him a daughter and four sons. The youngest was Mohandas, later Mahatma Gandhi.

The modest house in which Gandhi was born still stands,

three stories high. It had belonged to the Gandhi family for five generations.[3] He was born in a small room; a person has to crouch down while entering and leaving through the small door. Since Gandhi has been such an integral part of modern Indian history, it is difficult for Indians not to feel dazed, even a trifle overwhelmed, after setting foot in the room in which he was born.

Gandhi's mother belonged to the Pranami sect, founded by Prannath in the seventeenth century. Many positions that Gandhi assumed in later life, especially on the Hindu-Muslim question, are foreshadowed in this inheritance. The sect emerged after the decline of the Mughal Empire, whose last major emperor, Aurangzeb, ruled from 1658 to 1707. His harsh religious policies drove many Hindu rulers to rebel and ultimately to assert independence. One such ruler was King Chatrasal of Bundelkhand, who, though a Hindu, patronized the eclectic Prannath. Prannath insisted that his Hindu and Muslim followers dine together at initiation, and moved effortlessly between Hindu and Muslim sacred texts in his prayers and expositions. There was a Pranami temple in Porbandar, although Putlibai may have visited the Krishna temple with greater frequency on account of its proximity.[4]

Putlibai was pious by nature. Gandhi records in his autobiography that she would frequently observe long fasts during the rainy season without allowing illness to interrupt her. During one rainy season, Gandhi wrote years later, "she vowed not to have food without seeing the sun. We children on those days would stand, staring at the sky, waiting to announce the appearance of the sun to our mother. Everyone knows that at the height of the rainy season the sun often does not condescend to show his face. And I remember days when, at his sudden appearance, we would rush and announce it to her. She would run out to see with her own eyes, but by that time the fugitive sun would be gone, thus depriving her of her meal.

'That does not matter,' she would say cheerfully. 'God did not want me to eat today.' And then she would return to her round of duties."[5]

Hindu sacred texts sometimes provide genealogies of teachers, and some of the most ancient genealogies recount the names of the teachers by mentioning their mothers. Some scholars have suggested that this may be so because the names of the fathers were not known, hinting at a primitive promiscuity; but traditional commentators offer a very different explanation. According to them, the spiritual teachers are mentioned by referring to their mothers because the mother plays a decisive role in the spiritual development of the child. This was certainly true in the case of Mahatma Gandhi.

II

Gandhi himself acknowledges that two stories from Hindu lore left an indelible mark on him as a child, that of Shravana Kumar and that of King Harishchandra. Gandhi first became aware of Shravana Kumar by accidentally reading about his life of devotion to his parents in a book purchased by his own father. Later Gandhi also saw the story of Shravana Kumar's life enacted in a play by itinerant showmen, who carried placards depicting his life. One placard showed the son, Shravana Kumar, carrying his blind parents on a pilgrimage to holy places in two baskets attached to a pole slung on his shoulder. The depiction of filial piety impressed the child, who saw in it an example worthy of emulation. Gandhi first learned of the other story, that of Harishchandra, through its enactment by a dramatic company, which he was permitted to attend. Harishchandra was a king who made enormous, even tragic, sacrifices to keep his plighted word. His story, vaguely reminiscent of the testing of Job, also moved Gandhi. Harishchandra personified for him the ideal of devotion to truth.

Myths—morality tales by another name—mold our lives. A myth may not be literally true, but it may be fundamentally or morally true. Gandhi's life frequently demonstrates how myth intersects with biography. Such points of intersection are apparent in his later life.

It is only in the light of the story of Shravana Kumar, and the impact it had on Gandhi, that we can even begin to understand Gandhi's enduring regret that he was not with his father when his father died. Gandhi, who was with his wife at the time, writes: "The shame, to which I have referred in a foregoing chapter, was this shame of my carnal desire even at the critical hour of my father's death, which demanded wakeful service. It is a blot I have never been able to efface or forget, and I have always thought that, although my devotion to my parents knew no bounds and I would have given up anything for it, yet it was weighed and found unpardonably wanting because my mind was at the same moment in the grip of lust."[6] He refers to this incident as a double shame because his wife was in an advanced stage of pregnancy.

The consequences of his devotion to his parents were not always depressing. In one particular case they were positively uplifting. Gandhi and a relative became addicted to smoking in early adolescence. At first they contented themselves with the stubs left by an uncle given to that indulgence, but soon they began pilfering pennies from the pocket money given to the servants. Having to do this on the sly rankled. Their despair even drove them to contemplate suicide. They chose a temple for the purpose and planned to consume poisonous weeds they had found in the jungle to bring about the desired end, but their courage failed them at the crucial moment, and they discovered that it was easier to contemplate suicide than to commit it. The ordeal cured them of the addiction, though not of the habit of stealing. These events happened when Gandhi was twelve or thirteen, but Gandhi stole again, when he was fifteen. He took some gold out of his brother's armlet to pay a debt the brother had incurred.

The later theft was more than Gandhi could bear, and he resolved never to steal again. But making a promise to himself was not enough. Gandhi also felt compelled to confess to what he had done. He chose to do so in writing and handed his confession to his father, who was confined to bed with an illness. As his father read the note, "pearl-drops trickled down" his father's cheeks, "wetting the paper" when they landed. It was an agonizing moment for Gandhi. Then his father closed his eyes in thought and tore up the note. This experience convinced Gandhi that a "clean confession, combined with the promise never to commit the sin again . . . is the purest type of repentance."[7]

Just as Shravana Kumar was Gandhi's exemplar, so was King Harishchandra, the upholder of truth. Gandhi's commitment to truth manifested itself when he was a student in the form of a refusal to cheat. The class was told to spell a number of words by the British education inspector, one of which was "kettle." Gandhi had misspelled it, but when his teacher prompted him to cheat, that is, to correct his spelling by looking at his neighbor's slate, Gandhi refused to take the cue. He thought that teachers were supposed to prevent the students from copying.[8]

III

The combined moral synergy of devotion to parents, epitomized in the figure of Shravana Kumar, and devotion to truth, epitomized in the figure of Harishchandra, ultimately led Gandhi to give up his experiments in eating meat, a practice into which he had been lured by reformist zeal: "I wished to be strong and daring and wanted my countrymen to be such, so that they might defeat the English and make India free."[9] He undertook this experiment at the urging of a friend and partly also under the influence of the doggerel then current among the schoolboys:

Behold the mighty Englishman.
He rules the Indian small,
Because being a meat-eater
He is five cubits tall.[10]

The first time he ate goat's meat, Gandhi had a horrible nightmare that the goat was bleating inside him, but he overcame his scruples, believing that if the whole country began eating meat, the English would be overcome.[11]

This expression of reformist zeal required constant dissimulation, for his parents were devout worshippers of the god Vishnu and were therefore vegetarians. Gandhi finally concluded that although he might be introducing reform by eating meat, deceiving and lying to one's parents was much worse than not eating meat.[12] Devotion to truth and to parents won out in a kind of moral double victory, paralleling his double shame.

When one nation suffers defeat at the hands of another, the defeated nation is filled with self-doubt, just as the victorious nation brims with confidence. The defeated people want to know what went wrong and how it might be rectified. In this case, a handful of Britons ruled over three hundred million Indians. To account for it, some Indians accepted the schoolboys' doggerel as true: the British were robust meat eaters, and the Indians were weak vegetarians. The explanation, however, was superficial. The real reason underlying their failure was lack of unity, and once the people of India rallied around Gandhi later in his life and gained some semblance of unity, they were able to dislodge the British.

2

Child Marriage

I

It will probably surprise many readers that Gandhi was married at the age of thirteen, and it might be an occasion for even greater surprise that Gandhi was betrothed thrice prior to his marriage. Two girls chosen for him died in turn, and he married the third.[1] The name of his wife was Kasturbai.

Gandhi felt excited by the prospect of his marriage. He rebelled instinctively when exposed to the practice of untouchability as a child but had no such reaction to his "child marriage" and participated enthusiastically. His father had been injured in a road accident while traveling to Porbandar, where the marriage was solemnized, but he attended despite the injuries.[2]

In describing the rites associated with his marriage, Gandhi mentions *kansar* and *saptapadi*. The first term need not detain us long. It refers to a sweet preparation the pair feed each other at the end of the ceremony, perhaps in the hope that the banquet of marriage will always provide them with the dessert of romance.

The second term is crucial. It refers to the seven steps—saptapadi—taken by the bride and the bridegroom around a fire, a circumambulation at the completion of which they are deemed to be husband and wife. The fire, which is ceremoniously lit, is supposed to be the celestial witness of the wedding, along with the numerous human beings present. This core ceremony is ancient, going back to at least the middle of the second millennium BCE.

The seven steps are laden with symbolism. Each step is sometimes taken to stand for a decade, so the marriage is supposed to unite the couple happily for seventy years, the biblical threescore and ten standing for married life rather than life itself. A more imaginative leap is involved in associating each step with a lifetime. Marriage is thus an alliance that is supposed to last seven lifetimes—a mutual commitment that might seem excessive. What the seven steps denote in either case is lifelong companionship. According to a common expression in Sanskrit, friendship between the virtuous is formed by merely taking seven steps together or by merely exchanging seven words. For marriage, which is undertaken in Hinduism with many ends in view, saptapadi highlights the key element of companionship.

II

Marriage is a major rite of passage, and so it was for Gandhi. If getting married is an event, leading a married life is perhaps best viewed as an ongoing event. Small wonder, then, that being married played a major role in the development of Gandhi's moral and spiritual life. This becomes evident when we compare Gandhi's views about marriage as a young teenager with his views after he had become an adult. Although Gandhi gleefully participated in his wedding, he later reproached his father for marrying him off at such a tender age. As an adult, Gandhi considered it his obligation, as a "worshipper of Truth," to record his marriage as a "painful duty." He not only pities himself for his lot but congratulates those who escaped an early wedding and criticizes a practice he had himself embraced.[3]

Social reformers in India often found themselves in a moral predicament and deserve our sympathy, especially when they were acutely aware, as Gandhi was, that they should practice what they preach. It is not always possible to be precociously sensitive to the shortcomings of one's own tradition. And the force of Indian tradition was sometimes so strong that even elderly statesmen succumbed to it. M. G. Ranade (1842–1901) was a famous advocate of allowing widows to marry, but to his great chagrin, his father, to whom he was devoted, insisted that he marry a virgin after the death of his first wife, and he did so.[4]

Not only did Gandhi get married enthusiastically, he also performed his conjugal duties enthusiastically, so much so that he describes himself as a lustful, if faithful, husband. How did he form his ideas regarding conjugal fidelity? Gandhi identifies two sources: popular pamphlets read during his youth, which discussed conjugal love and similar subjects, and his own passion for truth.[5] An omission here is striking. Gandhi does not mention the name of Rama, the god he was so devoted to, in the context of conjugal fidelity. One of the reasons Rama is looked up to in the Hindu tradition is because he is seen as an upholder of family values. He was totally devoted to his wife, Sita, even through a long period of separation. Sita had complete control over his sexuality, even as Kasturbai had complete control over Gandhi's.

Gandhi's faithfulness was not achieved without struggle. He mentions four occasions when he almost slipped; three can be clearly identified in his autobiography. While still in India he was induced to visit a brothel but was "struck dumb in the den of vice" and retreated. Later, while in England, he had another close shave when he visited Portsmouth to attend a conference. And on his way to take up a job in South Africa, he was struck dumb again in a den of vice, this time in Zanzibar, where he ended up as the result of a favor from the captain, who had taken a liking to him.[6]

On all these occasions, Gandhi saw himself as having been saved by divine intercession, at least when he viewed these incidents in retrospect. We may wonder how clear an idea of God's ways Gandhi had as an adolescent, and yet Gandhi, in recalling the first incident, not only stated that "God in his infinite mercy protected me from myself" but launched into a discussion of fate, free will, and providence. When he was in England, he admits, he understood "only vaguely . . . that God had saved me on the occasion." He nevertheless also added: "On *all* occasions of trial He has saved me. I know that the phrase 'God saved me' has a deeper meaning for me today, and still I feel that I have not yet grasped its entire meaning." After the Zanzibar incident as well, Gandhi writes, "the incident increased my faith in God."[7]

III

Gandhi's efforts to stay within the bounds of marriage and not to stray seem to reveal the dialectical nature of his ethical theism. The two pillars of Gandhi's spiritual life were morality and theism. We saw that Gandhi ultimately rejected child marriage, a rejection that contained a strong moral element.

He describes the custom of child marriage as "cruel." When he describes himself as playing the husband, we can sense an undercurrent of loathing at sexual indulgence early in one's teens. He saw no "moral argument in support of a preposterously early marriage."[8]

Gandhi's theistic dialectics also played out in interesting ways. Gandhi had faith that he was saved by God, and being saved by God increased his faith. He writes that God saved him in his moral trials but goes on to claim that God saved him in *all* his trials; that is, God protected his morals as part of a more comprehensive insurance. This argument seems to involve, from a biographer's point of view, an element of reading his later full-blown convictions back into earlier incidents, as if the earlier happenings were foreshadowing his subsequent convictions.

Such retrodiction is puzzling, even baffling. But Gandhi may have a point. According to "high mystical theory," it is God who turns his face toward us before we turn our face toward God. As someone once said to the famous eighth-century Islamic woman mystic, Rabia, "I have committed many sins. If I turn in penitence towards God, will He turn in mercy towards me?" "Nay," she replied, "but if He shall turn towards thee, thou wilt turn towards Him."[9] It is as if our gaze turns toward another person after the other person has begun to look at us.

Perhaps God does not so much choose the equipped as he equips the chosen.

IV

The bonds of matrimony are said to be so heavy that it takes two, and sometimes three, to carry them. The third party, in the case of Gandhi, seems to have been God. The presence of a third party ultimately affects the relationship between the original two. For Gandhi, it led not to divorce but to the cessation of marital relations, when Gandhi took the vow of celibacy. His criticism of child marriage ultimately became a criticism of marriage itself, which he describes as a fall.[10] In this unlikely way, the child became the father of the man. Gandhi seemed to think that marriage and sex made one morally porous. He accepted that he had been divinely protected in keeping his marital vows, but when he vowed to realize God, then God-realization demanded that Gandhi abandon marital relations altogether. How this ascending dialectic proceeded will become clear in later chapters—we shall see Gandhi groping for God instead of seeing God groping for him—but at the moment we must ask a preliminary question: When and how did God, to whom he attributed such saving power, enter his life?

····

3

▲▲▲▲

God Enters
Gandhi's Life

I

God did not make a dramatic entry into Gandhi's life; belief
infiltrated gradually, almost imperceptibly, in stages. Gandhi
was easily scared as a child and refers to his fear of ghosts
and spirits on more than one occasion. When he confided
these fears to Rambha, who had been his nurse since he was
three, she told him: "There are no ghosts, but if you are afraid,
repeat the name of Rama." So Gandhi began repeating the
name of Rama to get rid of his fear of ghosts and spirits. He
adds that although this experiment was short-lived, "the good
seed sown in childhood was not sown in vain."[1] The seed was
nourished by his memorization of some hymns in praise of
Rama.

The seed thus sown and nourished sprouted in his adolescence, which he entered with his fears of ghosts and spirits intact. By the time he entered high school, at the age of eleven, he was haunted by the fear of thieves and serpents as well, and terrified of darkness. He could not sleep without the light on in his room and does not hesitate to describe himself as a coward. He was stalked by fear, that dark room where negatives are developed.[2] His wife, Kasturbai, on the other hand, was totally free of such fears. Thus shame was added to the cauldron of his adolescent emotions.

That Gandhi was brought to God by fear may raise a few eyebrows, for fear is not a lofty sentiment, although fear of God may qualify as such. But Gandhi was brought by the fear of goblins to God. Hindu theology, however, is comfortable with the idea that negative emotions yield positive consequences in a theistic context. The popular Hindu text on devotion, the *Bhagavata Purana,* says on this point: "Therefore, one should concentrate one's mind on the Lord so completely— either through inveterate enmity or through total freedom from it (that is, through steady and continuous devotion), or through *fear,* friendship or love, that he [or she] can think of nothing else." Not only fear, then, but even hostility toward God can lead to salvation. In fact, the same text, in the same statement, presents the same person as saying, right after the sentence quoted above: "I am myself convinced that even through sustained devotion a man [or a woman] cannot so completely merge himself [or herself] in the Lord as through inveterate enmity."[3]

In Hindu theism, it is enough to be theocentric to set in motion the elastic machine of divine grace: a person does not even have to be a theist! Any emotional charge in relation to God, positive or negative, so long as it electrifies one's being, acquires salvific potency.

Gandhi admittedly used the word Rama as a psychological crutch in his childhood and early adolescence, but he hints at a more mature appropriation of it in later life. This process began when, around the age of thirteen, he was introduced to the *Ramayana*. The original epic, in Sanskrit, is known as the *Ramayana* of Valmiki, but versions of it are available in almost all of India's major languages, including in the language now called Hindi. The author of this Hindi version is Tulsidas (c. 1532–1623); it is thus popularly known as Tulsidas's *Ramayana*, although its proper name is *Ramacaritamanas*, or "Lake of the Deeds of Rama." To understand the role of the *Ramacaritamanas* in Gandhi's life—it is this Hindi version to which he was introduced—we must comprehend its immense and continuing popularity. It has been claimed, on good grounds, that no figure has so profoundly influenced as many Indians as Tulsidas (with the possible exception of the Buddha), and that his work is probably better known in North India than the Bible is in any Western country.[4]

A certain halo surrounds the book and those who recite it, which Gandhi saw and recognized. The person he heard recite it was Ladha Maharaj.[5] Ladha Maharaj had reportedly cured himself of leprosy by offering leaves to Lord Shiva, then, when the leaves were cast off, applying them to the affected parts and by repeating the name of Rama. His faith had made him whole; he had not used any medicine to heal himself. The story may or may not be true, but those who heard him believed it. His body was free from leprosy when Gandhi saw him.

As the example of Ladha Maharaj illustrates, the key to the effectiveness of the recitation is the charisma of the reciter. The verses are first sung and then explained, and they are now broadcast on television as well. So it is not irrelevant that Ladha Maharaj possessed a melodious voice and was carried away by devotional fervor as he recited the couplets and quatrains. And what is perhaps even more important is that he carried the listeners along with him.[6]

This reappropriation of Rama by Gandhi through the *Ramacaritamanas* was a lasting one. Reverence for Rama runs like a sacred thread through his life to the very end. "Rama" was the last word to escape his lips when he was felled by the assassin's bullets. Gandhi repeated the name of Rama when he was dying, as he had when he was a fearful child.[7]

For Gandhi, the name of Rama had to be internalized so completely that a person could repeat it even while asleep. The repetition did not have to be verbal once it was "enshrined in the heart." When he was asked whether for him the name Rama stood for a particular incarnation of God in Hindu mythology, or for the formless God—he was asked this a number of times—he cited the well-known Hindu devotional statement that the *name* of Rama, whatever its referent, is more potent than Rama himself. At one point, however, he did try to address the question directly: "I worshipped Rama as Sita's husband in the first instance, but as my knowledge and experience of Him grew, my Rama became immortal and omnipresent. This does not mean that Rama ceased to be Sita's husband; but the meaning of Sita's husband expanded with the vision of Rama. This is how the world evolves. Rama cannot become omnipresent for the man who regards him merely as the son of Dasharatha. But for the believer in Rama as God, the father of the omnipresent Rama also becomes omnipresent—the father and son become one. It may be said that this is all a matter of imagination. 'To each man according to his faith,' is all that I can say."[8]

III

The story of Rama's deeds, apart from the sound of his name, influenced Gandhi powerfully. One incident in the *Ramacaritamanas* involves Rama's determination to see that his father kept his promises despite the extreme inconvenience of honoring them. The life of Rama's father had twice been saved by one of his wives during battle, and on each occasion he offered her a boon. She took a rain check each time. When Rama was about to be crowned the heir apparent, she invoked those two boons, demanding that (1) Rama be sent into exile for fourteen years and (2) her own son be crowned heir apparent instead of Rama. The king hesitated; the courtiers demurred. Rama, however, insisted that promises made by the father be kept. He chose to renounce the throne and go into voluntary exile—all for the sake of truth, interpreted as promise keeping. Rama defends his position in a couplet known to millions by heart:

> In our royal line, we have heard,
> We give our life but keep our word.

Gandhi's refusal to eat meat while in England, despite being vigorously pressed by a well-wisher to do so, also echoes the example of Rama. When Rama was being urged to disregard the promises his father had made to one of his queens, he was told that the word given by his father to a woman in a besotted moment should not be allowed to interfere with matters of state. Similarly, Gandhi's interlocutor urged: "What is the value of a vow made before an illiterate mother, and in ignorance of the conditions here [England]? It is no vow at all. It would not be regarded as a vow in law. It is pure superstition to stick to such a promise." The same sort of argument was made to Rama. But Rama did not budge. Neither did Gandhi. He in fact alludes to Rama in recalling the occasion.[9] What is also significant here is the understanding of truth involved in these situations. We are used to associating the word "truth" with *telling* the truth; the Hindu understanding of it includes this sense but associates the word "truth" (*satya*) primarily with *upholding* the truth. And one major way of upholding the truth is honoring one's vows. Keeping promises is being truthful.

Years later, Gandhi lost his life for insisting that the Indian government honor a promise to the Pakistani government. The Indian National Congress and the Muslim League had accepted, in the summer of 1947, what is known as the Mountbatten Plan (named after the viceroy who promoted it). According to the plan, British India was to be divided into the two independent dominions of Pakistan and India on August 14 and 15, respectively, in 1947. The partition naturally involved a division of assets. India's payment to Pakistan would be made in three installments, two of which had been already paid when war broke out over Kashmir, after its ruler officially acceded the province to India, on October 29, 1947. The Indian government held up the release of the third installment of the payment. The two nations were at war now; paying it would amount to funding an active enemy. Gandhi, however, insisted that the promise be kept and went on a fast to the death to make the point. The Indian cabinet met again three days later, changed its decision, and released the amount.

On the very day Gandhi went on a fast to ensure this outcome, the man who would assassinate Gandhi began making his plans. Gandhi began his fast on January 13, 1948. He had many reasons for undertaking it, but the one that rankled most in the mind of his assassin-to-be, Nathuram Godse, was Gandhi's insistence that the government of India should stop withholding payment of the 550 million rupees due to Pakistan. It was also on January 13, 1948, that Godse named his brother's wife and his collaborator's wife as beneficiaries of his life insurance policy in case he lost his life in attempting to take Gandhi's.[10]

Gandhi laid down his life for a promise not even made by him, just as Rama went into exile to honor a promise not made by him.

▀▀▀

4

▄▄▄▄

Gandhi in
London

I

After completing his studies in India, Gandhi left for London
to become a barrister. He stayed in London for three years,
from October 1888 until June 1891, and lost no time in head-
ing back for India once his studies were over.[1] Gandhi's single-
minded stay in London and his precipitate return to India
from London after obtaining his jurisprudence degree have
tempted some scholars to view his stay there as essentially
professional in nature but otherwise of not much significance.[2]
The spiritual biographer of Gandhi, however, must dwell on
it in more detail. Almost 10 percent of his autobiography is
devoted to this impressionable period of his life. He arrived
in England just after he had turned nineteen, and Gandhi

himself, as well as his biographers, have noted how the seeds of what would later bear fruit were sown during his London years.[3]

The events leading up to Gandhi's trip to England are perhaps as significant as the trip itself on account of the hurdles he had to overcome to undertake the trip. These included, first of all, opposition within his own household once such a trip had been proposed by an old Brahmin advisor to the family. His mother was afraid that he might go astray while abroad. Three vows administered to him by a Jaina monk took care of her opposition: he promised to abstain from meat, wine, and women while in England. Then Gandhi had to overcome the opposition of his community, known as the Modh Banias.

The word Bania is used for people belonging to the sociological category of Vaishyas, ranked third after the priests and scholars (Brahmins) and warriors and rulers (Kshatriyas) and above the laboring class (Shudras). The Vaishyas constitute a class, which consists of distinct castes, and Gandhi belonged to the Bania caste, whose geographical origins could be traced to the city of Modhera in North Gujarat, which explains their designation as Modh Banias. The various castes in India by now had begun observing restrictive rules on interdining and intermarriage, which constituted an important element in their self-understanding as Hindus, and the Modh Bania caste community thought that Gandhi would not be able to live in England without breaking these rules and compromising his religion.[4]

Even "at the green age of eighteen," to use Louis Fischer's expression, and despite his respect for authority, which Robert Payne attributes to his having had a powerful father, Gandhi not only decided to face the challenge posed by the community but to face it down. In later life he wondered how he had mustered up the courage to appear before the caste council when summoned to do so. Gandhi told the council forth-rightly that in his opinion, it was not against their religion to go to England. The statement is a remarkable one to make before a caste council, which is supposed to lay down the religious code of conduct. In effect, he was telling the council that he was going to act according to his own conscience. The source of his confidence was a solemn promise to his mother to abstain from the three things that his caste community feared most.[5]

The head of the council declared Gandhi an outcaste, but according to Gandhi, the order had no effect on him.[6] It did, however, affect his brother-in-law, who was handling the money for the trip to England and who was now afraid to hand it over to Gandhi for fear of attracting the penalty of associating with him. The problem was solved ingeniously. Gandhi borrowed the money from a friend, and the brother-in-law cleared the debt on his behalf!

Gandhi sometimes claimed in later life, when he cast his lot with the untouchables, that he was one of them on account of his own excommunication, although he did try to mend fences with caste members upon his return from England. One section of the caste, however, was never reconciled to him, nor he to them: "I would not so much as drink water at their houses." As one biographer points out, he lauded himself for his own "non-resistance."[7]

We can here identify two features of Gandhi's spiritual profile that will be on display throughout his life: his self-reliance when it came to deciding what was authentic in matters of religion, and his ambivalent attitude toward caste, some aspects of which he disowned and some he owned up to.

But Gandhi overcame these hurdles and went to London, wearing a string of beads around his neck where his mother had placed it as a parting gift.[8] He wore it for many years, giving it up only when it broke.

II

While in London, Gandhi both encountered moral challenges and acquired greater familiarity with world religions, including his own. His great moral challenge was to maintain the vows he had made to his mother. The one against wine was easy to keep, but his insistence on vegetarianism involved numerous trials and complications. Even before he set out for England, Gandhi tells us that one thing had taken deep root in him: "the conviction that morality is the basis of things, and that truth is the substance of all morality."[9] This conviction reflected the consensus of the entire Indic religious tradition—Hinduism, Buddhism, Jainism, and Sikhism—that while spirituality may be more than morality, it cannot be less. A moral order, usually referred to as karma, undergirds the universe. According to the concept of karma, our personal destinies are closely linked to the moral quality of our lives. Gandhi's originality lay not in this conviction but in the new applications he found for it.

As we saw, promise keeping was a form of truth for Gandhi. It is this aspect of truth that he had to hold on to and define for himself while in London. Keeping his vows involved hardships, such as occasional hunger and, at times, humiliation. Once, while dining at a posh restaurant prior to going to the theater, he inquired whether the soup had meat in it, whereupon his Indian host angrily told him that he was not fit to eat in good restaurants and had better eat elsewhere. Gandhi cheerfully obeyed, but he had to go to the theater hungry since the vegetarian restaurant nearby had closed.[10]

In fact, Gandhi's vegetarian vow was responsible for a lifestyle change during his stay in London. His adoption of a new mode, described as an aberration, had significant social consequences. Gandhi writes that to compensate for the social clumsiness involved in insisting on vegetarianism, he cul-

Gandhi in London

tivated accomplishments that would make him fit for polite society. In short, he set out to become an English gentleman. He donned a new suit made in Bond Street and took lessons in dancing, French, and elocution. For the last pursuit Bell's *Standard Elocutionist* was recommended to him, but it ultimately served more as an alarm bell or prompt. It induced introspection. Gandhi asked himself whether he was going to spend the rest of his life in England, and if not, what was the point of learning elocution and dancing?[11]

Gandhi soon realized that he was trying to learn things that either had no use in India or could be learned in India, and the following Confucian insight came to him: "If my character made a gentleman of me, so much the better. Otherwise I should forgo the ambition." His biographer Louis Fischer thinks that this short-lived experiment, a spin-off from his vegetarianism, was especially consequential so far as his inner life was concerned: "At first, Gandhi had thought he would become an 'Englishman.' Hence the fervor with which he seized the instruments of conversion: clothes, dancing, elocution lessons, etc. Then he realized how high the barrier was. He understood he would remain Indian. Therefore he became Indian."[12] Vegetarianism thus ended up reinforcing his Indianness, albeit circuitously.

While Gandhi was trying to become an Englishman, and later, he kept a scrupulous account of his expenses, as if proper bookkeeping for him was a form of truth, like promise keeping. Gandhi belonged to the class of merchants, who are supposedly adept at keeping accounts, so one way of looking at this activity would be to say that Gandhi was merely acting like a Bania. On the other hand, it could be suggested, in the spirit of this book, that scrupulous bookkeeping could well have constituted one facet of that multifaceted virtue that he described as truth. This interpretation of truth may not be as glamorous as some others, but it seems firmly within Gandhi's moral orbit.[13]

Not only did the attempt to observe the vow of vegetarianism affect Gandhi's life as he lived it in London, but it also had major implications for his moral and spiritual life. While grappling with his vegetarianism, Gandhi was led into clarifying for himself what it meant to be truthful in observing a vow. Since Gandhi had promised his mother that he would abstain from meat, he needed to define what meat was. He came across three definitions of meat in England: (1) the flesh of birds and beasts, a definition that permitted a person to eat fish and eggs; (2) the flesh of all living creatures, a definition that permitted a person to eat eggs; and (3) all living beings as well as their products, a definition that excluded both eggs and milk.

How was Gandhi to decide which of these three meanings was the right one for him, especially after he had experimented with eating eggs for a while? After some reflection, Gandhi became convinced that his mother's definition—number 3—was the definition that bound him. It did not include eggs, so Gandhi gave up eggs. This solution led Gandhi to formulate a hermeneutical principle that could serve as the litmus test for identifying the correct meaning of a pledge when it was in doubt. Gandhi writes: "Interpretation of pledges has been a fruitful source of strife all the world over. No matter how explicit the pledge, people will turn and twist the text to suit their own purposes. . . . One golden rule is to accept the interpretation honestly put on the pledge by the party administering it. Another is to accept the interpretation of the weaker party where there are two interpretations possible. Rejection of these two rules gives rise to strife and iniquity, which are rooted in untruthfulness. He who seeks truth alone easily follows the golden rule. He need not seek learned advice for interpretation. My mother's interpretation of meat was, according to the golden rule, the only true one for me, and not the one my wider experience or my pride of better knowledge might have taught me."[14]

<h2 style="text-align:center">III</h2>

Gandhi's other vow, that of celibacy, was also tested while he was in England.

On his way to England, in Aden, he ran into a pimp and dismissed him. Once in England, on a vacation in Ventnor, on the Isle of Wight, the daughter of the landlady of the boarding house he was staying in had induced him to take a walk. This was probably his maiden encounter with a maiden, and Gandhi found it hard to keep up with his vigorous companion. This encounter might be placed in the category of innocent flirting, but there was another occasion when Gandhi did not "escape scatheless."[15] This time he was befriended by an elderly widow he met on a trip to Brighton who took it upon herself to matchmake. Back in London he found himself being introduced to young nubile women and was often left alone with one of them. Initially, Gandhi did not hesitate to pass himself off as a bachelor, although he was married and the father of a son. But when he sensed that the elderly widow might be introducing him to the young ladies with marriage in mind, Gandhi acquainted her with the true state of affairs through a letter, assuring her that if, upon the receipt of the letter, she found Gandhi unworthy of her hospitality, he would not take it amiss. Thus Gandhi removed what he calls the "canker of untruth," and they continued to see each other.[16]

These were minor skirmishes in comparison to the situation that developed in Portsmouth, where Gandhi had gone to attend a conference. One evening while there, Gandhi sat down with a friend to play a rubber of bridge with the landlady of the house he was staying in. They indulged in raillery, which soon crossed over into ribaldry, with Gandhi joining in. The situation was about to get out of hand when he remembered his vow and fled the scene. He went to his room, "quaking, trembling, and with beating heart, like a quarry escaped from its pursuer."[17] He recalls this as the first occasion on which a woman other than his wife had moved him to lust.

IV

Gandhi's stay in London was consequential not just morally but religiously as well, when we use the word "religion" to denote religious systems such as Hinduism, Islam, and Christianity.

Gandhi was afforded glimpses of the various religions while still at school in Rajkot, India, on account of the ecumenical interests of his father. Gandhi also later referred to the religious ferment that he would experience in Pretoria, South Africa.[18] It is revealing that he refers to his exposure to religious pluralism by his father's side in India by the expression "glimpses of religion," and uses the expression "religious ferment" to describe his encounter with religious pluralism in South Africa, but chooses the expression "acquaintance with religions" when he writes about his experience of religious pluralism in England.[19] In a way, then, London was a junction on the religious railway line from Rajkot to Pretoria. It is as if Gandhi was exposed to religious pluralism in three stages: to some in his home in India, to more during his sojourn in London, and to active engagement with it later in South Africa.

One important consequence of Gandhi's stay in England was that it enabled him to overcome his growing dislike of Christianity. The source of his aversion lay in his adolescent memories of Christian missionaries standing at a corner near his high school and pouring abuse on Hindus and their gods. Gandhi found their goings-on unbearable. He also learned that when a Hindu in town embraced Christianity, he was not only baptized but made to eat beef, drink liquor, and put on Western clothes. So far as Gandhi was concerned, "a religion that compelled one to eat beef, drink liquor, and change one's own clothes did not deserve the name."[20]

But that was India. In England, Gandhi met a good Christian from Manchester in a vegetarian boarding house who talked to him about Christianity. Gandhi narrated his Rajkot recollections to him, which he was pained to hear. He was himself a vegetarian, he did not drink, and he pointed out to Gandhi that although many Christians were meat eaters and did drink, neither was enjoined by Scripture. He also urged Gandhi to read the Bible.[21]

Gandhi did just that.

It has been claimed that more people in India have been converted to Christianity by reading the first three chapters of Genesis than in any other way. Gandhi did not have that kind of experience reading Genesis, but the New Testament made a definite impression on him, and the Sermon on the Mount went straight to his heart.[22]

Gandhi thus began to develop a feeling for Christianity during his stay in London and during trips abroad. Although he does not comment on British churches, he did attend services at them.[23] The churches of Paris, in contrast, made a profound visual impression on him, and he wrote, after he saw people "kneeling before the image of the Virgin," that "the feeling I had then has since been growing on me, that all this kneeling and prayer could not be mere superstition; the devout souls kneeling before the Virgin could not be worshipping mere marble. They were fired with genuine devotion and they worshipped not stone, but the divinity of which it was symbolic. I have an impression that I felt then that by this worship they were not detracting from, but increasing, the glory of God." At one point, he and a fellow Gujarati, Narayan Hemchandra, called upon Cardinal Manning to pay their respects.[24]

Curiously, though a theist, Gandhi attended the funeral of the famous atheist Charles Bradlaugh, who died on January 30, 1891. But he attended not because he approved of atheism but because he approved of heroism. Around that time, Thomas Carlyle's book *Heroes and Hero-Worship* had been recommended to Gandhi. He read the chapter on the hero as a prophet and came to know of Muhammad's greatness, bravery, and austerity.[25]

The newly founded movement of Theosophy made a deeper impact on Gandhi than Christianity, however, and led him to further explore his own Hindu background. Theosophy was a movement founded by the Russian Madame Helena Petrovna Blavatsky and the American Colonel Olcott. Together they established the Theosophical Society in New York in 1875. That it later moved its center to Adyar, India, provides a good indication of its orientation, for it sought to infuse the West with Eastern wisdom. It was also esoteric and ecumenical, and its members believed in the mystical and the paranormal, through which they thought they had special access to the Secret Doctrine received through the "Mahatmas" in Tibet. Gandhi attended some of its meetings and met not only Madame Blavatsky but also Annie Besant, who had joined the society amid controversy. Gandhi admits to following, with great interest, the controversy about her conversion.[26] The controversy was caused by her decision to join the Theosophical Society at a time when Madame Blavatsky was being publicly accused of being an imposter and a charlatan for claiming to have privileged access to so-called Tibetan masters, among other things. But if Madame Blavatsky was in love with Tibet, Annie Besant was "in love with India."[27] Gandhi read her book, *How I Became a Theosophist.*

Theosophy may have influenced Gandhi more than he perhaps realized, apart from re-introducing him to a major text of his own tradition, the Bhagavad Gita. The Theosophical Society was irenic and eclectic in its attitude toward the various religions, a congenial attitude that Gandhi reflected and that must have confirmed his own childhood experience in adopting a respectful attitude toward all religions. Gandhi had a fascination for what many would consider fringe movements, Theosophy among them, which aimed to reconcile religions. A few years later, in 1894, we find him writing in support of a movement called Esoteric Christian Union to the *Natal Mercury;* it also sought to reconcile all religions.[28] Gandhi's attempt, in later life, to make a fringe position mainstream probably cost him his life.

Gandhi did not join the society, pleading inadequate knowledge of his own religion, but he recalls reading Madame Blavatsky's *Key to Theosophy* at the insistence of Theosophist friends and remarks that the book stimulated in him the desire to read books on Hinduism. It also disabused him of the notion, fostered by the missionaries, that Hinduism is rife with superstition.[29] Hinduism was often reviled in England in the nineteenth century as a gross superstition, especially by the missionaries, to justify missionary activity in India and to generate funding.

Gandhi was helped in his desire to learn more about Hinduism by two Theosophists who happened to be related. They invited Gandhi, toward the end of his second year in England, to read the Bhagavad Gita with them in its English translation by Edwin Arnold, entitled *The Song Celestial.* Gandhi's reaction to the invitation is revealing: "I felt ashamed, as I had read the divine poem neither in Sanskrit nor in Gujarati.

I was constrained to tell them that I had not read the *Gita,* but that I would gladly read it with them." Once read, "the book struck me as one of priceless worth. The impression has ever since been growing on me with the result that I regard it today as the book *par excellence* for the knowledge of the Truth. It has afforded me invaluable help in my moments of gloom. I have read almost all the English translations of it, and I regard Sir Edwin Arnold's as the best. He has been faithful to the text, and yet it does not read like a translation. Though I read the *Gita* with these friends, I cannot pretend to have studied it then. It was only after some years that it became a book of daily reading."[30]

Thus we encounter here once more an illustration of the archetype of the "stranger" (in this case, strangers), who reveals the treasure hidden at one's own hearth.[31]

V

We should not overlook the immediate relevance of the Bhagavad Gita to Gandhi's life in London. In the first chapter of the Bhagavad Gita, the hero, Arjuna, becomes nervous at the prospect of battle and describes his condition as follows:

> My limbs sink, my mouth dries up
> My body trembles and my hair stands on end.[32]

Something similar used to happen to Gandhi in London when invited to speak. On one occasion, as he describes it, he had stood up to read his speech, "but could not. My vision became blurred and I trembled, though the speech hardly covered a sheet of foolscap." The speech was finally read out by someone else. Gandhi displayed what we might call the Arjuna-syndrome again when he made his debut in a small cases court in India: "I stood up, but my heart sank into my boots.

My head was reeling and I felt as though the whole court was doing likewise."[33]

Gandhi ultimately overcame his nervousness, just like Arjuna, but not yet. For now, the Bhagavad Gita confirmed the life of restraint he was leading in London. His favorite verses from that book were drawn from the second chapter, which ask one to withdraw one's mind from sense objects.

> If one
> Ponders on objects of the sense, there springs
> Attraction; from attraction grows desire,
> Desire flames to fierce passion, passion breeds
> Recklessness; then the memory—all betrayed—
> Lets noble purposes go, and saps the mind,
> Till purpose, mind, and man are all undone.[34]

What is really significant is the context of these verses. They are part of an answer to the question What are the characteristics of a spiritually realized person?—a question that Gandhi doubtless related to profoundly, for he would one day strive to become a spiritually realized person himself.

5

Gandhi and Raychand

I

Gandhi returned to India from England in 1891, law degree in hand. When he inquired about his mother from his elder brother, who had come to Bombay to receive him, he was told that she had died only a few weeks before, just after receiving the news of his success at the bar exam, which had made her cry.[1] The family had decided to conceal the fact of her illness from Gandhi, to whom the news came as a shock. His mother was forty at the time.

Gandhi took the loss stoically and did not dwell on it, although he admits that the grief he felt at his mother's death exceeded what he felt at his father's.[2]

His mother was perhaps the first guru-figure Gandhi had

in his life, which is confirmed by his statement that "the out-standing impression my mother has left on my memory is that of saintliness." He also describes her as profoundly religious. Saintliness and religiosity are two attributes that, in turn, would be applied to Gandhi himself. According to the Tantrika tradition of India, one's mother is one's best guru, and this maxim may have been realized in the case of Gandhi. She was, after all, his first spiritual exemplar and teacher, and he had spent his time in England keeping his vows to her. How profound her impact on Gandhi must have been may be judged by his response when he was asked in 1947 to express his views on the proposed Universal Declaration of Human Rights: "I learned from my illiterate but wise mother that all rights to be deserved and preserved came from duty well done. Thus the very right to life accrues to us only when we do the duty of citizenship to the world."[3]

Gandhi soon met a man who filled the spiritual vacuum created in his life, as it were, by the passing away of his mother. His name was Raychand (or Rajchandra), and he was twenty-two at the time. A surviving photograph shows him sitting on a curved Victorian chair with his hands placed on his knees. He has large eyes and dense eyebrows and is wearing a long dhoti and a heavy turban.[4] A jeweler by profession, he was rich, well-read, and married. He was also a follower of Jainism and a poet.

Raychand was introduced to Gandhi on the day after Gandhi's return to India by a friend, Dr. Mehta. Raychand was a relative of Dr. Mehta's. The meeting of Gandhi and Raychand is not difficult to imagine. Here was a freshly minted British-trained (but recently bereaved) barrister, twenty years old, in Western garb, ready to be launched on a legal career, come face to face with a traditional, self-confident, affluent twenty-two-year-old jeweler, in Indian dress, who was also a poet and a scholar. Despite the apparent contrast, Gandhi took to Raychand instantly; his very first meeting convinced him that Raychand was a person of great character and learning.[5] Curiously, though, what was on display at their first meeting was Raychand's intellectual prowess rather than his spiritual gifts. Gandhi, when told about Raychand's prodigious memory, tested it by providing him with a list of words to repeat, a list that exhausted Gandhi's vocabulary in European languages, only to hear him repeat them in the precise order in which they had been given. In fact, Raychand was known as a *Shatadhvani*—as someone who could attend to a hundred things simultaneously, perhaps an early incarnation of a multitasker.

Gandhi admits to being impressed but clarifies that it was not so much Raychand's intellectual prowess as his spiritual earnestness that drew him. He writes: "The thing that did cast its spell over me I came to know afterwards. This was his wide knowledge of the scriptures, his spotless character, and his burning passion for self-realization." Perhaps we could add God-realization as well, for the lines that were always on his lips were a prayer to detect God even in such quotidian acts as laughing and playing. For Raychand, God was the thread upon which even the ordinary events of life were strung, although Jainas are formally nontheists.[6]

II

The lives of Gandhi and Raychand became even more of a study in contrast once Gandhi began living in India. Between his return from England in 1891 and his departure for South Africa in 1893, he was struggling to find his feet, in contrast to Raychand, who stood firmly on his own in every way.

When Gandhi returned to India, the fortunes of the Gandhi family were at a low ebb. His brother had run afoul of the British agent in Rajkot and could never aspire to restore his family's influence there. Gandhi tried to start a law practice in Rajkot, but it went nowhere. He then tried to start one in Bombay, but this ended in disaster. He got butterflies in his stomach when he rose to represent his client in Small Causes Court and was struck dumb. He returned the client's fee. He also tried to make peace with the Bania community, which had excommunicated him, and underwent ritual atonement, but not everyone was satisfied, and the ban remained in force in Bombay. In short, Gandhi was a "briefless barrister," to use his own words. Given Gandhi's situation, it is quite possible that he wanted someone to look up to.[7]

Raychand, by contrast, was the very picture of self-assurance. He conducted transactions involving large amounts of money, was a connoisseur of pearls and diamonds, and found no business problem too difficult to tackle. Despite this gulf in their professional circumstances, Gandhi enjoyed close relations with him, although no business or other ties bound them. Whenever Gandhi saw him, Raychand would engage him in a serious conversation on religious matters, even though Gandhi was groping and could not even claim to be seriously interested in a religious discussion. Still, Gandhi found his talk absorbing. He writes: "I have since met many a religious leader or teacher. I have tried to meet the heads of various faiths, and I must say that no one else has ever made on me the impression that Raychandbhai did. His words went straight home to me. His intellect compelled as great a regard from me as his moral earnestness, and deep down in me was the conviction that he would never willingly lead me astray and would always confide to me his innermost thoughts. In my moments of spiritual crisis, therefore, he was my refuge."[8]

While Gandhi was thus struggling to establish himself as a lawyer, something unexpected happened. He was invited by a firm in South Africa, Dada Abdulla and Company, to come to Durban to advise them in a legal suit. Apparently one of the partners in Porbandar, Gandhi's birthplace, had recommended Gandhi for the job. Gandhi accepted the offer and left for Durban in 1893. Gandhi and Raychand remained in touch after Gandhi left for South Africa, where he went through a period of what he himself describes as "Religious Ferment." He found himself in a religiously plural environment, one in which both his Christian and his Muslim friends were trying to convert him. Gandhi was not fully committed to Hinduism at the time, for if he did not find Christianity perfect, neither did he find Hinduism to be so: its defects were quite apparent to him. Gandhi mentioned the issue of untouchability at this point, as well as wondered whether the Vedas were indeed the inspired word of God, and whether the Bible and the Qur'an were any less so.[9]

Gandhi turned to the guru-like Raychand for advice in the midst of this ferment, which had two dimensions: a particular one and a comparative one. The particular one was related to his attitude toward his own inherited religion, Hinduism. The comparative one was related to his attitude toward all the other religions.

Gandhi explicitly identifies the role Raychand played in the context of his Hinduism when he writes in his autobiography: "I expressed my difficulties in a letter to Raychandbhai. I also corresponded with other religious authorities in India and received answers from them. Raychandbhai's letter somewhat pacified me. He asked me to be patient and to study Hinduism more deeply. One of his sentences was to this effect: 'On a dispassionate view of the question I am convinced that no other religion has the subtle and profound thought of Hinduism, its vision of the soul, or its charity.'"[10]

Religious traditions are sometimes characterized by a tension between purity and charity. It is quite striking, and in its own way prophetic, that Raychand identified charity as a feature of Hinduism, for it could be argued that Hinduism is prone at times to sacrificing charity for purity. This is especially in contrast to Buddhism, which might be considered to exhibit an opposite tendency, namely, a willingness to sacrifice purity for charity. The same could be said of Christianity, when contrasted with Judaism. The prophetic element would then consist of Gandhi's future strivings to render Hinduism more "charitable" than he found it. The key point to note here nevertheless is that Gandhi had once again turned to Raychand in a spiritual crisis.[11]

Raychand may have also played a role in determining Gandhi's attitude toward other religions. Gandhi thanked his Christian friends for rousing him from his "dogmatic slumber" and for awakening him to a religious quest and leading him to the comparative study of religions.[12] Gandhi emerged from this study as a religious pluralist. The term "pluralist" may require a word of explanation. It is used to denote the view, in interfaith dialogue, that all religions are valid avenues for approaching the ultimate reality or God. That view is thus to be distinguished from the exclusivist view, that only one's own religion is salvifically potent, and from the inclusivist view, according to which other religions could play some role in salvation, but only a preparatory one.

If Robert Payne is right in suggesting that "Raychand was the first to suggest to Gandhi that no religion was superior to another, for all religions were concerned to bring the worshipper in the presence of God," then Gandhi's association with Raychand probably also played a role in shaping his views in relation not only to Hinduism but other religions as well.[13] In recommending Hinduism to Gandhi in particular while accepting no one religion as superior to any other in general, Raychand may seem to be contradicting himself. But the two positions are really two sides of the same coin. If it is not necessary to change, then it is necessary not to change.

The original letter that Gandhi wrote to Raychand in his moment of spiritual crisis is not traceable, but the questions put by Gandhi to Raychand have been reconstructed from Raychand's reply, in a book on him in Gujarati.[14] Gandhi appealed to him, in a long letter, for answers to "twenty-seven questions, some concerned with Hinduism, others with Christianity. What is God? What is the soul? What is salvation? What is duty? Who wrote the *Vedas* and the *Bhagavad Gita*? What will finally happen to the world? Who were Brahma, Vishnu and Siva? Is there any merit to be gained by sacrificing animals to the gods? Can we obtain salvation through faith in Rama and Krishna? Can a man be reborn as an animal, a tree, a stone? Were all the Old Testament prophecies fulfilled in Christ and was He an incarnation of God? If a snake were about to bite me, should I allow myself to be bitten or should I kill it?"[15]

The last question is itself as intriguing as the answer that Raychand offered to it. To us the answer seems obvious, but Payne argues that it "had a special significance to Gandhi, for they had already debated it at length. The truly perfect *sunyasi* [renunciant] must be devoid of fear, in total self-command of his own emotions. He must pass through life's most dangerous passages in the certain belief that he is under God's direct protection. It followed that if he encountered a lion in the forest, he would simply walk up to it, and if a snake attacked him he would pay no more attention than if a moth had lightly touched his hand. Shrimad Rajchandra replied sensibly: 'The question is not what I would wish you to do, but what you would wish your choice to be. That choice will depend on the degree of your illumination and enlightenment.'"[16]

We can form some idea, from their correspondence, in which Gandhi interrogated Raychand on such diverse issues, of the extent to which Gandhi continued to look upon Raychand as his spiritual mentor even after he had left India.

IV

The spiritual influence of Raychand on Gandhi may be traced in two other areas. In Gandhi's first public speech in South Africa, which was also his first public speech ever, he encouraged four pursuits: "Tell the truth even in business; Adopt more sanitary methods; Forget caste and religious divisions; Learn English."[17] Some biographers have traced Gandhi's urge to be didactic ultimately to Raychand. Raychand apparently held the view that it was not enough to be virtuous oneself; it was also part of one's duty to bring others to virtue. He certainly held this view about people one was responsible for. His example involves a son whom the father caught drinking. The father is justified, according to Raychand, in smashing the cup the son was drinking from and the wine bottle and, further, all the wine bottles the son concealed but which now the father could lay his hands on. The son may feel hurt by the conduct of the father and consider him heartless, but the father should not mind, because he has the son's good at heart. Biographers have noted that sometimes Gandhi tended to behave in this manner toward his own sons, with alarming consequences.[18]

Another area in which Raychand's influence has largely gone unnoticed has to do with Gandhi's vow of celibacy. This is surprising since Gandhi alludes to it himself. He recalls praising Mrs. Gladstone's devotion to her husband in that she insisted on preparing tea for her prime minister husband even in the House of Commons. When Gandhi eulogized conjugal devotion of this kind, Raychand asked him whether Gandhi would place her devotion above the devotion of someone who was not related to Mr. Gladstone and yet was equally devoted to him. Although the words sounded harsh to Gandhi, he admits to being gripped by them irresistibly. He openly states that it was as a result of this conversation that he began to realize the importance of having a platonic relationship with his wife. It is worth noting that a conversation that took place between two married people ended up in a tacit endorsement of celibate ecstasies.[19]

We also need to remind ourselves that Raychand was a Jaina and that Jainism has been historically influential in Gujarat. It exerted a profound influence on Gandhi through the person of Raychand, whose liberal views reflected the well-known Jaina doctrine of *anekantavada,* or the manifoldness of truth, with its tolerant connotation.[20] Gandhi may have been influenced by Jainism more subliminally in at least two other ways, both having to do with food. The first is vegetarianism. We know that Gandhi came from a family of vegetarians, but this very fact may well reflect the influence of Jainism in the region. According to the distinguished Jaina scholar Padmanabh S. Jaini, "Vegetarianism is the hallmark of the Jaina." He also maintains that Jainism "certainly contributed much to the eventual triumph of vegetarianism throughout the subcontinent."[21]

The other Jaina influence pertaining to food involves fasting. Jaini commences his book on the Jaina path of purification with the almost contemporary description of a fast unto death undertaken by a Jaina mendicant who finally passed away on September 18, 1955. The story easily brings to mind Gandhi's long fasts for self-purification of stunning duration.[22] Although fasting is a regular feature of the Hindu way of life, it is rarely carried to the extremes that we find in Jain-

Gandhi and Raychand

ism and in Gandhi. For Gandhi's use of fasting as a nonviolent form of protest, however, we may have to fall back on the Hindu tradition, wherein priests and housewives often resort to it as a mode of protest. A display of voluntary suffering is far more effective than mere words as a way of touching another's conscience.

V

Gandhi and Raychand were both in their early twenties when they met, but Gandhi survived into his seventies whereas Raychand died in his early thirties. While in South Africa, Gandhi learned from a friend in May 1901 that Raychand had passed away after a lingering illness, perhaps consumed by his extraordinary gifts. By this time Gandhi was a full-fledged public worker and hardly had the time to mourn.[23]

When Gandhi was jailed in 1909 in Pretoria, during his first satyagraha campaign, he was sustained spiritually by reading not only the Upanishads, Ralph Waldo Emerson, and Leo Tolstoy but also the poems of Raychand. Payne writes that in jail, sitting on the polished asphalt floor, Gandhi recited in the half-darkness:

> The sky rings with the name of the Invisible,
> I sit rapt in the temple, my heart filled with gladness.
> Taking up a Yogic posture, the face immovable,
> I have pitched my tent in the abode of the
> Inscrutable.

Gandhi would recite these verses day and night, and when he felt the dark pterodactyl of despair descending on him, he would banish it with the lesson that Raychand had taught him: "Let the mind be always rapt in joy."[24]

Raychand felt that a compassionate person would do his or her utmost to keep someone from being hurt. Gandhi wrote about him that the "grief which we feel at the death of our own brother or sister he used to experience at the existence of suffering and death in the world. If someone argued that people suffered from their sins, he would ask what drove them to sin." Robert Payne notes that in "the logical mind of Rajchandra, there was not a single hurt, not a single cry of pain, which could not be prevented if men were compassionate enough. But there was a price to be paid for these victories: a man of true compassion would inevitably suffer unendurable torment."[25]

Gandhi's life was destined to illustrate this agonizing moral truism.

VI

The relationship of Gandhi with Raychand raises an important question in a spiritual biography of Gandhi: Was Raychand Gandhi's guru? And if not, why not?

Robert Payne writes in the context of their original meeting that it "came just at the time when Gandhi, uprooted from London and grief-stricken by his mother's death, needed someone he could trust and admire. He desperately wanted a *guru,* someone who could speak to him with grave authority on spiritual matters." It is also a tantalizing fact that Gandhi brings up the question of a guru while writing about Raychand. After paying a handsome tribute to him, however, Gandhi goes on to say:

> And yet in spite of this regard for him I could not enthrone him in my heart as my Guru. The throne has remained vacant and my search still continues.
>
> I believe in the Hindu theory of Guru and his importance in spiritual realization. I think there is a great deal of truth in the doctrine that true knowledge is im-

possible without a Guru. An imperfect teacher may be tolerable in mundane matters, but not in spiritual matters. Only a perfect *gnani* deserves to be enthroned as Guru. There must, therefore, be ceaseless striving after perfection. For one gets the Guru that one deserves. Infinite striving after perfection is one's right. It is its own reward. The rest is in the hands of God.[26]

We are led to ask a delicate question: Why did Gandhi not accept Raychand as his guru?

The biographers of Gandhi have grappled with this issue. Robert Payne maintains that Raychand could never quite assume that role because of temperamental differences between them, although Raychand did open the way to self-knowledge for Gandhi. Louis Fischer seems to offer two responses. He suggests that "Raychand lacked the perfection Gandhi sought in a Guru," but he additionally offers Gandhi's sense of independence as an explanation and writes, "In the presence of prominent men he [Gandhi] felt respect, humility, awe, but, wrapped in these sentiments, he sometimes became impervious to their thoughts. With all his diffidence he was spiritually independent. Ideas came to him occasionally through books but chiefly through his own acts. He remade himself by tapping his own inner resources."[27]

Gandhi perhaps provides the clue to an answer in his remarks on the role of a guru in Hinduism. He states that a guru must be a *jnani* (spelled *gnani* in Gandhi's autobiography). A jnani is one who *knows* the ultimate reality, while *both* Raychand and Gandhi were seeking it. When they met, Raychand was perhaps more advanced in his search. That is why he made such an impression on Gandhi.

While Gandhi had guru-like figures in Raychand and perhaps his mother, he had no guru. He was, rather, his own guru.

····

6

▀▀▀▀

Gandhi's Conversion
Experience

I

To recapitulate: Gandhi had left for London at the age of
eighteen to obtain a degree in law and returned to India
three years later, in 1891. While trying to find his professional feet in India, he was engaged by an Indian firm in
South Africa, Dada Abdulla and Company, to represent it
in a lawsuit. He set sail for South Africa as their legal advisor
in April 1893.

It was during his stay in South Africa that he had what we
can call a conversion experience.

An experience that transforms one's life radically and
lastingly is often referred to as a conversion experience in the
psychology of religion. It is often either a spiritual experience

in itself or one with lasting spiritual consequences. Gandhi underwent such an experience in South Africa while traveling from Durban to Pretoria on behalf of the company that employed him. At the time there was no direct rail link between the two cities, and part of the journey had to be covered by horse-drawn coach. A train went from Durban to Charlestown, then travelers took a coach to Standerton to catch the train for Pretoria.

Mahatma Gandhi boarded the train from Durban. What happened next is a well-known part of Gandhiana and is best described in Gandhi's own words.

The train reached Maritzburg, the capital of Natal, at about 9 p.m. Beddings used to be provided at this station. A railway servant came and asked me if I wanted one. "No," said I, "I have one with me." He went away. But a passenger came next, and looked me up and down. He saw that I was a "coloured" man. This disturbed him. Out he went and came in again with one or two officials. They all kept quiet, when another official came to me and said, "Come along, you must go to the van compartment."

"But I have a first class ticket," said I.

"That doesn't matter," rejoined the other. "I tell you, you must go to the van compartment."

"I tell you, I was permitted to travel in this compartment at Durban, and I insist on going on in it."

"No, you won't," said the official. "You must leave this compartment, or else I shall have to call a police constable to push you out."

"Yes, you may. I refuse to get out voluntarily."

The constable came. He took me by the hand and pushed me out. My luggage was also taken out. I refused to go to the other compartment and the train steamed away. I went and sat in the waiting room, keeping my hand-bag with me, and leaving the other luggage where it was. The railway authorities had taken charge of it.[1]

Finally, after informing the general manager of the railways and Dada Abdulla of the incident, Gandhi decided to take the next available train. Before he left the next day, the Indian merchants in Maritzburg came to see him in response to a telegram from Dada Abdulla. Gandhi reached Charlestown safely, but another trial was in store for him during the long coach journey to Standerton. The white man in charge of the coach did not want Gandhi to sit with the white passengers because Gandhi was a "coolie," as Indians were contemptuously called, and made him sit on the coach box while he himself sat with the passengers. At one point during the ride, the man got the urge to smoke and, wanting Gandhi's seat on the coach box for himself, demanded that Gandhi sit on the footboard of the coach box. When Gandhi protested, he was almost shoved off the coach and had to cling to the brass rail, feeling as if his wrists would break. Eventually the passengers inside the coach interceded on Gandhi's behalf, and he was able to stay put on the coach box, but the experience made him wonder if he would reach his destination alive.[2] He reached Pretoria without further incident.

Let us revert now to the cold night he spent shivering at the Maritzburg station. Are we justified in calling what happened a conversion experience? It certainly was one in Gandhi's own estimation. Many years later, Dr. John R. Mott, a Christian missionary in India asked Gandhi, "What have been the most creative experiences in your life?" Gandhi identified the night in the Maritzburg station.[3]

Gandhi's Conversion Experience

Gandhi had suffered indignities at the hands of the ruling white elite before. Once previously, when living in the city of Rajkot, he had pleaded with the local British agent on behalf of his brother. The agent did not take kindly to Gandhi, although Gandhi had met him in England, so he had Gandhi physically removed from his office. Gandhi ends the chapter recounting the story, significantly entitled "The First Shock," with a simple but charged statement: "This shock changed the course of my life." He does not pause to tell us how exactly it changed his life. Autobiographically speaking, he shares more with the reader about what went on in his mind after the shocking incident at Maritzburg. In fact, his multivolume biographer D. G. Tendulkar says of this incident what Gandhi said of his encounter with the British agent in Rajkot: "This experience changed the course of his life." Let us remind ourselves that after being ejected, Gandhi could have returned to the train and found a place for himself in a third-class carriage. But he chose to spend it in the station waiting room. The room was cold, and his overcoat was in his luggage, but for fear of being insulted again Gandhi did not ask for it. So Gandhi sat by himself, shivering and brooding.[4]

What did Gandhi brood about?

"I began to think of my duty," he writes. "Should I fight for my rights or go back to India, or should I go on to Pretoria without minding the insults, and return to India after finishing the case? It would be cowardice to run back to India without fulfilling my obligation. The hardship to which I was subjected was superficial—only a symptom of the deep disease of colour prejudice. I should try, if possible, to root out the disease and suffer hardships in the process. Redress for wrongs I should seek only to the extent that would be necessary for the removal of the colour prejudice."[5]

It is difficult not to be struck by the restrained trajectory of his thought in the face of the indignity he had just experienced. Gandhi thinks not of how to vent his anger but of how to do his duty. He thinks not of revenge but of justice, implying that to seek revenge is to become unjust in the pursuit of justice. And in the pursuit of such justice, he speaks not of inflicting hardships on the oppressor but of suffering hardships himself in the process. As Louis Fischer notes correctly, "That frigid night in Maritzburg the germ of social protest was born in Gandhi," but we also need to take note that that protest had to be nonviolent. Gandhi had intuited that night what he was to articulate later:

> Man and his deed are two distinct things. Whereas a good deed should call forth approbation and a wicked deed disapprobation, the doer of the deed, whether good or wicked, always deserves respect or pity as the case may be. "Hate the sin and not the sinner" is a precept which, though easy enough to understand, is rarely practised, and that is why the poison of hatred spreads in the world.
>
> This *ahimsa* is the basis of the search for truth. I am realizing every day that the search is vain unless it is founded on *ahimsa* as the basis. It is quite proper to resist and attack a system, but to resist and attack its author is tantamount to resisting and attacking oneself. For we are all tarred with the same brush, and are children of one and the same Creator, and as such the divine powers within us are infinite. To slight a single human being is to slight those divine powers, and thus to harm not only that being but with him the whole world.[6]

The basic principles of what Gandhi was to describe as "Satyagraha," or holding on or clinging to truth, are all here *in nuce.* First of all, one's cause must be just, that is, true. And second, one should press it, but without employing violence. A person should undergo suffering if necessary, rather than inflict violence in the process of pressing for justice. Ahimsa is the principle of doing no harm to any living being.

III

A person, after a conversion experience, continues to physically inhabit the same world but begins to live psychologically in a different one.

7

Out of Africa

After reaching Pretoria, Gandhi decided to get in touch with every Indian in the city. As a first step toward achieving this goal, he called a meeting of all Indians. By and large they were Muslims, as Pretoria had only a small Hindu population. Once they assembled, the formerly tongue-tied Gandhi delivered his first speech ever. The leaven of the conversion experience at Maritzburg had begun to produce its effect. In his speech, he urged his listeners to be honest and clean, to rise above caste and religious differences, and to learn English.[1] In other words, if they desired to be treated properly, they must deserve it. Other meetings followed, and Gandhi soon became acquainted with all the local Indians.

Gandhi then pursued the issue raised by his adverse experiences during his trip from Durban to Pretoria, protesting that the disabilities under which the Indians labored were not justified under the railway rules. He received a reply to the effect that first- and second-class tickets would be issued to "properly dressed" Indians. The decision whether they were properly dressed or not rested with the station master.[2] Although Gandhi notes that this was far from "adequate relief," biographers note that although the railway's response was open to interpretation, it represented progress, and Gandhi felt encouraged, and the Pretorian Indians proceeded to form a permanent organization.[3]

In due course, the lawsuit that had brought Gandhi to South Africa in the first place was settled through arbitration. Gandhi had now been in South Africa for a year and was ready to return to India. Dada Abdulla arranged a daylong farewell party in his honor. It was during the festivities that Gandhi's attention was drawn to an item in a newspaper entitled "Indian Franchise." It drew attention to a bill, pending before the House of Legislature, which if passed, would deprive Indians of their right to elect members to the Natal Legislative Assembly. Everyone present at the party, including Gandhi, was taken aback.[4]

What Gandhi and others did not know was that about 250 free (as distinguished from indentured) Indians in Natal had the right to vote as British subjects, for they met the wealth qualification, and now this right was going to be abrogated. Gandhi told Dada Abdulla: "This Bill, if it passes, will make our lot extremely difficult. It is the first nail in our coffin. It strikes at the root of our self-respect." Gandhi said this hesitantly as he was about to leave, but the gravity of the situation was not lost on others. Gandhi was persuaded to delay his departure by a month to help direct the community.

"The farewell party was thus turned into a working committee," Gandhi noted later without irony.[5]

Preparations were made to submit a "monster petition" to the secretary of state for the colonies and to draw the attention of the Indian public to the issue.[6] A permanent body, the Natal Indian Congress, was formed in 1894 to sustain the movement. While agitation was in progress, the government proposed a new measure that affected the rights of the indentured Indians (as distinguished from the free Indians). The distinction between these two classes arose in the 1860s. When it was discovered that there was much scope for sugarcane cultivation in Natal, labor was recruited from India under what was known as the indenture system. The recruits were committed to working for five years on stipulated terms, after which they could return to India at the expense of the contractor. They could also do so after spending an additional five years as free laborers. Many chose to become permanent residents in Natal. Soon, however, the Indian laborers wore out their welcome, for they became successful enough to compete with white laborers. One white man put the matter candidly: "It is not the vices of Indians that Europeans in this country fear but their virtues."[7]

Under the new proposal, the laborer could return to India upon the expiry of the indenture period, or sign a fresh indenture every two years, or pay an annual "poll" tax of twenty-five pounds—an exorbitant figure. Gandhi suggests, but is not certain, that the campaign of the Natal congress against the tax had the amount reduced to three pounds. The congress, however, was determined to obtain complete remission.[8]

When Gandhi visited India in the middle of 1896, he drew the attention of the Indian public to the conditions of their compatriots in South Africa. Many whites in South Africa felt that his actions were disparaging to whites. On his return to South Africa in 1897, only quick action by the wife of the superintendent of police, who spotted Gandhi, and quick thinking by the superintendent himself ensured his safety after he was virtually assaulted. A crowd had already begun to chant: "Hang old Gandhi/On the sour apple tree."[9]

With the Natal Act of 1897, the attempt to disenfranchise free Indians was abandoned; the fees for indentured Indians had already been reduced: the agitation had brought results. Gandhi expressed his appreciation to the larger South African community by forming an Indian ambulance corps during the Boer War of 1899–1902. Its services were twice rejected, but the government relented when it found that the Boers were on the march, corpses were piling up, and the wounded were not being cared for.[10] The corps was disbanded in 1900, after reinforcements arrived from England.

Gandhi left for India in 1901, but the South African Indian community telegraphically summoned him to return in view of the impending visit of the British colonial secretary. Gandhi returned, but his pleas for redress were "answered with chilling evasiveness" by the secretary.[11]

Gandhi was now living in Johannesburg.[12]

The British, after they won the Boer War, also wanted to win the peace. It was a Boer leader, General Louis Botha, who soon became the prime minister of the Union of South Africa, and another Boer general, Jan Christiaan Smuts, who became the minister of finance and defense. Because the whites still feared competition from the Indians, the Transvaal government set up an Asiatic department to deal with them—which meant, initially, to keep them as far down as possible. It pursued its policy of suppression throughout 1904–1906. Then the Zulu Rebellion occurred. Gandhi considered himself a loyal subject of the British Empire at the time and wrote to the governor expressing his willingness to form an Indian ambulance corps, as before. The offer was immediately accepted.[13] Gandhi led a medical corps of twenty-four Indian volunteers.

Although Gandhi has recently been accused of being anti-black, his experience, as he reports it, contravenes that notion. "My heart was with the Zulus," he writes, "and I was delighted, on reaching headquarters, to hear that our main work was to be the nursing of the wounded Zulus. The Medical Officer in charge welcomed us. He said the white people were not willing nurses for the wounded Zulus, that their wounds were festering, and that he was at his wits' end. He hailed our arrival as a godsend for those innocent people, and he equipped us with bandages, disinfectants, etc., and took us to the improvised hospital. The Zulus were delighted to see us. The white soldiers used to peep through the railings that separated us from them and tried to dissuade us from attending to the wounds. And as we would not heed them, they became enraged and poured unspeakable abuse on the Zulus."[14]

It was during the long marches undertaken by the medical corps that Gandhi began to reflect on his duties as a public worker. These reflections ultimately led him to undertake the vow of celibacy, so that, in Louis Fischer's words, "a new Gandhi faced the South African Government" when on August 22, 1906, the *Transvaal Government Gazette* published a proposed ordinance requiring all Indians (above the age of eight) to be fingerprinted and to carry a certificate of registration that they would be required to produce on demand. The proposal disturbed the Indian community greatly. It applied to women also, who could now be accosted by policemen at will. Indians also feared that if passed in Transvaal, the law would be adopted by other states.[15]

II

A meeting of all South African Indians was called on September 11, 1906 (a date also destined for significance more than a century later) at the Imperial Theatre in Johannesburg. Those present swore in the name of God not to obey the anti-Indian ordinance if it became law.[16]

The government was to be resisted. But how?

This is when the word *satyagraha* was created to describe the method to be used. Here is how Gandhi recounts its genesis:

> The principle called Satyagraha came into being before that name was invented. Indeed when it was born, I myself could not say what it was. In Gujarati also we used the English phrase "passive resistance" to describe it. When in a meeting of Europeans I found that the term "passive resistance" was too narrowly construed, that it was supposed to be a weapon of the weak, that it could be characterized by hatred, and that it could finally manifest itself as violence, I had to demur to all these statements and explain the real nature of the Indian movement. It was clear that a new word must be coined by the Indians to designate their struggle.
>
> But I could not for the life of me find out a new name, and therefore offered a nominal prize through *Indian Opinion* to the reader who made the best suggestion on the subject. As a result Maganlal Gandhi coined the word "Sadagraha" (Sat = truth, Agraha = firmness) and won the prize. But in order to make it clearer I changed the word to "Satyagraha" which has since become current in Gujarati, as a designation for the struggle.[17]

The principles of satyagraha came into play as the agitation proceeded. Soon after the Indians' "spiritual baptism" in satyagraha at the Imperial Theatre, the Transvaal government exempted Asian women from the need to register for identification certificates and attendant fingerprinting. Although no one could not be certain that the change was a result of the agitation, Indians began to feel that Gandhi's tactics might be working.[18]

Since the other objectionable provisions remained in place, Gandhi decided to visit London with a view to preventing royal assent from being given to the legislation. On his way back to South Africa from London, he received a cable from Lord Elgin saying that the legislation would not be sanctioned. This was a trick, however, for on January 1, 1907, Transvaal ceased to be a crown colony; its legislation no longer needed royal approval. True to form, it proceeded to put the Asiatic Registration Act into effect on July 31, 1907. Gandhi formed the Passive Resistance Association (later renamed the Satyagraha Association) in response. Followers who refused to comply were arrested and imprisoned. A principle of satyagraha comes into play here—although the British government had tricked Gandhi, Gandhi did not lose confidence in the British. A follower of satyagraha gives one's opponent a long rope to hang itself with!

General Smuts, the minister in charge of Indian affairs, entered the picture at this point. He promised that the government would repeal the law and free all prisoners if the Indians registered voluntarily. Gandhi accepted the proposal. Now a second principle of satyagraha came into play: willingness to negotiate and compromise. This compromise almost cost Gandhi his life. A Pathan, Mir Alam by name, accused Gandhi of selling out and swore to kill the first person to register. Indeed, as soon as Gandhi entered the registration office, Mir Alam knocked him unconscious, and his companions kicked and beat Gandhi up. The police and some Europeans who happened to be passing by came to Gandhi's rescue, and he was carried to the office of an English friend, the Reverend Doke.[19] Here is a biographer's account of how events unfolded after that.

Out of Africa

When he regained consciousness, the Reverend Joseph J. Doke, a bearded Baptist idealist, was bending over him. "How do you feel?" said Doke.

"I am all right," Gandhi answered, "but I have pain in the teeth and ribs. Where is Mir Alam?"

"He has been arrested with the other Pathans," Doke said.

"They should be released," Gandhi murmured. "They thought they were doing right, and I have no desire to prosecute them."

Gandhi was taken to the Doke home, and the wounds in his cheek and lip were stitched. He asked that Mr. Chamney, the Registrar for Asiatics, be brought to him so he could give his fingerprints without delay. The process hurt Gandhi physically; every movement was painful. Chamney began to weep. "I had often to write bitterly against him," Gandhi declared, "but this showed me how man's heart may be softened by events."[20]

However, General Smuts refused to honor his word. He produced a bill that validated voluntary certificates but kept the provision for compulsory registration.

One of the principles of satyagraha now produced its effect. This principle required a person to trust an opponent. If the opponent betrayed the trust, then the person who had not, stood on higher moral ground. According to Gandhi, "one of the virtues of Satyagraha" is that "it uncovers concealed motives and reveals the truth. It puts the best possible interpretation on the opponent's intentions and thereby gives him another chance to discard baser impulses. If he fails to do so, his victims see more clearly and feel more intensely, while outsiders realize who is wrong."[21] Placing one's trust in the opponent unmasks the opponent in due course.

The inflamed Indian public now put the certificates to flame on August 16, 1908, at the Hamidia Mosque in Johannesburg. Some reporters compared this act to the Boston Tea Party.

Indians also decided to challenge the ban on their immigration into Transvaal. Now another principle of satyagraha came into play, that there is nothing furtive about it; the opponent is advised of one's moves in advance. Gandhi notified the government of the intention of the Indians to test its law by choosing a Parsi Indian to defy it. The tester was not stopped. Then a larger group moved in. Seventy-five people ended up in jail, along with Gandhi, when the government swung into action.

For the next two years the confrontations let up as the governments of Natal, Transvaal, Orange Free State, and Cape Colony worked toward constituting a Union of South Africa. The union had to be approved by the British government, and Gandhi visited London in 1909 in the hope of securing rights of citizenship for Indians. He was unsuccessful. The union became a reality in 1910. In the meantime, Gandhi's Phoenix Settlement was flourishing, and a Tolstoy Farm came into being in 1910 as a result of the generosity of a Jewish friend. These communal farms proved helpful in the satyagraha movement, because they could accommodate the families of the satyagrahis while the good fight was being fought.

In the autumn of 1912, the Indian political leader Gopal Krishna Gokhale visited South Africa and received assurances from both Botha and Smuts that the two laws that had proved galling for the Indians—the compulsory registration in Transvaal and the three-pound poll tax in Natal—would be repealed soon. Nothing came of these assurances.

Then, in 1913, the Cape Supreme Court ruled that only marriages solemnized by Christian rites would have legal status. Gandhi felt that this "decision had instantly made all Indian wives except Christian ones concubines or common-law wives, and their children illegitimate."[22] This law, now added to the list of the Indians' grievances, inadvertently highlights another aspect of satyagraha. A satyagrahi seeks the remedy of *specific* acts of injustice, as opposed to attacking injustice generally. Indians in South Africa were subjected to racism; the satyagraha was, however, conducted against specific instances of it and not against racism more broadly.

Dealing with one specific instance and then another sometimes makes satyagrahis' victories cumulative. The original trigger for what was later called satyagraha was the legislation in 1894 proposed to prevent *free* Indians from voting. Later that year the movement was enlarged to include the demands of *indentured* Indians as well, when their contractual terms were altered. The proposed fingerprinting in 1905 originally applied to all Indians but ultimately involved only men. The ruling on marriage, in 1913, affected women, drawing them within the ambit of satyagraha. Now they, too, could court arrest by violating unjust laws.

III

In 1913, Gandhi decided to openly break the law forbidding the movement of Indians across state lines. One group, which included his wife, Kasturbai, crossed over from Natal to Transvaal; the government arrested and jailed them. A group of eleven "sisters" who crossed from Transvaal into Natal were not stopped, however, and were allowed to march to Newcastle. There they persuaded the Indian miners to go on strike.

This strike changed the scale of the movement. Large numbers of people now became involved: five to six thousand. Gandhi decided to break the law himself by marching into Transvaal with a group. They stopped on the border at Charlestown, just inside the Natal border. Gandhi informed the government of his intentions, in keeping with the tradition of satyagraha, and on November 6, 1913, led over two thousand men, women, and children into Transvaal. Toward the end of the first day, as they headed for Tolstoy Farm, Gandhi was arrested but then released. Over the course of the next four days, Gandhi was arrested three times. The march continued until it was stopped at Balfour and the marchers were transported back to Natal and to the mines.[23]

The news of the march made headlines in Britain and India. The South African government, under international pressure, released Gandhi and set up a commission of inquiry. That was not a solution. Not only did the commission have no Indian members, but some of the members were known for their anti-Indian stance. So Gandhi planned a protest march against the commission. Just then, however, the European railway workers throughout South Africa went on strike, an act that threatened the survival of Botha's government.[24] At this point Gandhi called off his protest march, on the ground that a satyagrahi does not take advantage of an adversary when the adversary is in trouble. This is another principle of satyagraha.[25]

The railway strike required the imposition of martial law. Smuts finally summoned Gandhi for negotiations. Smuts had reneged earlier on his promises, and Gandhi's friends warned him against putting off the march again, reminding him of what had been done in 1908, when Smuts sponsored a law that validated voluntary certificates but did not rescind compulsory registration. Gandhi quoted a Sanskrit verse to the effect that "forgiveness is the ornament of the brave."[26]

The negotiations, concluded on June 30, 1914, were embodied in the Indian Relief Bill. According to the agreement, (1) Hindu, Muslim, and Parsi marriages were to be deemed valid; (2) the three-pound tax on indentured laborers in Natal was abolished and arrears were canceled; and (3) the indenturing of Indians from India was to cease by 1920. Indians still could not move from one province to another, but Indians born in South Africa could enter the Cape Colony. Thus, although the agreement involved a compromise, Gandhi saw it as a victory for the satyagraha movement.[27] He regarded it as the "Magna Carta" of South African Indians because it removed the racial taint and represented a move toward achieving racial equality. Perhaps Gandhi's assessment of its significance is what came to matter most. For Gandhi, the law vindicated the technique of satyagraha. He wrote in the *Indian Opinion,* a paper he had started in South Africa, that satyagraha "is a force which, if it became universal, would revolutionize social ideals and do away with despotisms and the ever-growing militarism under which the nations of the West are groaning and are being almost crushed to death and which fairly promises to overwhelm even the nations of the East."[28]

Many have suggested that Gandhi kept developing and refining the ideas he had formed in South Africa for the rest of his life.[29]

IV

How and why did satyagraha work? Perhaps what an officer under Smuts said in a jocular vein contains the seed of an answer: "I do not like your people, and do not care to assist them at all. But what am I to do? You help us in our days of need. How can we lay hands upon you? I often wish you took to violence like the English strikers, and then we would know at once how to dispose of you. But you will not injure even the enemy. You desire victory by self-suffering alone and never transgress your self-imposed limits of courtesy and chivalry. And that is what reduces us to sheer helplessness."[30]

8

Spiritual Warfare

I

Gandhi left South Africa for good toward the end of 1914, arriving in India with the new year. His political mentor, G. K. Gokhale, had extracted a promise from Gandhi that he travel around India to get acquainted with the country firsthand before embarking on public life there. Gandhi acted on this advice, but as he traveled, he was shadowed by a poor peasant from the district of Champaran in Bihar, who pleaded with Gandhi to pay a visit to his hometown to see for himself the oppressed state of the peasantry. Gandhi finally visited Champaran in 1917 and says that when he met the peasants of Champaran, he felt that he was standing face to face with God, ahimsa, and truth. The visit resulted in Gandhi's first satyagraha against the British in India, in which he exposed the exploitation of the peasants by the British planters and secured redress against it.[1]

At this point Gandhi still had faith in the British Raj.

Gandhi's attitude toward British rule over India changed with the passage of time, however. He had promoted recruitment in the British army during the First World War on the ground that if India benefited from the British connection, it must contribute its fair share to the war effort. The massacre, by the British army, of unarmed civilians in 1919, in Amritsar, Punjab, shook his confidence in the British. Nevertheless, although Gandhi continued to nonviolently protest against the actions of the British government in India, he did not call for complete independence from the British until January 26, 1930, when he demanded Purna Swaraj: complete independence.[2] *Swaraj* had earlier meant self-rule within the British Empire. Gandhi had finally stopped trembling before the precious mystery of the British Raj.

How was he going to achieve complete independence? He had sought to achieve self-rule within a year in the 1920s, but it had not materialized. A decade later he upped the ante.

When Rabindranath Tagore, the other great Indian of his time, visited him at his Sabarmati Ashram in Ahmedabad on January 18, several days before his call for Purna Swaraj, and asked him what he had in mind for the country that year, Gandhi replied that he was furiously thinking night and day but did not see any ray of light coming out of the surrounding darkness. Gandhi was planning to achieve complete independence by waging a war against the British Raj, and he planned on winning it—without conventional weapons.[3] How was Gandhi going to start such a war? How was he going to fire the first salvo?

Gandhi was given to hearing his inner voice on such occasions, and it had spoken. The war would be waged by marching to the seashore, to a place called Dandi, and making salt. The act would break the Salt Law, according to which all salt was subject to tax and could not be obtained freely. Gandhi wanted it for free. He had not used salt in six years, but the salt tax had now become a metonym for exploitive British rule over India. Every human being needs salt, and the British were monopolistically profiting from it. Incredible as it sounds, Gandhi proposed to "overthrow the Empire with a pinch of salt."[4]

Salt was to be the gunpowder with which he would blow up the Raj.

II

Gandhi set out from his Sabarmati Ashram on the morning of March 12, accompanied by male and female inmates of the ashram: seventy-nine volunteers. The police had been notified of their names in advance, in keeping with Gandhi's code of spiritual warfare. The procession extended for nearly two miles by the time Gandhi left Ahmedabad.

The core group kept walking—and walking. It walked two hundred miles in twenty-four days. When Gandhi arrived at Dandi on April 5, his small ashram band had grown into a nonviolent army several thousand strong. The attention of the entire nation, from pauper to prince, was riveted on him. Some of his contemporaries deemed his trek comparable to Napoleon's march to Paris on his return from Elba.[5]

The first night was spent in prayer. The next day Gandhi walked to the beach early in the morning accompanied by his followers and picked up some salt left by the waves. The poet Sarojini Naidu, who was standing by his side, proclaimed oracularly: "Hail, Deliverer." The same day he also issued an appeal to the world: "I want world sympathy in the battle of Right against Might."[6]

Spiritual Warfare

Gandhi withdrew from the scene after performing his gesture of defiance. But his gesture proved to be the proverbial spark that ignited a raging fire. This nonviolent war had an effect even on regular troops. A few days later, Peshawar fell into the hands of the so-called Red Shirts, the Pathan followers of the Gandhian noncooperation movement led by Khan Abdul Ghaffar Khan, who had earned the sobriquet "Frontier Gandhi." When two platoons of the second battalion of the 18th Royal Garhwali Rifles were sent to establish order three days later, they refused to fire on the protesting crowd of Muslims and broke rank, although all the soldiers involved were Hindus. The city was in the hands of Khan and his Red Shirts from April 24 to May 4. It was retaken with the help of Gurkhas—soldiers from Nepal—but the British realized that the Indian military could no longer be depended on to do their bidding.[7] British rule over India depended on the military. The British had to win every time from now on to keep India in subjection; the Indians had to win only once to be free.

On May 4, Gandhi was arrested at a village near Dandi, called Karadi. As he was about to be led off, Gandhi remembered that he had begun the salt march with a Vaishnava hymn to Rama, the incarnation of Vishnu, who assumed the guise of a young hero when he descended on earth. There was time for a short prayer, and so he and his companions intoned the hymn to the divine hero:

Oh Rama! Lord of the dynasty of Raghus!
Thou, an ideal king, an ideal husband of the ideal
    wife Sita,
Thou art verily the Redeemer of the fallen and the
    sinful.[8]

With Gandhi incarcerated, the command of the spiritual war was assumed by Sarojini Naidu, under whose leadership twenty-five hundred volunteers planned to nonviolently seize the saltworks at Dharasana, 150 miles north of Bombay. The actual confrontation took place on May 21. We have two accounts from the same eyewitness—the American correspondent Webb Miller. One is the press dispatch sent right after the event; the second constitutes part of his autobiography, written half a dozen years later. Both are worth sharing given the rarity of an eyewitness account of how a nonviolent battle, waged as part of spiritual warfare, actually unfolds.

This is the account Webb Miller transmitted over the wires right after the event.

> Mme. Naidu called for prayer before the march started and the entire assemblage knelt. She exhorted them: "Gandhi's body is in jail but his soul is with you. India's prestige is in your hands, you must not use any violence under any circumstances. You will be beaten but you must not resist; you must not even raise a hand to ward off blows." Wild, shrill cheers terminated her speech.
>
> Slowly and in silence the throng commenced the half-mile march to salt-deposits. A few carried ropes for lassoing the barbed-wire stockade around the salt pans. About a score who were assigned to act as stretcher-bearers wore crude, hand-painted red crosses pinned to their breasts, their stretchers consisted of blankets. Manilal Gandhi, second son of Gandhi, walked among the foremost of the marchers. As the throng drew near the salt pans they commenced chanting the revolutionary slogan, *Inqilab Zindabad* [Long live the revolution!], intoning the two words over and over.
>
> The salt-deposits were surrounded by ditches filled with water and guarded by four hundred native Surat Police in Khaki shorts and brown turbans. Half a dozen British officials commanded them. The Police carried

lathis—five foot clubs tipped with steel. Inside the stockade twenty-five native rifle-men were drawn up.

In complete silence the Gandhi men drew up and halted a hundred yards from the stockade. A picked column advanced from the crowd, waded the ditches, and approached the barbed-wire stockade, which the Surat Police surrounded, holding clubs, at the ready. Police officials ordered the marchers to disperse under a recently imposed regulation which prohibited gathering of more than five persons in any one place. The column silently ignored the warning and slowly walked forward. I stayed with the main body about a hundred yards from the stockade.

Suddenly, at a word of command, scores of native police rushed upon the advancing marchers and rained blows on their heads with their steel-shod *lathis*. Not one of the marchers even raised an arm to fend off the blows. They went down like ten-pins. From where I stood I heard the sickening whacks of the clubs on unprotected skulls. The waiting crowd of watchers groaned and sucked in their breaths in sympathetic pain at every blow.

Those struck down fell sprawling, unconscious or writhing in pain with fractured skulls or broken shoulders. In two or three minutes the ground was quilted with bodies. Great patches of blood widened on their white clothes. The survivors, without breaking ranks, silently and doggedly marched on until struck down. When everyone of the first column had been knocked down, stretcher-bearers rushed up unmolested by the Police and carried off the injured to a thatched hut which had been arranged as a temporary hospital.

Then another column formed while the leaders pleaded with them to retain their self-control. They marched slowly towards the police. Although everyone knew that within a few minutes he would be beaten down, perhaps killed, I could detect no signs of wavering or fear. They marched steadily with heads up, without the encouragement of music or cheering or any possibility that they might escape serious injury or death. The police rushed out and methodically and mechanically beat down the second column. There was no fight, no struggle; the marchers simply walked forward until struck down. There were no outcries, only groans after they fell. There were not enough stretcher-bearers to carry off the wounded; I saw eighteen injured being carried off simultaneously, while forty-two still lay bleeding on the ground awaiting stretcher-bearers. The blankets used as stretchers were sodden with blood.[9]

And this is what Webb Miller wrote in his autobiographical account published in 1936. It begins with an introductory note:

Just before Gandhi's arrest on May 5, 1930, at Karadi, near Dandi, he announced his intention of raiding the Dharasana Salt Works about 150 miles north of Bombay. With Gandhi in jail, Mrs. Sarojini Naidu—close associate of Gandhi and Indian poetess—assumed the leadership and went to the site with 2,500 volunteers. Webb Miller, well-known foreign correspondent for the United Press, heard about this projected salt raid on May 21, and wrote the following eye-witness account.[10]

Here is the account found in its later version.

After witnessing two serious riots at the Wadala salt pans in the suburbs of Bombay, I received on the eve-

Spiritual Warfare

ning of May 20, 1930, an important tip from a friendly Gandhian sympathizer. He told me they were planning the biggest demonstration yet at Dharasana, about a hundred and fifty miles north of Bombay.

"Sarojini Naidu, the famous Indian poetess, is leading a non-violent demonstration against the big salt pans near Dharasana. The nearest railway station is Dungri. It is an isolated spot and you will have to take your own food and water. You'd better telegraph Mme. Naidu to provide transportation from Dungri, otherwise you will have to walk many miles. Be sure to take an adequate supply of bottled water, because the water from native sources is unhealthy for white men."

... Dungri consisted of a little huddle of native huts on the dusty plain. There were no means of transportation because Mme. Naidu had not received my telegram. I could find nobody who spoke English. By repeatedly pronouncing the word "Dharasana" and pointing questioningly to the horizon, I got directions and set off across country on foot through cactus hedges, millet fields, and inch-deep dust, inquiring my way by signs.

After plodding about six miles across country lugging a pack of sandwiches and two quart bottles of water under a sun which was already blazing hot, inquiring from every native I met, I reached the assembling place of the Gandhi followers. Several long, open, thatched sheds were surrounded by high cactus thickets. The sheds were literally swarming and buzzed like a beehive with some 2,500 Congress or Gandhi men dressed in the regulation uniform of rough homespun cotton *dhotis* and triangular Gandhi caps, somewhat like American overseas soldiers' hats. They chattered excitedly and when I arrived hundreds surrounded me, with evidences of hostility at first. After they learned my identity, I was warmly welcomed by young college-educated, English-speaking men and escorted to Mme. Naidu. The famous Indian poetess, stocky, swarthy, strong-featured, barelegged, dressed in rough, dark homespun robe and sandals, welcomed me. She explained that she was busy marshaling her forces for the demonstration against the salt pans and would talk with me more at length later. She was educated in England and spoke English fluently.

After reproducing the press dispatch in his autobiography, Webb continues.

At times the spectacle of unresisting men being methodically bashed into a bloody pulp sickened me so much that I had to turn away. The western mind finds it difficult to grasp the idea of nonresistance. I felt an indefinable sense of helpless rage and loathing, almost as much against the men who were submitting unresistingly to being beaten as against the police wielding the clubs, and this despite the fact that when I came to India I sympathized with the Gandhi cause.

Several times the leaders nearly lost control of the waiting crowd. They rushed up and down, frantically pleading with and exhorting the intensely excited men to remember Gandhi's instructions. It seemed that the unarmed throng was on the verge of launching a mass attack upon the police. The British official in charge, Superintendent Robinson of Surat, sensed the imminence of an outbreak and posted his twenty-five riflemen on a little knoll ready to fire. He came to me, inquired my identity, and said: "You'd better move aside out of the line of shooting. We may be forced to open fire into the crowd." While we were talking one of the

Gandhiites, a young university student, ran up to Robinson, his face contorted by rage, tore open his cotton smock, exposing his bare breast and shrieked: "Shoot me, shoot me! Kill me, it's for my country!" The leaders managed to calm the crowd.

The Gandhi men altered their tactics, marched up in groups of twenty-five and sat on the ground near the salt pans, making no effort to draw nearer. Led by a coffee-colored Parsi sergeant of police named Antia, a hulking, ugly-looking fellow, detachments of police approached one seated group and called upon them to disperse under the non-assemblage ordinance. The Gandhi followers ignored them and refused even to glance up at the *lathis* brandished threateningly above their heads. Upon a word from Antia the beating recommenced coldly, without anger. Bodies toppled over in threes and fours, bleeding from great gashes on their scalps. Group after group walked forward, sat down, and submitted to being beaten into insensibility without raising an arm to fend off the blows.

Finally the police became enraged by the non-resistance, sharing, I suppose, the helpless rage I had already felt at the demonstrators not fighting back. They commenced savagely kicking the seated men in the abdomen and testicles. The injured men writhed and squealed in agony, which seemed to inflame the fury of the police, and the crowd again almost broke away from their leaders. The police then began dragging the sitting men by the arms or feet, sometimes for a hundred yards, and throwing them into ditches. One was dragged to the ditch where I stood; the splash of his body doused me with muddy water. Another policeman dragged a Gandhi man to the ditch, threw him in, then belabored him over the head with his *lathi*. Hour after hour stretcher-bearers carried back a stream of inert, bleeding bodies.

I went to see Mme. Naidu, who was directing the subleaders in keeping the crowds from charging the police. While we were talking one of the British officials approached her, touched her on the arm, and said: "Sarojini Naidu, you are under arrest." She haughtily shook off his hand and said: "I'll come, but don't touch me." The crowd cheered frantically as she strode with the British officer across the open space to the barbed-wire stockade, where she was interned. Later she was sentenced to prison. Manilal Gandhi was also arrested.

In the middle of the morning V. J. Patel arrived. He had been leading the Swaraj movement since Gandhi's arrest, and had just resigned as President of the Indian Legislative Assembly in protest against the British. Scores surrounded him, knelt, and kissed his feet. He was a venerable gentleman of about sixty with white flowing beard and mustache, dressed in the usual un-dyed, coarse homespun smock. Sitting on the ground under a mango tree, Patel said: "All hope of reconciling India with the British Empire is lost forever. I can understand any government's taking people into custody and punishing them for breaches of law, but I cannot understand how any government that calls itself civilized could deal as savagely and brutally with non-violent, unresisting men as the British have this morning."

By eleven the heat reached 116 in the shade and activities of the Gandhi volunteers subsided. I went back to the temporary hospital to examine the wounded. They lay in rows on the bare ground in the shade of an open, palm-thatched shed. I counted 320 injured,

many still insensible with fractured skulls, others writhing in agony from kicks in the testicles and stomach.
The Gandhi men had been able to gather only a few
native doctors, who were doing the best they could
with inadequate facilities. Scores of the injured had
received no treatment for hours and two had died. The
demonstration was finished for the day on account of
the heat.[11]

III

Gandhi had devised a new form of warfare. It was not unique
in that no killing was involved, for some of the protesters, the
soldiers in his army, were killed. It was unique in that his
soldiers would not kill; his soldiers would die, but they would
not kill.

9

Touching the
Untouchable

I

The success of the salt march led to negotiations between Gandhi and the viceroy of India. This prospect filled Winston Churchill with disgust. He could not bear the "nauseating and humiliating spectacle of this one-time Inner Temple lawyer, now seditious fakir, striding half-naked up the steps of the Viceroy's palace, there to negotiate and parley on equal terms with the representative of the King-Emperor."[1] The negotiations went ahead nevertheless and ultimately led to a Round Table Conference to discuss India's political future, held in London in 1931. Upon arriving in London, Gandhi was asked by a reporter what he thought of Western civilization. "I think it would be a good idea," he famously replied.[2]

Gandhi's wit and charm was on display throughout the visit, but the visit itself proved fruitless in advancing the cause of Indian independence.

In hopes of making some gains, Gandhi revived the civil disobedience campaign in January 1932. The British response was to offer limited self-government through elections at the provincial level, but in a way, Gandhi thought, that was calculated to divide Hindu society and weaken the nationalist challenge. The British proposed a separate electorate for the Depressed Classes (a politically correct euphemism for people otherwise considered untouchables). A separate electorate meant that a certain number of seats would be set aside for the untouchables in the provincial legislatures, to be filled through votes cast only by the untouchables.[3] This move was welcomed by their leader, Dr. B. R. Ambedkar, who had also attended the Round Table Conference.

Gandhi, too, sought the well-being of the untouchables, but through moral transformation rather than electoral isolation. The two approaches to the problem of untouchability were now at odds, and Gandhi decided to stake his life on a spiritual rather than a purely political solution by undertaking a fast to death against the separate electorate and the division of Hindu society.

II

To understand the depth of Gandhi's feeling in the matter, we need to recognize the nature of his opposition to untouchability and his approach to its solution. Unlike many outsiders, and some insiders, who might think that untouchability is integral or intrinsic to Hinduism, Gandhi considered it an excrescence. His opposition to it was rooted in morality and spirituality. An incident that occurred when he was twelve and in his second year at high school is revealing. His family had employed a scavenger—an untouchable—named Uka to clean the latrines. Gandhi became friendly with him. When Gandhi was asked to purify himself ritually whenever he touched Uka physically, he protested to his parents that this was wrong. Uka, he said, was a human being like any other. We need to bear in mind Gandhi's devotion to his parents to grasp the full weight of his protest. Gandhi's loving mother provided a uniquely maternal solution to the dilemma. All he needed to do was to touch his Muslim friend to get rid of the pollution, for Muslims were not subject to the taboos of the Hindu religion.[4]

Gandhi's sensitivity about untouchables is also revealed by a notorious incident in later life, when he was living in Durban. The clerks in Gandhi's office stayed with him in a house where chamber pots were used to deal with human waste. The clerks, who had virtually become members of his household, cleaned their own chamber pots, but Gandhi's family attended to the matter in the earlier days of their stay. Gandhi's wife did not quite like this but acquiesced in it. Then a Christian clerk joined Gandhi's office, whose parents had been untouchables. To clean the chamber pot of an untouchable proved too much for her, and she chided her husband, even as she complied with his request, to the point of breaking into tears. This upset Gandhi no end. He not only wanted her to carry the pot but wanted her to carry it cheerfully. They had an altercation. Gandhi lost his temper and dragged her to the door to throw her out of the house, whereupon she rebuked him for exploiting her helplessness in a foreign land and asked him to stop making a scene.[5]

Gandhi's opposition to untouchability was not the product of Western education. His uncompromising views in the matter were already in place in early life and were confirmed by his study of Hindu scriptures. The untouchables are sometimes described as a fifth *varna* (class), but the Hindu scriptures mention only four varnas as constitutive of society. The Bhagavad Gita places the Brahmin and the *bhangi* (scavenger) on a par. Gandhi found himself at a loss to understand how Hindus could countenance the practice of untouchability in the face of such textual evidence.[6]

Gandhi believed in removing the practice by personal example and moral suasion. He writes that even when he was "wavering between Christianity and Hinduism," "even then I believed that untouchability was no part of Hinduism; and that, if it was, such Hinduism was not for me." While he admitted that "Hinduism does not regard untouchability as a sin," he believed that "Hinduism has sinned in giving sanction to untouchability."[7] He even declared at the Round Table Conference: "I would far rather that Hinduism died than that untouchability lived."[8]

How Gandhi's preferred method of persuasion worked out in real life is evident in the course of the conversation the author Ved Mehta had with a Gandhian disciple named G. Ramachandran:

> "I was a young fellow of seventeen," he [Ramachandran] says. "The princely state of Travancore, where I was living, was convulsed by revolutionary activity. It was the early twenties, when Bapu [Gandhi] and his Constructive Workers were lighting fires everywhere, and in Travancore the lowly, downtrodden untouchables suddenly started walking on roads that for centuries had been reserved for high-caste Hindus. The Maharaja arrested hundreds of them. Bapu arrived, and the untouchables organized a rally to hear him speak. My parents wouldn't give me permission to attend it, but I slipped out of the house without their knowledge and got my first look at Bapu from a distance through a tremendous crowd. That was enough."

"What impressed you so much?"

"The crowd was chanting '*Mahatma Gandhi ki jai!*' but as soon as Bapu raised one finger they fell silent. He could control vast crowds, sometimes numbering millions, just by raising his finger. The magic of the man's finger was what affected me."

Ramachandran, who has small, nervous hands with thin fingers, raises his right hand and holds up his forefinger. "The crowd expected Bapu to attack the Maharaja, but practically the first thing he said was, 'I've come here on pilgrimage to help the Harijans [untouchables] gain their self-respect, but I've also come here to pay my respects to your great Maharaja.' You could see that the people were stunned and were beginning to turn hostile. They would have stoned him, but Bapu was able to control them with his magic finger. Within a few days of the rally, Bapu had persuaded the Maharaja to allow the untouchables to walk on the roads. That's my favorite fable for our times. But no one listens to me."[9]

Gandhi was leading a comprehensive campaign to eradicate untouchability. He campaigned for temples to be opened to Harijans, the name by which they preferred to be called.[10] Sometimes caste Hindus would protest his actions, even going on hunger strikes or engaging in a satyagraha against him. In one case, in later life, he had to face a satyagraha at the hands of the Harijans themselves.[11]

III

The events of 1932 brought the two approaches, spiritual-moral and legislative-electoral, to a head, because Gandhi saw the latter as an attempt to undo the former. The British had already driven a wedge between the Hindus and the Muslims through the device of separate electorates. Now Gandhi saw the separate electorate proposal as a "sinister British plot" to divide the Hindus the same way. To protest against what was known as the Communal Award, he now prepared to undertake a fast to death in his prison cell—his ninth fast.[12] When the British prime minister, Ramsay MacDonald, failed to understand the reason for fasting over an award whose goal was "solely to prevent the depressed classes, who admittedly suffer from terrible disabilities today, from being able to secure a limited number of representatives of their own choosing," Gandhi answered that he did not expect the British prime minister to be well informed in this respect and that what was at stake was the Hindu religion.[13]

Many Indians were mystified by the fast as well, including Pandit Nehru. He had little use for what he called Gandhi's "religious and sentimental approach to a political issue" and lamented Gandhi's having chosen a "side issue for his final sacrifice." But Nehru changed his opinion after a while, recalling Gandhi's knack for doing things at the psychological moment.[14]

As the news of Gandhi's fast spread through the country and people began to realize that he might die, the nation's conscience was stirred. People were not concerned about the technical legislative details; they felt that Gandhi's life was at risk because they had not treated the untouchables properly, and they began to make amends. Special feasts were organized at which caste Hindus broke bread with the untouchables. Nehru's own orthodox mother accepted food at the hands of an untouchable. More and more temples opened their doors to them. The word "miracle" is often used to describe the effect his fast had, which took everyone by surprise.[15]

People do not resist change so much as they resist being changed.

IV

In the meantime, untouchable leaders had been pressing Dr. Ambedkar to relent on the matter of a separate electorate, arguing that if Gandhi died and the untouchables were blamed for his death, it would prove disastrous for the untouchable cause. Ambedkar was persuaded to negotiate but declared: "I want my compensation."[16] It came in the form of increased seats in the legislature for the untouchables in exchange for not insisting on a separate electorate. The agreement is known as the Yervada Pact, after the name of the jail where Gandhi was incarcerated.

It took almost five days for the arrangements to be finalized, and Gandhi's health was sinking. Nor would Gandhi break his fast unless the British accepted this arrangement in lieu of the Communal Award. The text of the agreement between him and Ambedkar was telegraphed to London, the British prime minister was summoned from a party to go over it, and the British government accepted it, all within a few hours.

Kasturbai then handed Gandhi a glass of orange juice.

The Nobel Laureate Rabindranath Tagore was the one prominent Indian who had immediately grasped the revolutionary potential and significance of Gandhi's fast, both of which eluded not only Pandit Nehru but other politicians until they saw its results. Tagore traveled all the way from Calcutta to be with Gandhi and led the attendant group in prayer when Gandhi broke his fast. The verses he read then were from his book of poems, *Gitanjali,* which had won him the Nobel Prize:

When my heart is dry and parched, come with a
    merciful shower,
When grace has departed from life, come with a
    burst of song.[17]

Tagore had observed the puzzlement of the British at the
step Gandhi had felt compelled to take, and he explained it to
them in their own language by reminding them of their own
history: they had been prepared to perpetrate a bloodbath in
Ireland to prevent the dismemberment of the empire. He
asked: "Gandhi was immolating one person, himself, to prevent dismemberment of Indian society. This was the language
of non-violence. Is that why the West could not decipher it?"[18]

V

Discrimination against the former untouchables has not entirely ceased in modern India, so some might wonder whether
Gandhi was really successful in his campaign. He staked his
life for the abolition of untouchability, after all. Although ves-
tiges of the system remain to be rooted out, what Gandhi did
was to morally delegitimize the system. He tipped the scales
in favor of abolition decisively, and it no longer enjoys the
social and moral sanction it once had.

····

10

····

Fighting Fire
with Light

I

In 1934, Gandhi left the Indian National Congress. He had led it since the 1920s and was its sole spokesman at the Round Table Conference with the British in 1931. He had contested the Communal Award in 1932 at risk to his life. But he had come to the realization that the congress had adopted his policy of nonviolence out of expediency rather than conviction. He remained available for consultation, but his lack of formal connection with the congress meant that it could go its own way.

Still, the congress remained faithful to Gandhi's principles, by and large, even after he had formally left it. It participated in the 1937 elections under the Government of India Act, won handsomely, and went on to form ministries in eight provinces of British India by 1938. Then, in 1939, when the Second World War broke out, Viceroy Linlithgow declared that India was at war with Germany, without bothering to consult the congress.[1] Congress ministers resigned from office soon thereafter in protest.

As the war progressed, international affairs overshadowed national affairs. By 1942, Germany was planning to invade Britain, and Japan seemed poised to invade India. At this moment, Gandhi announced the Quit India movement. The British were asked to leave India "to God, or in modern parlance, to anarchy." The movement temporarily resulted in the largest civilian uprising in India since the Mutiny, or Great Rebellion, of 1857, but the uprising was suppressed as ruthlessly. Gandhi declined to accept responsibility for the violence that accompanied the uprising, but the British government was not convinced: it remembered that Gandhi had called for open rebellion. Now, however, the British focused on winning the war. India and its discontents would have to wait until the war was over.[2]

When the Allies won the war in 1945, the fate of India remained to be decided. For reasons still debated by historians, the Labour Party, which came to power in Britain after the war, resolved to "quit" India by April 1948 at the latest. There was a complication, however. The Muslim League, led by Muhammad Ali Jinnah, had, beginning in 1937, gained steady support for his plan for the formation of an independent country called Pakistan, a homeland for the Muslims of India, in the event of a British pullout. The league was now checkmating all efforts to work out a compromise short of that goal.

It achieved its goal in the Mountbatten Plan, proposed by Lord Mountbatten in the summer of 1947. With this plan the

British proposed the partition of India into two dominions along religious lines, but included a provision for the partition of the provinces of Punjab and Bengal along religious lines as well. The actual line of demarcation of these provinces was, however, made public only *after* the two dominions had come into being in the middle of August. Gandhi did not participate in the celebrations. Lord Mountbatten noticed his absence on the morning of August 15, when he described him as the architect of India's independence, and added: "We must miss his presence here today."[3] The uncertainty regarding the line of demarcation dividing the provinces of Punjab and Bengal had led to a feeling of acute insecurity among the religious communities in the areas where they were in a minority, and large numbers of people began migrating to areas where they would feel safe with the majority. Since Hindus were in a minority in Pakistan, and Muslims in India, this led to a two-way mass exodus. Both Punjab and Bengal were set to explode.

Gandhi spent the rest of his life trying to repair the damage caused by the partition of India to its political and social fabric.

II

Bengal was the scene of some of the worst communal rioting in August 1946, when the Muslim League launched its Direct Action. Gandhi was near Calcutta, in western Bengal, and when the first signs of trouble appeared, he went on a fast to maintain communal peace in Calcutta and, by extension, Bengal. Gandhi began his fast on September 1, 1947. A year earlier the city had witnessed a devastating Hindu-Muslim riot, and there were some initial disturbances in 1947, but by September 4 the situation had quieted down; there had been no disturbances for the past twenty-four hours. Such a desire to maintain peace took hold that five hundred policemen, including British police officers, went on a twenty-four hour fast in sympathy for the cause. The representatives of the various communities and urban organizations also pledged themselves to peace, but Gandhi wanted a promise in writing. They went into conclave and finally signed a pledge whose breach would result in an irrevocable fast unto death by Gandhi. On September 4, at 9:15 p.m., Suhrawardy, who was widely suspected of having instigated the riots the year before but who had now allied himself with Gandhi, handed a glass of sweet lime juice to Gandhi to signal the end of the fast, kneeling and weeping as he did so.

Bengal remained true to the pledge thereafter. No rioting took place there.[4]

Gandhi had put out one fire, but smoke was now rising in Delhi. A convoy fifty-seven miles long, one of several convoys of Hindus and Sikhs, was moving into India from Punjab. Hindus and Sikhs fleeing Western Punjab were seeking shelter in Delhi, and feelings were running high.

Gandhi arrived in Delhi from Calcutta only to find a city ready to erupt. So Gandhi began another fast, on January 13, 1948, this time for the sake of peace among the various religious communities in Delhi, as well as in order to press the Indian government to pay what it owed Pakistan after the division of assets between the two new nations. On January 17, he broke the fast after all the religious communities pledged to maintain the peace. At 12:25 p.m., Maulana Azad, a Muslim leader in the congress, handed Gandhi a glass of orange juice.[5]

By now, India was at war with Pakistan over Kashmir. Payment of assets was a very sensitive issue, for the funds could be used to finance hostilities against India. But as we saw earlier, Gandhi insisted that all promises, including this one, be kept. The famous nonagenarian Indian journalist Khuswant Singh was an eyewitness to the events surrounding Gandhi's

Delhi fast. What is impersonal history for us was still personal memory for him when he recalled that time in an interview years later: Gandhi "insisted that the Indian government pay the Pakistanis what it had agreed to do. Mobs of Sikhs and Hindu refugees stood at the gates outside baying for his blood. This did not bother him; the police had to guard him from the mob. On the third or the fourth day he started sinking. The same people then prayed for his life! How could you ever forget that? (*His voice breaks with emotion.*) At no stage did the man give a damn about his life. He staked it if he felt his call was just. I don't think the world has seen another person like that. We know nothing about our prophets: their lives are encrusted with myths and legends. But here was a man you saw doing what he preached."[6]

Although Gandhi was still widely revered, there were eddies of opposition. On the one hand, many Muslims were unhappy on account of his opposition to the formation of Pakistan; on the other, some Hindus and Sikhs felt that he had gone too far in insisting on the release of funds to Pakistan.

The day he began the fast for communal peace and the release of funds to Pakistan a radical Hindu set in motion a plot to assassinate him. Gandhi was aware of the danger to his life but declined all protection.

On January 29, 1948, he told his grandniece, Manubehn, around 10 p.m. as she was massaging his head with oil: "If I were to die of a lingering disease, or even from a pimple, then you must shout from the housetops to the whole world that I was a false Mahatma. Then my soul, wherever it might be, will rest in peace. If I die of an illness, you must declare me to be a false or hypocritical Mahatma, even at the risk of people cursing you. And if an explosion takes place, as it did last week, or if someone shot at me and I received his bullet in my bare chest without a sigh and with Rama's name on my lips, only then should you say that I was a true Mahatma."[7]

Fighting Fire with Light

According to the Hindu devotional tradition, uttering the name of God at the time of death is an infallible proof of sainthood.

The next day, at around 5:15 p.m., Gandhi lay dead, shot to death on his way to a prayer meeting, struck down by bullets to his bare chest, with the name of Rama on his lips.

III

This is how it happened. Gandhi was staying at the Birla House in Delhi (which has since been turned into a Gandhi museum). He came out for a prayer meeting, which was being held in the adjoining lawn. He was leaning on his granddaughters as he made his way through the crowd to the rostrum, when one Nathuram Godse elbowed his way through the crowd and came forward. One of the granddaughters, under the impression that he was going to touch Gandhi's feet, which would only further delay Gandhi, who was already arriving late, tried to hold him back, but he brushed her aside. Godse folded his hands before Gandhi, bowing as he did so, then fired three shots point-blank at Gandhi. The bullets found their mark on and below Gandhi's chest on the right side of the body. Gandhi faltered and fell, uttering the name of Rama.[8] Death came instantly.

The subcontinent was shocked into sanity. If the plot had succeeded, so had Gandhi. There was no communal rioting in either India or Pakistan for more than a decade after Gandhi's death.

part two

11

Mahatma Gandhi
and Ramana Maharshi

I

Hagiography in India has created a parallel universe of sorts, in which the political independence of India is seen as the result of an almost saintly conspiracy. Even the worldly Pandit Nehru has been projected as an ascetic who reincarnated himself as a favor to his father. It is claimed that Aurobindo, the fiery, almost violent nationalist, went into self-imposed exile in Pondicherry (then a French enclave) because he was divinely instructed that the person who would lead India to independence had already been selected and that his methods would be very different from Aurobindo's—a futuristic reference to the Gandhian nonviolent campaign against British rule over India. In this type of thinking, there is even the determined suggestion that the independence movement was partly a product of the presence of Ramana Maharshi at Arunachalam, in Tamil Nadu.[1]

That some people tried to mobilize spiritual resources to secure India's independence is not in doubt. T. Ganapati Sastri and T. K. Sundaresa Iyer set up Mahendra societies all over India, with a total of ten thousand members. The object of these societies was to win freedom for the country by devotional means: rituals, prayers, and penance.[2] The life, and lifestyle, of Mahatma Gandhi himself lends credence to this view. However, the preferred explanation for Gandhi's putative saintly influence has been cultural rather than spiritual. It has thus been argued that Gandhi was able to mobilize Indians in such a massive way because of his appeal as a holy person, to whose influence the Hindu psyche, or even the Indian psyche, may be particularly receptive.[3]

A historical biographer may understand Gandhi's appeal in terms of India's cultural ethos, which glorifies saintly life. But from a purely spiritual angle, the issue assumes a different shape. In the sober world of academia, it is human beings who supposedly have spiritual experiences. Looked at through the reversed telescope of a perspective that privileges the spiritual realm, human beings are spiritual beings having human experiences. This idea that people may be precipitates from another realm rather than projecting themselves toward it is a highly unusual way of viewing human life and spirituality but one that provides a fresh perspective on the life of Mahatma Gandhi.

II

When Gandhi was congratulated for acting on India's behalf, he declined credit, insisting that he was merely seeking his own salvation, or moksha. In this context, his relationship with Ramana Maharshi (1879–1950) is particularly intriguing, perhaps, ironically, because the two never actually met each other. Observers of the Indian scene have nonetheless been known to bracket them together. Sarojini Naidu, the freedom fighter and poet known as the nightingale of India, wrote: "We have two *Mahatmas* in India today. One is Ramana Maharshi, who gives us peace. The other is Mahatma Gandhi, who will not let us rest one moment in peace. But each does what he is doing with the same end in view, namely, the spiritual regeneration of India."[4]

This apparent inactivity of Ramana Maharshi and the apparent activity of Gandhi may seem contradictory at first, but the situation may have to be reassessed after taking the following incident, related about Ramana Maharshi, into account. An eighteen-inch-high Gandhi statue adorned a cupboard in a corner of Ramana Maharshi's ashram hall. One day a devotee told him that he was puzzled as to who should be his role model, the ever-active Gandhi or Maharshi Ramana, who just sits quietly. Ramana Maharshi turned to him, smiling broadly, and asked him, "Who told you that I am sitting quietly?" When the devotee appealed to the truth of what he saw with his own eyes, Ramana Maharshi asked: "Why do you think that what you are seeing with physical eyes is the truth?" When the devotee persisted with his inquiry, Ramana Maharshi asked him how he spent his time. Upon being told that the devotee was engaged in slum settlement, the uplift of untouchables (Harijans), and prohibition, Ramana Maharshi advised him to continue his work in the manner that Mahatma Gandhi recommended it should be performed— with devotion and detachment—for Gandhi had no interest in Indian independence if it were to be achieved by unspiritual or immoral means.[5]

Although Mahatma Gandhi never met Ramana Maharshi in person, some of his followers did, and this way Gandhi and Ramana did interact, though at one remove. What is remarkable about even such an interaction is that the basis of their interaction was spiritual; the issue of India's independence remained marginal. This comes out very clearly in a few contexts. One of them is provided by the meeting of two prominent followers of Gandhi with Ramana Maharshi on August 14, 1938, at his ashram in Tiruvannamalai, in Tamil Nadu. One of them was Dr. Rajendra Prasad, who went on to become the president of India. He was accompanied by Jamnalal Bajaj, a major supporter of the congress. The issue of Indian independence, or Swaraj, was touched upon toward the end of their meeting. The conversation then proceeded as follows. It is cited to indicate how Ramana Maharshi interacted with his interlocutors.

> D. [= Devotee]: Is the desire for *swaraj* [independence] right?

> M. [= Maharshi]: Such desire no doubt begins with self-interest. Yet practical work for the goal gradually widens the outlook so that the individual becomes merged in the country. Such merging of the individuality is desirable and the related *karma* is *nishkama* (unselfish).

> D.: If *swaraj* is gained after a long struggle and terrible sacrifices, is not the person justified in being pleased with the result and elated by it?

> M.: He must have in the course of his work surrendered himself to the Higher Power whose Might must be kept in mind and never lost sight of. How then can he be elated? He should not even care for the result of his actions. Then alone the *karma* becomes unselfish.

D.: How can unerring rectitude be ensured for the worker?

M.: If he has surrendered himself to God or to Guru, the Power to which he had surrendered will take him on the right course. The worker need no longer concern himself about the rectitude or otherwise of the course. The doubt will arise only if he fails to obey the Master in all details.

D.: Is there not any Power on earth which can bestow Grace on Its devotees so that they may grow strong to work for the country and gain *swaraj?* (Sri Maharshi remained silent. This, He later said, signified that such was the case.)

D.: Is not the *tapasya* [spiritual striving] of the ancient *mahatmas* of the land available for the benefit of its present-day inheritors?

M.: It is, but the fact must not be overlooked that no one can claim to be the sole beneficiary. The benefits are shared by all alike. (After a pause) Is it without such saving Grace that the present awakening has come into being? (Here Sri Bhagavan [the Maharshi] said that before His arrival in Tiruvannamalai in 1896, there was not any clear political thought in India. Only Dadabhai Nauroji had become an M.P. [member of Parliament]).

After a short pause, J.B. [Jamnalal Bajaj] said: Sri Rajendra Prasad is such a noble and selfless worker for the country that he has sacrificed a very lucrative career for this work. The country needs him. And yet he is not in good health, and is always weak and ailing. Why should there be such cruelty to such a noble son of the country?

(Sri Maharshi simply smiled a benign smile.)[6]

Ramana Maharshi almost downplays the issue of Indian independence and insists on maintaining a spiritual attitude throughout the discussion. This happens again during his discussion with some Congress Party members on September 28, 1938, of which we possess the following record.[7]

The party members handed over several questions to Ramana Maharshi: "1. How long is India destined to suffer bondage?; 2. Have not the sons of India made enough sacrifice for her liberation?; 3. Will India get freedom during Mahatma Gandhi's lifetime?"

The questions were not answered categorically. Sri Bhagavan simply remarked that Gandhi "has surrendered himself to the divine and works accordingly with no self-interest. He does not concern himself with the results but accepts them as they turn up." He added that such must be the attitude of national workers as well. When pressed for specific answers to the three questions, he kept drawing attention to the need for surrender to the divine, pointing out that such questions arise only because one has *not* surrendered to the divine. Questions about when independence might be achieved were glossed over repeatedly. Ramana Maharshi's final comment to the questioners was: "Follow the example of Gandhiji [*ji* is an honorific suffix] in the work of the national cause. 'Surrender' is the word." When, soon after this, some members of the Coorg Congress Committee sent a slip to Ramana Maharshi asking for a message, Ramana Maharshi said that the "same answer holds good here too. The message is contained in the word 'surrender.'"

Another context is provided by remarks published by Gandhi in his journal *Harijan* on March 11, 1939:

How mysterious are the ways of God! This journey to Rajkot is a wonder even to me. Why am I going, whither am I going? I have thought nothing about these things. And if God guides me, what should I think, why should I think? Even thought may be an obstacle in the way of His guidance.

The fact is, it takes no effort to stop thinking. The thoughts do *not* come. Indeed there is no vacuum— but I mean to say that there is no thought about the mission.[8]

Ramana Maharshi referred to these remarks two days later, saying how true they were and emphasizing each statement in the extract.[9]

The discussion spilled over to the next day, when he was asked: "Is not what Gandhiji describes the state in which thoughts themselves become foreign?" He replied in the affirmative, pointing out, "It is only after the rise of the 'I' thought that all other thoughts arise. The world is seen after you have felt 'I am.' The 'I-thought' and all other thoughts had vanished for him."[10]

The context of the interactions between the two was once again spiritual. What Ramana Maharshi and Gandhi specifically meant by having no thoughts may, however, not have been identical.

III

A third context is provided by the death of Mahatma Gandhi, to which Ramana Maharshi reacted poignantly. When Gandhi's favorite hymn, *Vaishnava Jana To*, was broadcast after Gandhi's death, he listened to it enveloped in sadness. When women in the ashram began chanting Gandhi's other favorite hymn, *Raghupati Raghav Raja Ram*, his eyes brimmed with tears. When reporters asked for his reaction to Gandhi's death, he choked up and could not speak. What is even more remarkable, indeed amazing, is that he drew a parallel between Gandhi and the God Gandhi worshiped: Rama. He alluded to an incident in the *Uttara Ramayana*—another version of the Ramayana—according to which Rama forgot to return to heaven after he had accomplished the earthly purpose of his incarnation, namely, the killing of the demon Ravana. So the gods sent one of themselves in the guise of an ascetic to remind him that his work was done and that he should now repair to heaven. Similarly, Ramana said, now that India's independence had been achieved, Gandhi's work was done, and so he had been "sent away."[11]

Despite his sympathy for Gandhi, however, Ramana Maharshi was so severely spiritual that his approach even seemed to sideline the Gandhian reformist agenda.

We know that Gandhi was a great reformer, especially known for his campaign against untouchability. But his efforts apparently made no deep impression on Ramana Maharshi, whose focus remained relentlessly spiritual. When asked "What is your opinion about Gandhiji's Harijan Movement?" Ramana Maharshi replied, "Ask him."[12] Ramana Maharshi refused to be drawn into a discussion of social issues of this kind and, when pressed, would insist on giving a spiritual turn to the discussion.[13] In this respect, we might say that Ramana Maharshi's spirituality differed from that of Gandhi. Although Ramana Maharshi was no less open than Gandhi to untouchables or people belonging to different faiths, his interest was focused elsewhere. Similarly, while Gandhi regarded celibacy as an important item in his spiritual repertoire, Ramana Maharshi, though he did not disapprove of it, rarely advocated it. Ramana and Gandhi converge more on the question of the appropriate diet for the spiritual life than on celibacy.

IV

One more comparison could be drawn, pertaining to the role of vicarious atonement of sins in the spiritualities of Ramana

Maharshi and Mahatma Gandhi. The *followers* of Ramana Maharshi have occasionally argued, on the basis of their interaction with him, that he seemed at times to take on the karmic burden of his disciples. We do not have an instance of Gandhi doing this, or seeming or saying that he was doing this, although we do have evidence of Gandhi doing something analogous—atoning for the sin or wrong committed by another. Intimations of this are present in his life in South Africa, where he established two centers of communal living, the Phoenix Settlement and the Tolstoy Farm. Children, whom Gandhi considered innately innocent, naturally formed part of the community. Boys and girls played and even bathed together, though under his "watchful eye." When he learned that a boy and a girl had indulged in sexual activity, he went on a weeklong fast to atone for their lapse. When they did it again, he went on a fifteen-day fast. What is significant here is that Gandhi fasted for the purification of others as well as himself.[14]

The same behavior occurred again, in India, in the context of his movement for the abolition of untouchability. In 1934, his opponent Pandit Lalanath was hit on the head with a lathi (staff) by one of Gandhi's followers when he was addressing a meeting at Ajmer condemning the Harijan movement. Gandhi promised to hold a penitential fast as soon as he reached his ashram. What is better known, however, is Gandhi's willingness to vicariously atone for the errant behavior of communities. In the 1920s, Gandhi went on a fast for self-purification in a Muslim household to atone for Hindu-Muslim riots. Gandhi was willing to atone in this way not just for contemporaneous wrongs on the part of individuals or groups but also for historical wrongs committed by groups. Gandhi's 1932 fast in protest over the Communal Award by the British on the issue of untouchability, often called the "epic fast," is well known. It lasted for six days. It is perhaps not as well known that he fasted again, in 1933, for twenty-one days, from May 8 to May 29, to vicariously atone for India's sin of untouchability.[15]

Gandhi describes the circumstances in which he undertook this penitential fast in intriguing detail. He had been brooding on the sin of untouchability and how it might be atoned for when he had what we might call a mystical experience:

> I had gone to sleep the night before without the slightest idea of having to declare a fast next morning. At about twelve o'clock in the night something wakes me up suddenly, and some voice—within or without, I cannot say—whispers, "Thou must go on a fast." "How many days?" I ask. The voice again says, "Twenty-one days." "When does it begin?" I ask. It says, "You begin tomorrow." I went off to sleep after making the decision. I did not tell anything to my companions until after the morning prayers.

The voice spoke on the night of April 28, 1933, commanding him to begin the fast on the following day, but for some reason Gandhi preferred to begin the fast on May 8. He spoke as one who had heard the authentic voice of God, and described it as an unconditional and irrevocable "heart prayer for purification of myself and my associates for greater vigilance and watchfulness in connection with the Harijan cause."[16]

There is a hint of something comparable in the life of Ramana Maharshi, according to his disciples, which involves not individual but collective atonement. G. V. Subbaramayya wrote, while reminiscing about Ramana Maharshi, that on April 25, 1942, Ramana Maharshi fell and fractured his right collarbone when he saw a dog chasing a squirrel and tried to prevent the attack with his walking stick. This incident coincided with the sudden withdrawal of the invading Japanese fleet from the Madras coast. Subbaramayya and some fellow devotees saw a parallel between the impending attack on India by Japan and the threat posed by the dog to the squirrel and believed that Ramana Maharshi had "averted the national disaster by taking it vicariously upon his person."[17]

V

Over and above the divergences and convergences between these two spiritual leaders—each considered a saint or holy man by many people—hovers the overarching fact that Ramana Maharshi saw in Gandhi a person who had completely and unequivocally surrendered to God, as Ramana Maharshi preached one should. On this point, he gave full marks to Gandhi. Such a wholesale endorsement of one living spiritual figure by another is rare in the annals of hagiography. The only other instance I know of is Nisargadatta Maharaj's open declaration that Ramana Maharshi and Jiddu Krishnamurthy had realized the ultimate truth.

12

Spiritual
Temptations

I

Saints are known to have been sinners; they consider themselves fallible but for God's grace. The temptations I wish to
speak of now are not the temptations of the flesh to which all
beings are subject. The subject of this chapter is a special
temptation to which saints are subject: the temptation to
serve. We might consider it a virtue and not a temptation,
but saints, at least those of a certain mold, have to rise above
seeking virtue and avoiding vice. It is not that saints have
to abandon virtue but that they must abandon the seeking
of it.

This is a subtle point. Gandhi was fully aware of and
freely admitted to his desire to serve. His meditation on this

point appears in a rather unlikely context. He was so turned off by the oppression to which cows were subjected in dairies, that in 1912 he forswore taking cow's milk.[1] This greatly upset his wife, who, like any other wife, wished to see her husband well-nourished. She therefore proposed that he take goat's milk instead.

Gandhi accepted the suggestion but not without some misgivings. Gandhi had forsworn milk. Drinking goat's milk, Gandhi felt, compromised his vow in two ways. (1) Although he had considered only the milk of the cow or the she-buffalo when he gave up milk, he felt that his vow implicitly covered the milk of all animals. (2) He held that milk is not part of the natural diet of a human being. Thus Gandhi felt both morally and medically compromised, and yet, to use his own expression, he "succumbed." Why did Gandhi succumb? The answer is best offered in his own words: "My intense eagerness to take up the Satyagraha fight had created in me a strong desire to live, so I contented myself with adhering to the letter of the vow only, and sacrificed its spirit"—but not without a guilty conscience. He goes on to say: "The memory of this action even now rankles in my breast and fills me with remorse, and I am constantly thinking of how to give up goat's milk. *But I cannot yet free myself from that subtlest of temptations, the desire to serve which still holds me.*"[2]

Western and Indian readers alike may find the point difficult to grasp, but perhaps Westerners more so, for many associate devotion to God with good deeds, certainly in the context of a saint. The Indian reader, however, may have heard enough about detachment to not be totally surprised by its application to good deeds.

One Westerner who seems to have grasped this Indic position is the Australian physicist Raynor C. Johnson (who approvingly quotes a friend as saying that "Gandhi did more for the people of India than all the yogis of his period put together").[3] Johnson discusses the case of a Swami who gives up doing good works because he was becoming attached to doing them. The account begins by describing the atmosphere, the "sense of strange power," in the room where the Swami was sitting.

> On the floor were seated two young ladies, an old gentleman, [who was] their father, and a young monk in yellow, crouching before the Maharshi as though bowed by his sanctity.
>
> The Holy one bade me be seated. "I am glad," he said, "that thy feet pain thee. That will start the easing of the pain in thy soul." . . . He turned to the others, "What was I talking about?—I remembered—the hospital which is a punishment for doing good." "How could that be my Lord?" questioned the old gentleman.
>
> "Even though, an old man, dost ask me that question also? Well—it all began one day about eleven years ago. I, who was meditating with a brother disciple under a big tree, decided to stop meditating and care for a man who had fallen sick by the roadside. He was a lean moneylender from Marwar, and he had come to Benares to make a rich gift to some temple in order to have his way to Heaven paved in solid gold. Poor fellow, he did not know that all the flowery good deeds done to catch the eye of God will in the end become the bitter fruits of desire.
>
> "I ministered to him until he recovered and could return to Marwar, to lend more money, I suppose. But the rascal did me an evil turn. He spread the news all along the way that if people fell sick near my big tree I took care of them. So very soon two more people came and fell sick at the prearranged place. What else

could my brother-disciple and I do but care for them? Hardly had we cured them when we were pelted with more sick folk. It was a blinding shower. I saw in it all a terrible snare: beyond doubt, I felt, if I went on tending the sick, by and by I would lose sight of God.

"Pity can be a ghastly entanglement to those who do not discriminate, and there I stood, with a wall of sick men between me and God. I said to myself, 'Like Hanuman, the monkey, leap over them and fling thyself upon the Infinite.' But somehow I could not leap, and I felt lame. Just at that juncture a lay disciple of mine came to see me; he recognized my predicament and, good soul that he was, he at once got hold of a doctor and an architect to set to work to build the hospital. Very strange though it seems, other illusions co-operated with that good man to help him—the money-lender, the first fellow I cured, sent an additional load of gold and built the day clinic. In six years the place was a solid home of delusion where men put their soul-evolution back by doing good. Shiva, Shiva!"

"But Master, I notice that your own disciples, boys and young girls, work there?" I put in my question.

"Yes, like these two young ladies here, other young people come to me to serve God. Well, youth suffers from a delusion that it can do good. But I have remedied that somewhat; I let them take care of the sick as long as God remains vivid and untarnished, but the moment any of my disciples shows signs of being caught in the routine of good works—like the scavenger's cart that follows the routine of removing dirt every morning—I send that person off to our retreat in the Himalayas, there to meditate and purify his soul. When he regains his God-outlook to the fullest, if he wishes,

I let him return to the hospital. Beware, beware: good can choke up a soul as much as evil."

"But if someone does not do it, how will good be done?" questioned the old gentleman in a voice full of perplexity.

"Live so," replied the Master in a voice suddenly stern, "live so that by the sanctity of thy life all good will be performed involuntarily."[4]

This unusual position also finds an echo in Buddhism, in the life of the famous twelfth-century Tibetan monk Milarepa, who was asked by his disciples, more than eight hundred years ago, whether "they could engage in worldly duties, in a small way, for the benefit of others." Milarepa replied:

> If there be not the least self-interest attached to such duties, it is permissible. But such [detachment] is indeed rare; and works performed for the good of others seldom succeed, if not wholly freed from self-interest. Even without seeking to benefit others, it is with difficulty that works done even in one's own interest [or selfishly] are successful. It is as if a man helplessly drowning were to try to save another man in the same predicament. One should not be over-anxious and hasty in setting out to serve others before one has oneself realized the Truth in its fullness; to do so, would be like the blind leading the blind. As long as the sky endures, so long will there be no end of sentient beings for one to serve; and to every one comes the opportunity for such service. Till the opportunity comes, I exhort each of you to have but the one resolve, namely to attain Buddhahood for the good of all living beings.[5]

The potential danger of spiritual narcissism that the reader might detect in these responses is mitigated in the context of theism, where the danger is more likely to assume the form of moral unilateralism. This angle on the issue is provided by Mother Teresa (1910–1997), in our own times, which is perhaps inches closer to Gandhi's, as best we can interpret his view from his life as he lived it. She said: "People are often unreasonable, illogical and self-centered; forgive them anyway. If you are kind, people may accuse you of being selfish and having ulterior motives; be kind anyway. If you are successful, you will win over some false friends and some true enemies; succeed anyway. If you are honest and frank, people may cheat you; be honest and frank anyway. What you spend years building, someone may destroy overnight; build anyway. If you find serenity and happiness, they may be jealous, be happy anyway. The good you do today, people often forget tomorrow; do good anyway. Give the world the best you have, and it may never be enough; give the world your best anyway. You see, in the final analysis, it is between you and God; it was never between you and them."[6]

II

The attitude toward doing good to society seems to undergo a kaleidoscopic shift when the mind turns toward God. A good example of this is provided by a mystic of modern India, Ramakrishna Paramahamsa (1836–1886), a household name in India, whose disciple Vivekananda founded a movement based on his teachings. Ramakrishna took a rather dim view of social reform in relation to God, although he was profoundly sensitive to social injustice. It could be that his view was based on the lurking suspicion that the attempt to alleviate the ills of others might be an attempt to avoid the formidable moral effort involved in reforming oneself. The example of Milarepa and others suggests that perhaps the greater danger consists of treating social reform as a substitute for spiritual effort. In a theistic context the issue raises the question, as Ramakrishna once asked ironically: "If you happen to meet God face to face, will you plead: 'God, please grant that I may dig a canal, build a school and found a hospital?'"[7]

It is as if a person starts on the Hindu-Buddhist spiritual path with our quotidian existence as the axis, then the wheel turns on the issue of good or bad karma, with other-regarding karma constituting good karma and self-regarding karma constituting bad karma. As the spiritual goal is approached, there is an axial shift from good or bad karma to attached or unattached karma, which might account for the otherwise alarming statement by mystics that a bad deed done without attachment is better than a good deed done with attachment. Augustine said: "Love God and do whatever you like," of which Martin Luther's statement "Sin boldly. Grace may abound" may be taken as a more sensational paraphrase. A seeker proceeds from karmically consequential or karmically differential action to karmically equal action.

But the next stage on the Hindu-Buddhist path is the hardest to come to terms with, when karmically equal action yields either to karmically neutral action or to no action at all. This spiritual state may be compared to the experience of zero gravity. The seeker who reaches this stage may have been exposed to some form of karmic gravity throughout his or her life, but is now free from its effects. From such a perspective, Gandhi's concern about his desire to serve may appear less baffling.

····

13

▄▄▄▄

Spiritual
Serendipity

I

There occurs a line in Mahatma Gandhi's autobiography that lacks the punch of some of his other lines and perhaps on that account has rarely been cited. Its significance should become apparent as this chapter unfolds. The line runs: *"It is my faith, based on experience, that if one's heart is pure, calamity brings in its train men and measures to fight it."*[1]

Gandhi wrote these words when he was living in Johannesburg, where the Indians were confined to a ghetto, known as a "coolie location." "Coolie" was the name by which Indians were contemptuously known, and "location" was a euphemism for their ghetto. The expression was in use throughout South Africa. While the Indians enjoyed only tenancy rights in coolie locations outside Johannesburg, they had ninety-nine-year leases in the city and therefore enjoyed proprietary rights. Conditions in the Johannesburg coolie location had become so unsanitary that the municipality wanted to destroy it, but first needed to acquire the land and pay compensation. Mahatma Gandhi became involved as the legal advisor of the Indian community. While matters were in a somewhat unsettled state—the municipality secured land ownership but had yet to provide suitable accommodations for the Indians to shift to—there was a sudden outbreak of the black plague, also known as pneumonic plague, which is even deadlier than bubonic plague.

The outbreak took place in the February of 1904, at a gold mine near Johannesburg, where a few Indians were employed. Twenty-three of them returned one evening to their coolie location in the grip of an acute attack. One of the Indians in the coolie location reacted promptly by breaking the lock of a vacant house and confining the patients to the venue, even as he informed the municipality and Mahatma Gandhi. The municipality moved the patients into a vacant godown made available for the purpose.

Gandhi makes his unpunchy but significant statement, cited above, when he recalls how four Indians joined him in helping the patients. Two patients survived this highly contagious plague. It so happens that these were among the three to whom Gandhi had administered his earth treatment, which involved the application of wet (mud) bandages to the heads and chests of the patients. Gandhi had prevented other people from attending to the patients out of fear of infection. He mentions one Mr. Ritch who came from a large family and was ready to help but was prevented from doing so because Gandhi did not want to expose him to risk. He was, however, allowed to attend to work outside the danger zone. The municipality also lent the services of a nurse, who would have been happy to serve the patients but was rarely allowed to touch them lest she catch the plague. She succumbed nonetheless, which led Gandhi to wonder how the two patients who survived and he, along with his team, came through unscathed. He was inclined to give some credit to his earth treatment, but Gandhi admits that his faith in it was not based upon solid evidence.[2]

Gandhi is thus rather tentative in making his statement; on the other hand, he writes elsewhere: "But the whole incident, apart from its pathos, is of such absorbing interest and, for me, of such religious value, that I must devote to it at least two more chapters."[3]

II

The question we need to ask is: What religious value did Gandhi derive from this incident? In our attempt to answer this question, we are led back to Gandhi's unadorned statement: "It is my faith, based on experience, that if one's heart is pure, calamity brings in its train men and measures to fight it."

Is Mahatma Gandhi hinting at some kind of a spiritual law here? It is difficult to say, and yet there is at least one other aspect of the situation that is tantalizing to pursue: the "experiments in earth treatment." In a subsequent chapter in his autobiography Gandhi writes:

This and other experiments enhanced my faith in such household remedies, and I now proceeded with them with more self-confidence. I widened the sphere of their application, trying the earth and water and fasting treatment in cases of wounds, fevers, dyspepsia, jaundice and other complaints, with success on most occasions. But nowadays I have not the confidence I had in South Africa and experience has even shown that these experiments involve obvious risks.

The reference here, therefore, to these experiments is not meant to demonstrate their success. I cannot claim complete success for any experiment. Even medical men can make no such claim for their experiments. My object is only to show that he who would go in for novel experiments must begin with himself. That leads to a quicker discovery of truth, and *God always protects the honest experimenter.*

This passage occurs in a chapter significantly entitled: "Whom God Protects."[4]

If we join these two dots, we can read Gandhi as implying that *when a calamity results from an honest experiment, then means and measures become available to overcome it if one's heart is pure.* Gandhi did not actually say this, but he does seem to imply it. In fact, in typical Gandhian fashion, praxis outpaces theory here if we take the following incident from Gandhi's later life into account.

III

After returning to India, Gandhi founded an ashram in Ahmedabad on May 25, 1915. It was unsurprisingly called Satyagraha Ashram. Gandhi had the option of settling in other cities, Hardwar or Calcutta, for instance, but he chose Ahmedabad because he thought he could perform more useful service from there, and friends had prevailed upon him to stay in the hope that financial help for his projects might be more forthcoming in Ahmedabad than elsewhere. Since an ashram is generally considered open to all, the possibility that an untouchable might apply for admission was discussed, but it was discounted by Gandhi's associates as unlikely.[5]

Within a few months of the ashram's coming into existence, the unexpected happened. Gandhi received a letter inquiring whether he would accept a pious untouchable family who wanted to join the ashram. Gandhi felt disturbed at first. He had not quite expected such a request, but the recommendation came from an unimpeachable source. When Gandhi discussed the matter with the current inmates, they welcomed the arrival.[6] The untouchable family, consisting of Dudabhai, his wife Danibehn, and their infant daughter Lakshmi, were admitted into the ashram and agreed to abide by its rules.

Their admission had serious repercussions. To begin with, the person in charge of the water-lift at a well from which the residents of the ashram also drew water objected to being polluted by drops of water from the bucket used by the ashram residents. He not only objected, he swore at and molested Dudabhai. When the residents did not react to his abuses and continued to draw water, the objector became ashamed and stopped bothering them. But soon a far more serious threat arose. One of the reasons Ahmedabad was chosen as the location of the ashram was that monetary help to run it might be available—and this hope was fulfilled to a certain extent—but now all monetary help stopped, and rumors of a social boycott swirled in the ashram air. Finally, Maganlal, a cousin of Gandhi's, told him: "We are out of funds and there is nothing for the next month." Gandhi replied quietly: "Then we would go to the untouchables' quarter."[7]

At this point, the spiritual law that Gandhi hints at seemed to kick in. What happened next is perhaps best described in Gandhi's own words:

> One morning, shortly after Maganlal had given me warning of our monetary plight, one of the children came and said that a Sheth [business magnate] who was waiting in a car outside wanted to see me. I went out to him. "I want to give the Ashram some help. Will you accept it?" he asked.

"Most certainly," said I. "And I confess I am at the present moment at the end of my resources."

"I shall come tomorrow at this time," he said. "Will you be here?"

"Yes," said I, and he left.

Next day, exactly at the appointed hour, the car drew up near our quarters, and the horn was blown. The children came with the news. The Sheth did not come in. I went out to see him. He placed in my hands currency notes of the value of Rs. 13,000, and drove away.

I had never expected this help, and what a novel way of rendering it! The gentleman had never before visited the Ashram. So far as I can remember, I had only met him once. No visit, no enquiries, simply rendering help and going away! This was a unique experience for me. The help deferred the exodus to the untouchables' quarter. We now felt quite safe for a year.[8]

Gandhi notes that God sent such help every time. His biographer Robert Payne is even more explicit. After narrating the incident, he wrote: "Such miracles were not uncommon and in time Gandhi came to depend on them."[9]

14

Beefing Up
Vegetarianism

I

Vegetarianism was a surprisingly major element in the spiritual life of Gandhi. In the years since Mahatma Gandhi was martyred, the world has grown more receptive to the idea of vegetarianism. Half a century ago the idea was more radical and less well received.

Gandhi was born into the Vaishya class, one of the four varnas (classes) in Hinduism; the Vaishya class is ranked third among the four. The hierarchy of varnas is based on moral and ritual purity, so it is the Brahmins, usually listed first among the four varnas, who are traditionally expected to be vegetarians. But if Gandhi was born into a family that was Vaishya by class, he was also born into a family that worshipped Vishnu.

Gandhi notes that his parents were particularly devout Vaishnavas, or Vishnu worshippers. They visited Vaishnava temples regularly, and the family had its own temples in addition to the public ones. One key ingredient of their piety was a strong abhorrence of eating meat, which the Vaishnavas shared with the Jainas, adherents of Jainism.[1]

We saw in an earlier chapter how Gandhi was tempted into eating meat by a friend who held out the prospect of becoming physically as strong as an Englishman if he did so, an Englishman's strength being attributed to his non-vegetarian diet. Gandhi gave up the experiment because it involved deceiving his parents, who never came to know that two of their sons had temporarily become meat eaters.[2]

His mother may not have known about this experiment, but she did ensure that Gandhi would not eat meat while in England. As we also saw earlier, she would not let Gandhi leave for London until he had pledged to abstain from wine, women, and meat while there.[3] It is worth noting that the vows to the Hindu Gandhi were administered by a Jaina monk, a fact that would hardly surprise anyone in India, where the religions of Indian origin were, and in good measure are, not compartmentalized the way Abrahamic religions are in the West.

The vow caused Gandhi, at least initially, great discomfort. While he was at sea, an English passenger made light of Gandhi's insistence on vegetarianism and said in a friendly way that it was so cold in England that Gandhi could not possibly live there without eating meat. The Englishman did make the finer point that he was not asking Gandhi to drink liquor, although he himself did so. Gandhi thanked him for his advice but made it plain that he would sooner return to India, if what the man said was true, than break his vow to his mother. His first few days in London were also made more difficult by his vow. Gandhi was homesick, England was an

Beefing Up Vegetarianism

alien country, and he was a novice at English etiquette. In this already fraught situation, he had to learn to deal with the *"additional inconvenience of the vegetarian vow."*[4] Gandhi found himself in a fix. England was hard to bear, but returning to India was out of the question. But Gandhi's inner voice had spoken. He must finish his three years of schooling and earn his jurisprudence degree.

Even after he had moved from his hotel to private quarters, the difficulties continued. But Gandhi stood his ground, and when he found a vegetarian restaurant, he attributed it to divine favor and had his first full meal.[5]

As Gandhi entered the restaurant, he noticed some books for sale, one of which was Henry S. Salt's *Plea for Vegetarianism,* which he bought for a shilling. He read it from cover to cover at the first opportunity and was quite impressed. It is as if he had regained the intellectual ground he had lost when his friend had brandished Bentham's *Theory of Utility* in an earlier discussion while trying to persuade him to eat meat. He states that until then he had abstained from meat for the sake of truth as represented by his vow, but from then on he was a vegetarian by choice. He blessed the day he had taken the vow in front of his mother. It now became his mission in life to promote vegetarianism.[6]

After being defensive about vegetarianism, Gandhi now went on the offensive. He admits to an extreme shyness throughout his stay in England, but his crusading zeal for vegetarianism proved an antidote. Although he led an otherwise quiet life, vegetarianism provided a vigorous outlet. He was so convinced of the need to promote vegetarianism that he founded his own Vegetarian Club in Bayswater. Dr. Josiah Oldfield became its president, Sir Edwin Arnold its vice president, and he himself its secretary. Sir Edwin Arnold is the well-known Victorian scholar whose translation of the Bhagavad Gita so impressed Gandhi. Dr. Josiah Oldfield, who is less well known, was the editor of the magazine *The Vegetarian*. More than fifty years later, he could still recall his first meeting with Gandhi, "a young, shy, diffident youth, slim and a little weakly," who had consulted him on a question of diet.[7]

Gandhi soon began to make his mark in vegetarian circles. Not only did he found a Vegetarian Club, but he also joined the London Vegetarian Society and went on to become a member of its executive committee. Gandhi was one of its official delegates to the conference at Portsmouth, in the UK, in 1891, which sought to create a Federal Union of Vegetarian Societies. He began to use his pen to promote vegetarianism and wrote articles for *The Vegetarian;* the first article he ever wrote was on vegetarianism in India. Gandhi began to speak in public as well. He delivered a speech on "the foods of India," about which *The Vegetarian* noted that he was "rather nervous in the beginning."[8]

Even during a flying visit to Paris to see the Great Exhibition of 1890, Gandhi located a vegetarian restaurant. While working for his law degree at the Inner Temple, he had to fulfill the obligation of "keeping terms," which involved attending at least six out of about twenty-four dinners at the university every term. Since these dinners included wine and meat, Gandhi often ate nothing. The only foods he could eat there were bread, boiled potatoes, and cabbage, which he did not like to begin with, but he gradually came to relish them and gained the courage to ask for more. The dinner provided for the "benchers," the Masters of the Bench—the senior officers of the Inn—was better than that for the students, so Gandhi joined a Parsi student in petitioning for the vegetarian courses that the benchers were served. After the request was accepted, they collected fruits and vegetables from the benchers' table.[9]

Gandhi not only retained his commitment to vegetarianism in South Africa but also became more passionate in promoting it. He carried out his missionary work in the only way he felt such activity should be carried out: (1) by personal example and (2) through discussions with other seekers of knowledge. There was a vegetarian restaurant in Johannesburg run by a German, which Gandhi patronized and helped drum up support for, but which closed down. A Theosophist started another and wanted to expand it. Gandhi lent her a thousand pounds on credit, a sum deposited with him by a friend. Gandhi realized within a few months that the amount would never be recovered, and made good the loss, learning the lesson that reforming zeal should not make one exceed one's limits. He frankly acknowledges that the sacrifice he made for the cause was not intended: he had to make a virtue of necessity.[10]

II

The real test for Gandhi came in India in 1901–1902, when he visited it while still settled in South Africa. His second son, Manilal, had a severe attack of typhoid combined with pneumonia, and a Parsi doctor recommended eggs and chicken broth. When Gandhi told him that the family were vegetarians, the doctor suggested milk diluted with water but did not think it would provide sufficient nourishment. He asked Gandhi to reconsider his decision on medical grounds. Gandhi replied that although the doctor was acting as he must, religious convictions were involved, so rightly or wrongly, he could not accept the advice. It was his personal conviction that a person may not do certain things even for the sake of survival, that there should be a limit even to what we may do to stay alive. In this case, the limit had been reached. If his child had been older, he would have consulted him on this point, but Gandhi had to make the decision, and he felt the burden of his responsibility to the full. Gandhi did request the doctor to visit from time to time to check the vital signs, to which he agreed.

Although Gandhi made the decision on behalf of his son, he did share his conversation with the doctor. The son concurred with the decision and asked Gandhi to try his hydropathic treatment.

The consequences when Gandhi applied Dr. Ludwig Kühne's treatment to his son are best narrated in Gandhi's own words.

But the temperature persisted, going up to 104 degrees. At night he would be delirious. I began to get anxious. What would people say of me? What would my elder brother think of me? Could we not call in another doctor? Why not have an Ayurvedic physician? What right had the parents to inflict their fads on their children?

I was haunted by thoughts like these. Then a contrary current would start. God would surely be pleased to see that I was giving the same treatment to my son as I would give myself. I had faith in hydropathy, and little faith in allopathy. The doctors could not guarantee recovery. At best they could experiment. The thread of life was in the hands of God. Why not trust it to Him and in His name go on with what I thought was the right treatment?

My mind was torn between these conflicting thoughts. It was night. I was in Manilal's bed lying by his side. I decided to give him a wet sheet pack. I got up, wetted a sheet, wrung the water out of it and wrapped it about Manilal, keeping only his head out and then covered him with two blankets. To the head I applied a wet towel. The whole body was burning like hot iron, and quite parched. There was absolutely no perspiration.

Beefing Up Vegetarianism

I was sorely tired. I left Manilal in the charge of his mother, and went out for a walk on Chaupati to refresh myself. It was about ten o'clock. Very few pedestrians were out. Plunged in deep thought, I scarcely looked at them. "My honour is in Thy keeping oh Lord, in this hour of trial," I repeated to myself. *Ramanama* [the name of God] was on my lips. After a short time I returned, my heart beating within my breast.[11]

Gandhi returned from the walk to discover that his son's fever had broken. He ends this emotion-laden chapter with the following words: "Today Manilal is the healthiest of my boys. Who can say whether his recovery was due to God's grace, or to hydropathy, or to careful dietary [*sic*] and nursing? Let everyone decide according to his own faith. For my part I was sure that God had saved my honour, and that belief remains unaltered to this day."[12]

That Gandhi's vegetarianism occupies an important place in a spiritual biography of Gandhi should be obvious by now. First of all, it illustrates how, in Gandhi's case, action often precedes "thought," or conviction. As Louis Fischer remarks on Gandhi's statement that Salt's treatise made him a vegetarian by choice, "In the beginning was the act, and only then the conviction." Gandhi's vegetarianism also illustrates how, within that conviction, there was scope for experimentation. Gandhi experimented with eggs as part of a vegetarian diet for a while, but gave them up upon concluding that his mother would have regarded eggs as meat. By eating them he was violating his vow. Gandhi's vegetarianism also serves to illustrate how his life, not just his spiritual life, was transformed by commitment. Even the shy Gandhi became a campaigner for vegetarianism, founded a society, wrote articles, joined other societies, even became a missionary. And finally, it became a matter between him and God.[13]

Gandhi placed his commitment to vegetarianism beyond its role in his life. He foresaw a day when humanity would rise above non-vegetarianism, just as it had risen above cannibalism.

That Gandhi traversed such a spiritual landscape, and even scaled such spiritual heights, while treading the path of vegetarianism is scarcely imaginable. Let us move on to the perhaps meatier topic of Gandhi's celibacy.

15

The Sex Life
of a Celibate

I

Mahatma Gandhi took a vow of celibacy in 1906.

Reaching that point did not come without struggle: Gandhi had been practicing celibacy "more or less" since 1901, but there were lapses. Gandhi notes that he failed twice despite his efforts to sleep separately from his wife or to retire for the night only after he was completely exhausted. Nevertheless, Gandhi felt that the successful adoption of the vow was the cumulative effect of unsuccessful striving.[1]

When Gandhi volunteered for medical work during the Zulu rebellion, he organized an ambulance corps, which served on the front from June to July 1906. The work of the corps consisted in nursing wounded Zulus. Gandhi often fell deep in thought while marching through the solitudes of the sparsely populated country.[2]

One train of thought centered on celibacy, or what is called *brahmacharya* in the Indic religious traditions of Hinduism, Buddhism, Jainism, and Sikhism. The word literally means "lifestyle that leads to the realization of the ultimate reality" (which is called *Brahman* in Hinduism), but it came to denote celibacy in these traditions, perhaps because it was considered an integral part of that quest. Gandhi grasped its meaning at both levels.

Gandhi's early reflections on the point contain only a hint of the spiritual nature of his resolve. If his wife had been expecting, he could not have undertaken his medical missions. His family obligations would have come in the way of serving the community. His conclusion was that to serve humanity with one's whole soul meant observing brahmacharya. Without celibacy, the conflict between serving the family and serving the community could not be satisfactorily resolved.[3]

After mature deliberation and full discussion with his co-workers, Gandhi took the vow of celibacy. Until that point Gandhi had not shared his thoughts on it with his wife. He obviously had to do so now. She had no objection.[4] Gandhi was thirty-seven at the time.

II

A vow is usually taken for moral or spiritual purposes, but was Gandhi's decision purely, or even primarily, a moral or spiritual one? Ostensibly it seemed so to Gandhi *in hindsight,* but Gandhi's motives, some biographers feel, are hard to decipher and perhaps were difficult even for him to fathom.[5]

Various motives, irrespective of whether he was conscious of them, could be assigned. One motive could indeed be the desire to be free to serve the community, for Gandhi clearly

The Sex Life of a Celibate

believed that his celibacy was a response to the call of public duty. An allied motive could be birth control. Gandhi speaks of his conviction that procreation, and the concomitant care of children, was inconsistent with public service. Kasturbai's health may also have played a role in the decision; she was anemic and had almost died from internal hemorrhaging. A gynecological operation brought her some relief but could not cure her anemia. Yet another factor could have been a feeling of dispassion and detachment. Gandhi wrote in the *Harijan* magazine on June 25, 1945, that when he was in South Africa, the sight of women had ceased to titillate him. Gandhi could also have been influenced by the importance attached to celibacy in Hinduism. The influence of Raychand could also have been a factor, as he placed disinterested love above conjugal affection. The *asrama* (stages of life) system within Hinduism could also have played a role, for Gandhi writes that during the marches in the South African desert, it occurred to him that he should now live the life of a *vanaprastha*, that is, of one retired from household cares.[6] Vanaprastha is the third of the four stages of life; in that stage a person begins disengaging from the world after having led a householder's life. The fact that Gandhi always felt guilty that his father could not die in his arms because he was in the arms of his wife at the time perhaps added a psychological dimension to the decision.

This list of factors enables us to recognize (1) that multiple factors underlay the vow; (2) that the factors may not be mutually exclusive; and (3) that cause and effect may have been telescoped. This last point is of special significance in a spiritual biography, but the first two may be dealt with first.

Although Louis Fischer notes an inconsistency between the desire to serve people and the desire to practice birth control, the two are not necessarily opposed. Gandhi considered that he would not have been able to serve the South Asian community with his ambulance corps if his wife had been pregnant. Fischer also wonders why Gandhi would have wanted to avoid having additional children. In the Phoenix community children were raised jointly. While this may be true, there remains the question of the personal responsibility felt for one's own children. Fischer, however, does make what seems to be both a sound and a profound observation when he writes: "In retrospect, Gandhi naturally did not attribute the chastity vow to his own physiology or to Kasturbai's, nor to his psychology. On the contrary, he identified effect with motive, and the effect was spiritual. The chaste life apparently reinforced his passion and determination to sacrifice for the common weal. Less carnal, he became less self-centered. He seemed suddenly lifted above the material. A new inner drive possessed him. Storms continued to rage within, but now he could harness them for the generation of more power."[7]

III

Gandhi experienced the salutary effects of the vow right away. Even the prospect of making the vow had filled him with a certain kind of exultation, although that statement was made in retrospect, so some retrodiction may be involved. Initially at least, Gandhi found the observance quite easy and says that the first change he made in his life was to stop seeking privacy with his wife.[8]

Even as Gandhi exults about the vow, he also mentions the necessity of observing "eternal vigilance." Gandhi does add, however, that formally taking the vow gave him a sense of freedom and a joy he had never felt before.[9]

Gandhi was both anxious and ecstatic about celibacy. He makes a startling statement in this context, however. He says: "The knowledge that a perfect observance of *brahmacharya* means realization of *Brahman,* I did not owe to the study of

The Sex Life of a Celibate

the shastras [scriptures]. It slowly grew upon me with experience. The shastric texts on it I read only later in life."[10] What is striking about these lines is that Gandhi's experience *preceded* his awareness of scriptural testimony. Usually people first follow the scriptural injunctions and then experience their positive effects. But Gandhi took action first, and that led to conviction, as with his vegetarianism.

IV

Both Gandhi's views and his vow regarding celibacy were tested severely in 1936.

The views were tested by Margaret Sanger, the well-known advocate of birth control, who sought an interview with him. She thought that her cause would benefit greatly if someone like Gandhi could be persuaded to endorse it. She ran into heavy weather while trying to do so. Two aspects of birth control particularly horrified Gandhi, the physical apparatus involved and the sexual license it allowed. Even when Sanger proposed that something so simple as a cotton swab dipped in lemon juice could serve as a contraceptive, Gandhi still considered the intervention unnatural. And having sex just for the sake of sex was an idea that Gandhi found revolting and quite contrary to his ascetic orientation. He insisted that women learn to resist their husbands and, if necessary, leave them. He failed to realize that such a step on a wife's part might drive the husband to do the same.[11]

Two major strands in Gandhi's response can be identified. One is that abstinence was the best and, for him, the only acceptable method of birth control. All techniques of birth control for Gandhi were contained in one word: abstain. He attributes abstention's lack of effectiveness to the fact that women could not say no to their men. He seems to blame women more than men here, probably because he felt that women were a cut above men when it came to exercising self-restraint, although he does not always spare men either. The second strand is his view that sex is simply evil. For him this meant that a married couple should unite sexually only for the sake of having children. When Sanger asked him if he thought this kind of restraint was possible, Gandhi replied: "I had the honor of doing that very thing, and I am not the only one."[12] He had in mind the birth of his youngest son, who was so conceived; the other sons were born on the "spurt of the moment." In maintaining this position Gandhi was perhaps unwittingly invoking a distinction made in the Hindu texts between sons who are conceived righteously (and hence *dharmaja*, or "born in virtue [*dharma*]") and those conceived out of passion (and hence *kamaja*, or "born of passion").

Sanger did not hesitate to push the point to its logical extreme and asked: "Then throughout a whole lifetime you expect the sexual union to take place only three or four times?" Gandhi's reply was yes: "People should be taught that it is immoral to have more than three or four children, and after they have had these children they should sleep separately. If people were taught this, it would harden into custom. And if the social informers [*sic*] cannot impress this idea on people, why not a law?"[13]

A law to ban sexual union not designed to have children? If commitment to an idea is to be judged by the extent to which one is prepared to push it, then Gandhi would probably pass that test here.

This encounter with Margaret Sanger, in which some argue she prevailed, was followed by a test of his vows, which came after an operation to remove teeth that had been troubling him. On January 18, 1936, he felt the stirring of sexual passion while recovering from the operation. Gandhi referred to this incident twice that year in his articles in *Harijan*, and as Robert Payne puts it, both times he wrote like a "man who has been struck by lightning out of a clear sky."[14] This is how Gandhi described his experience: "My darkest hour was when I was in Bombay a few months ago. It was the hour of my temptation. Whilst I was asleep I suddenly felt as though I wanted to see a woman. Well, a man who had tried to rise superior to the instinct for nearly forty years was bound to be intensely pained when he had this frightful experience. I ultimately conquered the feeling, but I was face to face with the blackest moment of my life and if I had succumbed to it, it would have meant my absolute undoing."[15]

He described his remedial response to his experience as well. "I was disgusted with myself. The moment the feeling came, I acquainted my attendants and the medical friends with my condition. They could give me no help. I expected none. I broke loose after the experience from the rigid rest that was imposed upon me. The confession of the wretched experience brought relief to me. I felt as if a great load had been raised from over me. It enabled me to pull myself together before any harm could be done."[16]

These words were from a man of sixty-seven who had attempted to remain chaste since 1899 and had taken an absolute vow of chastity in 1906. All these years he had thought he was in control only to suddenly discover that he was not.[17] What you are aware of, you are in control of; what you are not aware of controls you.

This doubt about control haunted him during the fateful days when India was partitioned, for what occurred during the night of January 18, 1936, was for him an intimation that he might have lost, or might be losing, the power to control events.[18] Later in life, when riots between the Hindus and the Muslims continued to spread despite his efforts, he was compelled to ask himself: Am I truly chaste?

To find the answer to this question he had to test himself, and he did. While Gandhi was in Sirampur, Bengal, his eighteen-year-old niece, Manubehn Gandhi, for whom Gandhi's now-dead wife had had a special affection, arrived to be with him. Nirmal Kumar Bose had volunteered his services to Gandhi as a personal secretary during Gandhi's tour of Bengal and was already with him. He reports that on the morning of December 12, 1946, when he entered Gandhi's room, he found them both in the same bed, talking. What were they up to?[19]

Gandhi was explaining to Manubehn the great experiment he was about to undertake, whose "heat would be great." He would walk through the troubled region from village to village *alone,* without any escort, placing his life entirely in the hands of the region's people, mostly Muslims.[20] But even as he said this, he was conducting another great experiment, whose "heat would be great" when people would come to know of it. By lying naked in bed with Manubehn he was testing his vow of celibacy by ascertaining whether the situation aroused any sexual stirring in him or her. He had to be so pure that even the other gender had no sexual reaction.

When Nirmal Kumar Bose wrote about this experiment after Gandhi's death, it created a sensation even though Gandhi had already publicly acknowledged it.[21] The question to ask is: What was Gandhi trying to achieve?

The answer is provided by Gandhi's boast that were he to be successful in his brahmacharya experiments, and prove what a potent celibate he was, he would be able to defeat Jinnah's attempts to partition India.[22]

Nirmal Kumar Bose warned Gandhi that he might be exploiting the young Manubehn, not consciously perhaps, but unconsciously, the way Freud had suggested. This was the first time Gandhi had heard of Freud, and he wanted to know more about him. In a sense, Gandhi always had what in Zen is called the "beginner's mind," an openness to learning new things. Years later, at one point in their conversation, Ved Mehta was to ask Nirmal Kumar Bose point-blank: "Have

The Sex Life of a Celibate

you told all you know about the brahmacharya experiments?" Bose replied that he "was never able to find out very much." He continued:

> None of the girls would talk to me—I'm considered an apostate. Anyway, the wish to be truthful died in our country with Gandhiji. It was never very strong, even among his disciples. Since Gandhiji never had any privacy—and in the camp everyone slept in one room—there could be no question of impropriety. Once, when he had been pestering the girls about how they felt about holding him during his shivering fits, I asked him, "What's so special about hugging an old man of seventy-seven to comfort him in the night?" He gave me the standard reply that he wanted to be so pure that he would be above arousing impure thoughts in anyone else.

When Mehta asked Bose why he hadn't talked further with Gandhi about Freud, Bose explained that he "was far from being an authority on Freud."[23]

And to the next question, "Do you think Gandhi ever succeeded in becoming completely sexless? Did he ever, in your opinion, become a perfect brachmachari?" Bose replied: "I don't think he succeeded in identifying completely with women—in reaching the bisexual state of, say, a Ramakrishna. If he had, I don't think he would have been so concerned about what the women who lay next to him were feeling. I do think, however, that there was something saintly, almost supernatural, about him." Bose here refers to the famous mystic Ramakrishna Paramahamsa, who is said to have identified himself so completely with women that he would even menstruate.[24]

Nirmal Kumar Bose objected to Gandhi's experiment on grounds of propriety as much as morality. Bose did not think it proper for a person of Gandhi's standing to indulge in such experiments. He also feared, as indicated earlier, that they involved the unconscious exploitation of the other person involved.[25]

V

Gandhi's experiments in celibacy, in the broadest sense, enabled him to share some insights on how best to maintain it. Four such insights seem significant.

The first is the realization that the instincts of eating and mating are connected and that the attempt to control one of these appetites involves controlling the other. Hence Gandhi's dietetic experiments had a medical as well as a moral component. He concluded from these experiments that a "*brahmachari*'s food should be limited, simple, spiceless, and, if possible, uncooked." Gandhi carries his logic further to claim that the removal of sexual passion as a rule involves fasting, which he regarded as indispensable for the observance of brahmacharya. It is as if Gandhi thought of food as foreplay. The second insight is that the mind is at the root of all sensuality. So although Gandhi emphasized the importance of controlling the palate in order to control one's passions, he makes it quite clear that the principal source of control is the mind.[26]

The third insight follows from the first two: celibacy involves a life devoted to God-realization. When Gandhi first took the vow, he did so with full faith in the sustaining power of God. Gandhi emphasized the role of the mind even above that of diet, but added that it is the "existence of God which makes even control of the mind possible."[27]

The final insight is the most intriguing. It is not so evident in his autobiography, which ends around 1921. In 1926, Gandhi made the following comment while expounding the Bhagavad Gita to ashram sisters: "A man should remain a man

The Sex Life of a Celibate

and yet should learn to become a woman; similarly a woman should remain a woman and yet learn to become a man." This so-called maternalism of Gandhi has been construed in different ways. Nirmal Kumar Bose connects it most explicitly with Gandhi's quest for celibacy. He argues that Indian mystics have long advocated that a man become a woman to overcome a longing for women, that is, sex. Bose does add, as pointed out earlier, that Gandhi's identification with women did not match the degree of identification achieved by the saint Ramakrishna. Bose maintains, nevertheless, that the feminization of Gandhi began as soon as he undertook his vow of celibacy. He also suggests that Gandhi's experiments in brahmacharya could be explained in this light, for they reflect the permanent need to test himself to ascertain how far he had advanced along the path to ultimate reality.[28]

Making such a connection requires that women be considered sexless creatures. Ved Mehta accordingly observes parenthetically: "Gandhi assumed that women got no pleasure from sex."[29] Mehta himself, however, relates the following account by Kaka Kalelkar, which seems to indicate that Gandhi may not have been that innocent:

Bapu [= Gandhi] used to tell a story about a European girl in South Africa—I forget her name. She was young and was living with Bapu as a member of his family. She suffered from headaches, and no medicine seemed to help. When she told this to Bapu, he said to her, "You must be constipated. I'll give you an enema." As he was preparing the syringe, she undressed and came up to him and embraced him. Bapu asked her, "Do you take me to be your father or your paramour?" She blushed with shame and backed away. Bapu was not the slightest bit disturbed in body or mind, and proceeded to give her the enema. Then he made her confess her transgression to friends and family, and saw to it that they respected her for her truthfulness. The few times in his brahmachari life when he did feel sexual excitement, he felt that public confession was the only way to expiate his sense of sin. I myself completely approved of his brahmacharya experiments, although I never agreed with him that sleeping with Manu in Noakhali was the ultimate test of his purity, because Manu was like a granddaughter to him. But then he didn't really need to experiment, to test himself, because his relationships with women were, beginning to end, as pure as mother's milk.[30]

Did he regard women as uninterested in sex? The answer seems to be no. It also seems that once the element of sex was removed from the equation between men and women by his vow of brahmacharya, women could interact with him, and he with them, in a manner not possible while the element was present.

The Bhagavad Gita,
Gandhi's Other
Mother

I

Gandhi's mother passed away shortly before his return to India from England in 1891. He referred to the Hindu sacred text the Bhagavad Gita as his "mother" in later life, presumably because it was a source of comfort and moral inspiration for him, just as his mother had been. He wrote in 1930, to the members of the Sabarmati Ashram from Yervada Jail, that he turned to his mother Gita whenever he found himself in difficulties, and up to now she had never failed to comfort him.[1]

What is the Bhagavad Gita, from which Gandhi drew such maternal solace and inspiration?

It is a text of seven hundred verses in the form of a dialogue between Krishna and Arjuna that takes place on the eve of the battle between two parties in a family feud. The battle ultimately involves casualties of such mythic proportions that it may be described as the ancient Indian equivalent of the world wars of modern times. The Mahabharata epic is literally "the great narrative of the battle of the Bharata tribe."[2] The cousins on either side are known as the Pandavas (the good guys, consisting of five brothers) and the Kauravas (the bad guys, consisting of a hundred brothers). The word Mahabharata is now used for both the event and the narrative that describes it—the second-longest epic in the world (after Tibet's *Gesar* epic), being eight times the length of the *Iliad* and the *Odyssey* combined.

The Bhagavad Gita forms a part of this grand narrative but is also a text unto itself. One of the interlocutors—Krishna— is identified as an incarnation of God within the Hindu religious tradition. So the dialogue is God speaking to humanity in the form of Arjuna, a hero in the larger epic. Arjuna faces moral and metaphysical dilemmas on the eve of the great battle, and Krishna acts as a guide to the perplexed man.

Krishna's pronouncements in the course of trying to resolve Arjuna's doubts end up offering a summary statement of the Hindu worldview. It remains a teasing fact that the Bhagavad Gita, sacred as it is, is not formally included within the category of "revealed texts" of Hinduism. This position is enjoyed by the Vedas, which are the Hindu equivalent to the Bible as revelation; the Bhagavad Gita is part of Hindu tradition.[3] Nevertheless, as a living religious text, the Bhagavad Gita surpasses the Vedas. The Vedas elicit awe, but not engagement; they are respected from a distance. It is the Bhagavad Gita that is read and recited. Its appeal is widespread; it is in the Bhagavad Gita that Hinduism comes closest to possessing a universal scripture. It may be read in two hours, or over a lifetime, or even over several lifetimes.

The text had already become endowed with salvific potency by the ninth century, when a king of Kashmir had it recited to him as he lay dying. Its reputation for facilitating such life transitions may explain why Gandhi's father began reading the text toward the end of his life and intoned some of its verses every day in prayer.[4]

II

Gandhi may have become aware of the high value placed on the text while in India, but he realized this value for himself while living in London, as we discovered in an earlier chapter.

Part of its fascination for Gandhi derived from the picture that Krishna paints of an ideal type. While instructing Arjuna on how to lead his life in the best possible way, Krishna presents as an ideal type someone established in transcendence in such a way as to rise above life's perplexities, in a manner reminiscent of Confucius's portrait of the *chun tzu* (*junzi*), or "nobleman." This ideal type is described in some detail at four places in the Bhagavad Gita.[5] Descriptions of a spiritually accomplished person are found scattered throughout the text, but at these four places the description gains a certain density. The name used for the ideal type varies, but the portrayal in all four cases is remarkably similar.

The first and the most extensive description is found in the second half of the long second chapter. Gandhi's favorite passage in the Bhagavad Gita forms part of this description. It was a section from this description that so captivated him when he first read it in Edwin Arnold's translation in London.[6]

Gandhi's faith in the Bhagavad Gita was based not just on this favorite part but extended to the whole text. I use the word "faith" advisedly because Gandhi would consider it a shortcoming of his, and not of the Gita's, if he was unable to live up to its ideal. At one point he describes his faith in the Gita as being as bright as ever.[7]

III

What, then, is the message of the Bhagavad Gita?

Gandhi was explicit. He states that the message is *anasakti* —selfless action. That is why, when he translated the Gita, he called it *Anasaktiyoga,* or "the yoga of selfless action."[8]

Any modern Hindu, if asked, would likewise describe selfless action as the message of the Bhagavad Gita. In doing so, the interlocutor may partly be following the trend set by Gandhi, but Gandhi himself, to a certain extent, was amplifying a trend initiated by B. G. Tilak (1856–1920), who established selfless action as the core teaching of the Bhagavad Gita by writing a commentary to that effect in 1911 while imprisoned by the British for spreading disaffection against their rule.

Tilak, who was a contemporary of Gandhi's political mentor, G. K. Gokhale, was Gandhi's predecessor in more ways than one. Although Gokhale was more moderate in his opposition to the British than Tilak was, both probably wanted the same thing but at different speeds. Some historians are even of the view that although Gandhi always claimed that Gokhale was his political guru, it was really Tilak's mantle that fell on Gandhi's shoulders, for Gandhi ultimately adopted Tilak's more radical program. When Gandhi was himself tried for sedition, the judge sentenced him to six years in prison, using the precedent set in Tilak's case, a comparison that Gandhi found flattering. The point, then, is that both Tilak and Gandhi, at some subliminal level, probably realized the appositeness of the message of selfless action for a people struggling for independence against the greatest empire the world had seen. The possibility of success was so remote that only a gospel of selfless action could, paradoxically, provide the motivation for engaging in such a struggle. Thus the convergence in their interpretations of the message of the Bhagavad Gita could well be more than a coincidence.

But the question remains: What kind of selfless action did the Bhagavad Gita preach? Was it meant to be violent or nonviolent? The soldier performs selfless actions, and so does the satyagrahi.

Although Tilak and Gandhi agreed that the Bhagavad Gita preached selfless action, they differed on whether it preached violent or nonviolent action.

The Hindu tradition, as a whole, tends to take the Bhagavad Gita literally. The setting of the text is martial, so such an interpretation becomes immediately plausible. It should not come as a surprise, therefore, that some revolutionaries (terrorists, in British parlance), when sent to the gallows by the British, did so with the Bhagavad Gita in their hands.

But the Bhagavad Gita in the hands of Gandhi was another story. Gandhi insisted on taking the text allegorically rather than literally. He wrote that even as early as 1888–1889, when he first became acquainted with the text, he felt that it was not a historical work but a metaphorical one. The battlefield was a metaphor for the perpetual duel in the human heart between right and wrong, and it had been depicted as physical warfare to add allure.[9]

Thus the great battle of the Mahabharata was, for Gandhi, a simulacrum of the great battle between good and evil that forever rages in the human breast. The Bhagavad Gita was a call to arms, an invitation to engage in this interior struggle. Gandhi produced some astute arguments to support his position. The main characters in the Mahabharata are often assigned supernatural origins, and Gandhi took this as a hint thrown by its author (or authors) that the text is to be taken allegorically. Moreover, selfless action could only mean nonviolent action, according to Gandhi, for it is our selfish attachments that cause us to turn violent.

The contest between the literal and the allegorical interpretation of the Bhagavad Gita ultimately involved Gandhi's very life. These two hermeneutical streams were represented in our times by Savarkar and Gandhi. V. D. Savarkar (1883–1966) was a champion of Hindu nationalism and, until he struck a deal with the British for his release from prison, an advocate of the violent overthrow of British rule. Unlike Gandhi, he was not altogether averse to the use of violence. His mantra—"Militarize Hindu-dom and Hinduize politics"—has still not lost its appeal. He met Gandhi briefly in London when he was also a student there, and some scholars argue that he is the veiled interlocutor in Gandhi's book *Hind Swaraj*, written in the form of a dialogue. Like Gandhi, he also was a great devotee of the Bhagavad Gita, which he knew by heart, even as it was Gandhi's ambition to memorize as many verses of it as he could. The stream of interpretation represented by Savarkar flowed through Nathuram Godse, who assassinated Gandhi. In fact, Savarkar was himself tried as Godse's co-conspirator, but he was acquitted for want of evidence.[10]

In the case of Gandhi and Godse, we thus have a paradox: victim and assassin both swearing by the same book, but each having his own interpretation.

V

Godse bowed to Gandhi before aiming his revolver at him. This is well documented. He later explained his behavior, in the courtroom of the historic Red Fort, on November 8, 1948. He bowed, he explained, because Arjuna had done likewise. Arjuna looked up to Dronacharya as his teacher, but Dronacharya had chosen to fight on the side of Arjuna's opponents, so Arjuna shot an arrow at the feet of Dronacharya to salute him as a teacher before, reluctantly, shooting a second arrow into his chest to kill him because he was siding with evil. Simi-

The Bhagavad Gita, Gandhi's Other Mother

larly, Godse looked upon Gandhi as a saint, so he bowed, but Gandhi had now turned to evil, so he then shot him dead.[11]

Godse's full statement at court is worth citing here. His words are remarkable as much for his acknowledgment of Gandhi's charisma as for the invocation of his own "inner voice."

> My respect for the Mahatma was deep and deathless. It therefore gave me no pleasure to kill him. Indeed my feelings were like those of Arjuna when he killed Dronacharya, his Guru at whose feet he had learnt the art of war. But the Guru had taken the side of the wicked Kauravas and for that reason he felt no compunction in finishing his revered Guru. Before doing so, however, he first threw an arrow at the feet of Dronacharya as a mark of respect for the Guru; the second arrow he aimed at the chest of the Guru and finished him. My feelings towards Gandhi were similar. I hold him first in the highest respect and therefore on January 30, I bowed to him first, then at point blank range fired three successive shots and killed him. My provocation was his constant and consistent pandering to the Muslims. I had no private grudge, no self-interest, no sordid motive in killing him. It was his provocation, over a period of twenty years, which finally exhausted my patience; and my inner voice urged me to kill him, which I did. I am not asking for any mercy.[12]

In his speech, he referred to both Gandhi and Savarkar. After mentioning the various leaders and scholars whose works he had studied, he spoke of studying the written and spoken words of Veer ("brave") Savarkar and Gandhiji more deeply, for their ideologies had contributed the most to shaping the thought and action of Indians during the previous thirty years.[13]

Godse left little doubt, however, about whose hermeneutical side he was on when it came to the Bhagavad Gita. He stated quite explicitly that he believed armed resistance to aggression could never be immoral. Rama had killed the demon Ravana, and Krishna had killed the demon Kansa. So, in his view, Gandhi displayed an amazing ignorance of the springs of human action in holding Krishna and Arjuna guilty of violence.[14]

Godse's strictures against Gandhi may seem harsh and a trifle overwrought, but it is clear that violent action was a valid option for him, and in line with the teachings of the Bhagavad Gita. Gandhi demurred.[15]

It seems as if Godse chose to use Arjuna as the model for his conduct—the warrior Arjuna fighting for his rights— while Gandhi used the description of the ideal spiritual person in the second chapter as his model.

VI

We are back to our question: What is the Bhagavad Gita's message? To ask that question is to raise yet another question: How do we determine the message of any sacred text? Every sacred text provides several hermeneutical options, so what determines which ones come to be championed?

People decide, for a host of reasons, what a text means to them. And they sometimes decide to interpret the text differently when their situation changes. Such an interpretation is usually carried out through a commentary (or a translation). Thus a person may change the meaning of a fixed text by offering a new commentary.

The Bhagavad Gita provides a good example of the operation of this process. In ancient India, the message of the Bhagavad Gita was primarily interpreted through the commentary of Shankara (ca. eighth century). Shankara was of the view that spiritual insight, rather than devotion or action, held the real key to liberation and that this was the message of the Bhagavad Gita. He used the word *jnana* to denote spiritual insight, or gnosis. His view was probably dominant until another sage-scholar, Ramanuja by name, appeared on the scene in the twelfth century. According to Ramanuja's interpretation, the Bhagavad Gita set forth devotion to God, or what he called *bhakti,* as a far more efficacious way of securing liberation. He held, contra Shankara, that bhakti, rather than Shankara's jnana, constituted the fundamental teaching of the Bhagavad Gita. These two main lines of exegesis prevailed in medieval times.

B. G. Tilak, in modern times, examined these views in the light of his own reading of the Bhagavad Gita and reached his own conclusion regarding its final teaching. According to him, the message of the Bhagavad Gita is that the best way to achieve liberation is not through spiritual insight, or jnana, as Shankara had maintained, or through devotion to God, or bhakti, as Ramanuja had asserted, but through action, or karma—more specifically, selfless action, or *nishkama karma,* as it is commonly called. Changing historical conditions may underlie these changing perceptions of a multivalent text.

Gandhi and Godse differed on whether selfless action could be violent.

VII

Both Gandhi and Godse claimed to be Hindus. Hinduism therefore has to be larger than both to embrace them both, the victim and the assassin. We could even argue that Gandhi, through his constant invocation of God and his description of the British Raj as satanic, and Godse, through his allusions to the characters of the Mahabharata, had raised contemporary history to a mythic, even apocalyptic, level.[16]

It is sometimes alleged, especially when the martial back-ground of the Bhagavad Gita is taken into account, that the text promotes war, although the Hindu religious tradition has rarely read it in this light, and according to Gandhi, it must not be read in this light. But if Krishna's/God's promise of redemption for humanity is to be taken seriously, then even Godse cannot be excluded from redemption, nor can Godse exclude Gandhi. Perhaps the Hindu tradition has intuited the message of the Bhagavad Gita to be that redemption is possible for anyone, in any situation, at any time, and in any manner.

Arjuna is offered spiritual redemption in the unlikeliest of places: a battlefield. Could, therefore, all the interpretations of the Bhagavad Gita not find their place in the soteriological economy of the divine? That a person is always free to choose freedom could well be the core message of the Bhagavad Gita.

17

Gandhi, God, and Goodness

I

How appropriate is it to present Gandhian philosophy in outline, after a discussion of his life and thought? Life and thought may be distinguishable in a biography, but they are inseparable in life. This point applies to the case of Mahatma Gandhi with special force and comes into clear focus when Gandhi's concept of contradiction is examined. We normally use the term in the sense of two facts contradicting each other, as in law, or two concepts or formulations contradicting each other, as in philosophy, or two statements contradicting each other, as in the everyday use of the term. Gandhi was sensitive to contradiction but not so much in these forms; rather, he noted contradictions between thought and life, between precept and practice. He memorably said: "My aim is not to be consistent with my previous statement on a given question but to be consistent with the truth as it presents itself to me at a given moment. I want to grow from truth to truth."[1] Some even see in his ongoing receptivity the secret of Gandhi's influence.

That he was less sensitive to other forms of contradiction is exemplified by an anecdote. A reporter once told him, "But you were saying the opposite thing two weeks ago," to which Gandhi replied: "Maybe I learnt something in the meantime." Gandhi's greater sensitivity to contradictions between life and thought is brought out by another anecdote. A couple, whose child was given to eating sugar in excess, took him to see Gandhi in the hope that if a person of Gandhi's stature asked him to desist, he would. Gandhi asked the couple to bring the child back a few weeks later. When they met again, Gandhi asked the child not to eat too much sugar. When the parents protested that if they had known this was all he was going to do, they could have been spared the extra trip, Gandhi replied: "I have reduced my own consumption of sugar in the meantime." Gandhi would have wholeheartedly approved of Albert Schweitzer's observation "Example is not the main thing. It is the only thing."

Let us revert from pedagogy to philosophy. Gandhi is one of those rare figures of modern times whose praxis gave rise to theory, rather than vice versa. In this respect, Gandhi presents a stark contrast to Lenin, who put Marxism into practice in a way dubbed Leninism. Although we have the life and thought of Gandhi, there is no such thing as Gandhism, even the possibility of which Gandhi disavowed. Thought arose out of life in Gandhi's case, as it does for people in general. So it might be better to say that for Gandhi, thought arose not just out of life but out of his life as he lived it with others. This point is possible to overstate, however. We know by now

Gandhi, God, and Goodness

that Gandhi had a marked experimental strain, which found expression in his life in fields as diverse as diet, dress, medicine, and ethics. But he always claimed to be experimenting in the spirit of a key moral idea like truth or nonviolence. So Gandhi was not so much an adventurer in the realm of thought as an experimentalist in search of new applications for a set of moral principles.[2]

This assessment runs the risk of going to the other extreme. Despite Gandhi's claim that truth and nonviolence are as old as the hills, did he have nothing new to teach?[3] It is widely admitted that Gandhi found new applications for old ideas. The point that calls for recognition is that Gandhi's ideas on God, truth, and nonviolence display signs of evolution. For instance, Gandhi himself states that even though truth came to him naturally, he had to cultivate nonviolence. This clearly implies a development of his thought along these lines.[4] But even in relation to truth, he admits to a shift in his position, especially in his understanding of its relationship to God. Gandhi began by identifying God with truth, but in 1929 he reversed the equation and identified truth with God.[5]

Gandhi recognized the fine distinction between the two statements and explained his reason for reversing them: denial of God we have known; denial of truth we have not. Even the atheist accepts the necessity of truth. Gandhi, in his long search for truth, found that other words he had employed, such as "love" or even "non-violence," could be interpreted equivocally, but he never found the possibility of a double meaning emerging in the case of truth. He found truth to be the most comprehensive unequivocal term among all the alternatives on which to take his stand.[6]

A similar development can be discerned in Gandhi's ideas about God. As mentioned in an earlier chapter, the word that Gandhi used most often for God was Rama. The word doubles in Hinduism both for a particular incarnation of God and for God in general, and Gandhi notes his transition from one sense to the other: "I worshipped Rama as Sita's husband in the first instance, but as my knowledge and experience of Him grew, my Rama became immortal and omnipresent. This does not mean that Rama ceased to be Sita's husband; but the meaning of Sita's husband expanded with the vision of Rama. This is how the world evolves."[7]

It seems true to say, nevertheless, that Gandhi's thought, on the whole, retains its fundamental outline, though with this kind of embroidering and amplification. The real difficulty in presenting the chief ingredients of the Gandhian philosophical worldview is not their development but rather the telescoping of his basic ideas into one another, probably because his theory was rooted in practice, and practice is multitextured and multilayered.[8]

II

The realm of Gandhian philosophy can be entered through many portals, and since this book bills itself as a spiritual biography of Gandhi, the word "spiritual" could itself provide a good point of entry, for Gandhian thought has been described as spiritual through and through. God is a spiritual rather than a physical entity for Gandhi, and for him, a human being possesses a spirit apart from the body. When we deal with others, we are dealing with other spirits, he would say, and conscience is the voice of the spirit within us.[9]

Gandhi described God as an indefinable, mysterious power that pervades everything and that can be felt but not seen. As an unseen power, it defies proof because it transcends the senses. Looking at space in relation to material objects helps explain this point. Material objects possess length, breadth, and height; they are tangible and material. Space, by contrast, does not possess these attributes. It is immaterial and without

Gandhi, God, and Goodness

length, breadth, or height, nor is it tangible. There is no material attribute which can be applied to space, and yet all material objects exist in space, and it pervades them. Gandhi admits in more than one place that he does not know God. He writes in the introduction to his autobiography that "*I have not yet found Him, but I am seeking after Him,*" and admits that "*I have not seen Him neither have I known Him.*"[10]

In the Farewell section of the autobiography, Gandhi acknowledges seeing flashes of truth, which he equates with God. It is interesting, however, that he chooses to focus on truth rather than God in concluding his narrative, and on ahimsa, the principle of doing no harm to living beings:

> My uniform experience has convinced me that there is no other God than Truth. And if every page of these chapters does not proclaim to the reader that the only means for the realization of Truth is Ahimsa, I shall deem all my labour in writing these chapters to have been in vain. And, even though my efforts in this behalf may prove fruitless, let the readers know that the vehicle, not the great principle, is at fault. After all, however sincere my strivings after Ahimsa may have been, they have still been imperfect and inadequate. The little fleeting glimpses, therefore, that I have been able to have of Truth can hardly convey an idea of the indescribable lustre of Truth, a million times more intense than that of the sun we daily see with our eyes. In fact what I have caught is only the faintest glimmer of that mighty effulgence. But this much I can say with assurance, as a result of all my experiments, that a perfect vision of Truth can only follow a complete realization of Ahimsa.[11]

He also wrote that since truth is the highest attribute of God, "I recognize truth by the name of Rama. In the darkest hour of my trial, that one name has saved me and is still saving me."[12] God was for him truth come alive.

In a sense, then, Gandhi invokes both the personal and the impersonal aspects of God, which should not be confused with the personal (*saguna*) and impersonal (*nirguna*) aspects of Brahman as the ultimate reality in Hinduism. Here Gandhi's position, in terms of this framework, is clear: he believes in a personal God, or *saguna Brahman*.[13] But this personal God can possess impersonal and personal dimensions. God is not, to Gandhi, a person like a human person but a living reality, as is clear from Gandhi's writings. A human person is also a living reality, but God is not a human person. What is meant by stating that God possesses both impersonal and personal dimensions is that God is both law and love. God, however, remains indefinable. A philosophical reason for this is provided by Gandhi's comparison of God to Euclid's point, which is said to possess no dimension. It has also been credibly proposed that Gandhi might have been reluctant to define the nature of God because everyone has a personal conception of God.[14]

Although God cannot be defined or known, it is possible to have access to God. Gandhi seems to suggest that God is accessible in two ways: by way of introspection and by way of selfless service—that is, by way of one's inner self and by way of the rest of creation. One can hear the voice of God within oneself. There is always the danger of hearing not the voice of God but one's own echo, but this does not mean that the voice of God cannot be heard. The higher the moral purity of one's life, the greater the probability that it is God's voice that is being heard.

Gandhi candidly claims to have heard the voice of God and asserts that others have heard God too, although he knows no way of proving it. For Gandhi, God would not be God if he became an object of proof in the hands of his creatures.

Gandhi, God, and Goodness

Gandhi even claims that "his voice has been increasingly audible as the years have rolled by," yet there is no way of proving this except through results.[15] Whether a voice is God's cannot be verified ex ante, only ex post.

The other way of accessing God is through his creation. That is why Gandhi states that in order to see the "Spirit of Truth" face to face, "one must be able to love the meanest creature as oneself."[16] For Gandhi, heights were meant to be looked at, not to be looked from. God existed in all things as their essence, and all things existed in God as modifications. It is not so much that those who want to draw close to God think any less of themselves. It is rather the case that they think of themselves less and of God and God's creation more.

It is as if the "impersonal" aspect of God could be approached through *truth* and the personal aspect through *love*, although we must remember that in Gandhian philosophy, truth is at times described as love, and love can hardly be impersonal. Gandhi explains his entry into politics in terms of this passion to serve the meanest creature: "That is why my devotion to Truth has drawn me into the field of politics; and I can say without the slightest hesitation, and yet in all humility, that those who say that religion has nothing to do with politics do not know what religion means."[17] We could misconstrue this statement if we forgot that for Gandhi, religion and morality were synonymous.

A word may not be out of place here on the interplay of the impersonal and the personal, which runs like a thread through Hindu and Gandhian thought. The use of the concepts appears forbiddingly philosophical at first sight, but much of the opaqueness disappears, and even turns into richness, when it is realized that their interplay reveals four tantalizing possibilities: (1) It is possible to have an impersonal attitude toward the impersonal, as when an anonymous scientist studies an unknown virus; (2) it is also possible to have a personal attitude toward the impersonal, as when a person "loves" truth or justice; (3) it is possible to have a personal attitude toward the personal, as when we love our children or as when a devotee loves God; and (4) it is also possible to have an impersonal attitude toward the personal, as when a judge presides over a case. Even this list does not exhaust the possibilities. The impersonal can sometimes act like a person, as when lightning strikes a sinner. Thus God can be both law and love.

III

What we have discussed so far about Gandhi's ideas of God, truth, and ahimsa is factual and autobiographical but largely noncontroversial, if somewhat philosophical. Controversy entered in a particular case. On January 15, 1934, the Indian state of Bihar was shaken by an earthquake in its northern parts. Gandhi was traveling in South India at the time. The telegram that Gandhi received from his lieutenant in Bihar, Dr. Rajendra Prasad, on January 21, reads: "Earthquake has wrought terrible havoc. . . . Death casualties anything between ten and fifteen thousand and countless injured. Indescribable damage to property. Appalling suffering." Telegraphic brevity fails to convey the apocalyptic nature of the disaster, which needs to be recognized to understand the way Gandhi interpreted an event that was probably caused by the movement of tectonic plates. But geological knowledge would have been small consolation for the residents in the towns and villages who had been reduced to destitution in three minutes.[18] To the person standing on the shaken ground, the earthquake must have seemed like the infliction of divine wrath, like the beginning of the end of the world.

It certainly seemed so to Gandhi. To the consternation of his more rational friends, Gandhi saw a vital link between the Bihar calamity and the untouchability campaign. The nuances of his belief, spelled out in the following passage, are important for an appreciation of the theology of the event in Gandhian terms.

> I share the belief with the whole world—civilized and uncivilized—that the calamities such as the Bihar one, come to mankind as chastisement for their sins. And when that conviction comes from the heart, the people pray, repent and purify themselves. I regard untouchability as such a grave sin as to warrant divine chastisement. I am not affected by the posers such as "why punishment for an age-old sin," or "why punishment to Bihar and not to the south," or "why an earthquake and why not some other form of punishment." My answer is that: I am not God. Therefore, I have but a limited knowledge of His purpose. Such calamities are not a mere caprice of the deity or nature. They obey fixed laws as surely as the planets move in obedience to laws governing their movement. Only we do not know the laws governing these events and, therefore, call them calamities or disturbances. Whatever may be said about them must be regarded as guesswork. But guessing has its definite place in man's life. It is an ennobling thing for me to guess that the Bihar calamity is due to the sin of untouchability. It makes me humble, it spurs me to greater effort towards its removal, it encourages me to purify myself, and it brings me nearer to my Maker. That my guess may be wrong does not affect the results named by me. For what is a guess to the critic or the sceptic is a living belief with me, and I base my future actions on that belief. Such guesses become superstitions, when they lead to no purification and may even lead to feuds. But such misuse of divine events cannot deter men of faith from interpret-

ing them as a call to them for repentance for their sins. I do not interpret this chastisement as an exclusive punishment for the sin of untouchability. It is open to others to read in it the divine wrath against many other sins.[19]

On the last point, he was even prepared to admit that those Hindus who opposed his campaign for the abolition of untouchability were fully justified in claiming that the earthquake was a punishment brought about by Gandhi's campaign against it.[20] In any case, for Gandhi, karma was woven so densely into the fabric of the universe that even natural events were moral events.

Rabindranath Tagore (1861–1941), the person who gave Gandhi the title Mahatma, by which he is known now, was appalled by this kind of logic. In a carefully crafted letter, in which he acknowledged immense gratitude to Gandhi for what he had done for his compatriots, he nevertheless expressed his "hurt" that Gandhi was promoting "unreason." His criticism was twofold: Gandhi's interpretation was morally pernicious, for even a human ruler will not make an ethical point so callously, and it was unscientific. Tagore felt compelled to state the scientific truism that physical events had physical causes.[21]

Gandhi responded by asserting that human knowledge is like a particle of dust in the face of God's laws, although he admitted that he did not know the laws' workings and asserted that God ruled him in the tiniest details of his life. Gandhi believed literally that not a leaf moves except by God's will. He agreed with Tagore (whom he addressed as Gurudev or Revered Teacher) that God does not interfere in the inexorable working of universal laws because he is law itself. For Gandhi, disturbances like droughts, floods, and earthquakes, though physical in origin, are "somehow" related to human

Gandhi, God, and Goodness

beings' morals. That is why he instinctively felt that the earth-quake was a punishment for the sin of untouchability. He added that if the instinctive connection that he felt was proven to be false, it would still have done some good for Gandhi and those who believed him.[22]

In his response to Tagore, he also addresses the elephant in the room, namely, the charge that he was indulging in superstition. Here he claims that such a belief would be superstition only if it led him to harm others.[23]

Gandhi and Tagore, regarded by many as the two great Indians of their time, were both theists, and their exchange needs to be examined critically and closely for the light it sheds on Gandhian thought by reciprocal illumination. The significance of the exchange really lies in the facets it reveals.

One facet is the moral earnestness of Gandhi's response. Even when Gandhi accepts that *ontologically* everything happens according to the will of God, he emphasizes that *morally* human beings are responsible for their own actions. Every movement we make on the surface of the earth is affected by the law of gravitation, but we cannot blame the law of gravitation if we trip and fall. We are responsible for our fall even if we hold God responsible for the law. Similarly, when Gandhi admits the possibility that the connection he has forged between the earthquake and untouchability may turn out to be ill founded, he points to the salutary moral effect of such a belief, inasmuch as it might provoke moral introspection and even purification. And he distinguishes his "speculation" from "superstition" because it draws him "nearer to god." So spirituality and morality for Gandhi go hand in hand; this would be one way of interpreting his dual emphasis on truth and nonviolence.[24]

Another facet of Gandhian philosophy is revealed when we revisit the dialectic between God and truth found in Gandhi, and his metathetical inversion of the statement from "God is

Truth," to "Truth is God." We saw earlier how the latter formulation possesses a more universal appeal. One way of moving further down this line of analysis would be to ask: Which consciousness—theistic consciousness or moral consciousness —is more universal? A little reflection suggests that perhaps moral consciousness should be considered more universal. Everyone may not agree on what is right and what is wrong, but everyone possesses a consciousness of right and wrong. To put it paradoxically, everyone possesses an identical consciousness, although the content of that consciousness may not be identical. We are led once again to the importance of moral consciousness in Gandhian thought.

Let us ask a further question: Is aesthetic consciousness more universal than moral consciousness? Even a child responds to musical beats, although the moral consciousness of the child may not have awakened yet. In that sense, aesthetic consciousness may be said to be even more universal than moral consciousness. But Gandhi did not travel further down that road, and beauty remained for him forever linked with truth and goodness.[25] We could tease the issue out even further by asking: Is aesthetic consciousness or sex consciousness more universal? We could, in some sense, argue for the greater universality of sex consciousness, which might help explain the development of tantra—the rituals and practices associated with sex—within Hinduism, Buddhism, and Jainism, but Gandhi did not go there, either.

Two other points of general significance emerge from the exchange between Gandhi and Tagore. Tagore here is the voice of the Enlightenment, of reason, and he sees danger in the voice of Gandhi becoming a voice of endarkment, of unreason, if Gandhi employs the kind of logic that connected the earthquake to untouchability. The assumption is that everything has to fall within the grid of reason or unreason, rationality or irrationality. But Gandhi, by emphasizing that

Gandhi, God, and Goodness

we, or science, may not know all that is to be known, seems to imply a broader grid, which we may identify as consisting of three terms: the rational, the irrational, and the non-rational. From this point of view, the great disservice of the Enlightenment, all its positive services notwithstanding, was to define modernity in terms of the first two referents alone, thereby conflating irrationality and nonrationality. This conflation might explain some of the ills of modern civilization. Gandhi's dissatisfaction with modern civilization, which is well known, may have been based partly on this instinctive realization. Our friendships, our family relationships, the world of art and literature, the sense of transcendence—all these are neither rational nor irrational: they are non-rational.

Gandhi's use of the earthquake to make a moral point may also indicate that there is a deep place in Gandhian philosophy for suffering. Gandhi even describes nonviolence as "conscious suffering." What Gandhi seems to be saying is that whenever the status quo is going to be disturbed, a status quo in the continuance of which there are vested interests, there is bound to be suffering. So the real question is: Who is going to do the suffering? Should we not accept suffering willingly? Because this is the question for Gandhi, love and suffering are almost inextricably bound up. We come to love not by finding a perfect person but by learning to see an imperfect person perfectly. The point of interest for us at the moment, however, is the Gandhian view that while reason may fail to carry conviction to the wrongdoer, suffering will not fail to convince.[26] There could also be an element of this in Gandhi's connection of the suffering caused by the earthquake with untouchability. The aftermath of an earthquake is suffering made visible. Very simply, Gandhi may have intended to make the invisible suffering of untouchability visible to the Hindus.

In the course of his exchange with Rabindranath Tagore, Gandhi makes a significant point from the perspective of his spiritual biography: "I have long believed that physical phenomena produce results both physical and spiritual. The converse I hold to be equally true."[27] Although Gandhi speaks here about the interaction between the physical or material realm and the spiritual realm, it is the distinction between them that provides the key to understanding his spiritual orientation.

IV

Our life, as we live it every day, discloses two features about the earthly world with which we are in constant contact and which are in constant contact with each other. First, the world possesses a material dimension; it consists of numerous material objects of different shapes and sizes—from the pen we write with, to the jet airliner in which we travel. Our physical bodies also belong to this realm. Second, the world possesses an immaterial dimension. This consists of our thoughts and feelings and, above all, our consciousness. These two dimensions are very different from each other, but we are constantly, if not consciously, in contact with both. The material and the immaterial worlds are obviously also in constant contact themselves.

If we approach these facts of life philosophically, then three major philosophical tendencies can be traced to them. Philosophers sometimes insist that one of these dimensions is a by-product of the other, so the two can be reduced to one. Those who claim that the immaterial dimension can be reduced to the material espouse what is called materialism, which covers a wide range of opinions, all the way from scientific materialism, which reduces all immaterial phenomena to matter, to Marxist materialism, which reduces historical developments to material and economic forces. Some philosophers make the opposite claim, namely, that the material world can be reduced to the immaterial. This philosophical position is generally referred to as idealism, which also covers a gamut of positions, ranging from the idealism of George Berkeley, to the schools of idealism found in Hinduism, Buddhism, and even Confucianism. The modern Western world essentially subscribes to materialism. Asian thought, and especially Indian thought, possesses a pronounced idealistic orientation in this philosophical sense. These two positions represent a durable conundrum of philosophy: Are things because of the mind, or is the mind a mind because of things? A third group of philosophers refuse to reduce one to the other and accept the dual reality of both matter and spirit. These philosophers thus subscribe to what is best described as a fundamental dualism.

In order to see the relevance of this distinction between materialism and idealism in the context of Gandhi, we have to take it into account religiously rather than philosophically. Gandhi flirted with philosophy all his life, but he never embraced it. Religion, however, was a matter of life and death to him—or even more important than that.

The way the distinction plays out in religion makes it possible to offer a credible natural or material account of the universe, as well as a spiritual or theistic account of it. The universe hangs before us in the form of a huge question mark, as it were, demanding an explanation. It was the spiritual or theistic explanation that, by and large, prevailed in the premodern age. The rapid progress of science in the past few centuries has now also produced a credible natural or material explanation of the universe as a rival to the explanation provided by religion. If one is not committed to either of the two positions in advance, then it may not be unfair to say that we now possess *two* fairly credible accounts. Of the two, Gandhi opted for what we might call the spiritual and theistic account, with full awareness of the existence of the natural account.

A seemingly innocent paragraph in his autobiography illustrates the point. When his ten-year-old son Manilal contracted typhoid, the doctor recommended eggs and chicken broth, a recommendation that ran counter to Gandhi's belief in vegetarianism. So Gandhi instead relied on hydropathy. The whole incident is covered earlier in this book; what we need to take into account here is the passage with which Gandhi concludes the pertinent chapter in his autobiography. It was also cited earlier: "Today Manilal is the healthiest of my boys. Who can say whether his recovery was due to God's grace, or to hydropathy, or to careful dietary and nursing? Let everybody decide according to his own faith. For my part I was sure that God had saved my honour, and that belief remains unaltered to this day."[28]

For Gandhi, just as both a credible natural account and a credible theistic account *of the universe* are possible, similar rival accounts of what *goes on in this universe* are also possible. Gandhi alludes to both accounts of the universe and then favors the theistic for himself.

The word "faith" in the quoted passage is crucial, enabling us to conclude the chapter by indicating the real significance of the word "spiritual" in the expression "spiritual biography." If two possible explanations are equally plausible, then choosing one has to be an act of faith. If proof were available either way, then faith would no longer be involved. This book has been an attempt to demonstrate how, when presented with such choices, Gandhi *chose* to emphasize the spiritual dimension rather than the material, and with what consequences.

····

18

▰▰▰

Demythologizing and Analyzing Gandhi

I

The spiritual biography of a person like Gandhi, with its sustained focus on the spiritual, runs the risk of turning into a hagiography. The spiritual, however, constitutes only one of many dimensions of a person's life and personality. In other words, we need to run a reality check in order to gain a balanced perspective on Gandhi.[1] Gandhi needs to be demythologized, and not just because he may have been mythologized— deliberately and falsely projected as something he was not—but also because it might be easy to get carried away at times by his larger-than-life achievements.

How such developments might occur can be gauged from an incident in Gandhi's life, narrated by someone who has been described by another writer on Gandhi as the author of "perhaps the best general biography of Gandhi." Louis Fischer writes:

> At Dacca, in Bengal, a man of seventy was brought before Gandhi. He was wearing Gandhi's photograph around his neck and weeping profusely. As he approached the Mahatma, he fell on his face and thanked Gandhi for having cured him of chronic paralysis. "When all other remedies failed," the poor man said, "I took to uttering Gandhiji's name, and one day I found myself entirely cured."
>
> "It is not I but God who made you whole," Gandhi rebuked him. "Will you not oblige me by taking the photograph off your neck?"[2]

Of such stuff are hagiographies made, but Gandhi himself demythologizes this incident by attributing the supposed miraculous healing to God. In doing so, Gandhi cleaves to an official theological line. A statement in the New Testament (Acts 4:12), which is often taken as a proof-text for proselytization in Christianity, runs: "For there is no other name under heaven given among human beings, whereby we must be saved." Krister Stendahl points out that the statement is made by Peter in answer to the accusation that he had performed a miracle in his own name. Peter answers by exclaiming: "Heavens no, in no other name is there salvation but Jesus." The response from within the Hindu and Buddhist traditions would be somewhat similar—that it is the person's own faith that secures the effect. In the anecdote, it is the person's faith in Gandhi (and not Gandhi himself) that is at work.[3] Of course, we may wonder how Gandhi could arouse such faith when we cannot.

Gandhi demythologizes himself, but we have yet to demythologize Gandhi.

Let us begin by placing under a critical lens what is considered by common consent to be Gandhi's greatest achievement, namely, leading India to political independence from Britain through nonviolent means. It could be questioned whether this outcome was brought about nonviolently. Skeptics point out that the amount of bloodshed and bad blood that accompanied the arrival of India's independence was enormous. The Partition, with which Indian Independence was Siamese-twinned, cost anywhere between half a million to a million lives and displaced another fourteen million people.[4] The skeptical thrust here is even more powerful when pushed forward, for the American Civil War cost almost as many lives. Would not it have been better for India to have undergone a civil war, cruel as that may sound? Civil war may still have ended in a partition, but then at least the people of India would have been reconciled to the existence of Pakistan. That they are not reconciled to it may be gauged by the way the slightest praise for its founder, Muhammad Ali Jinnah, rocks the country and puts the political careers of those praising him in jeopardy, as demonstrated not so long ago in the case of the leader of the Bharatiya Janata Party, L. K. Advani.[5] And who is to say that an attempt at secession would have succeeded?

Such a counterfactual critique, involving the ifs of history, though suggestive, is hypothetical rather than substantial in nature. According to a more substantial version of this critique, the nonviolent independence movement was a mere shadow play behind which lay forces of realpolitik that determined the outcome. Gandhi and the viceroy, or the Indian National Congress and the British Raj, were engaged in prolonged, choreographed shadow-boxing while the real action took place elsewhere. The argument moves along several lines, but they converge. The main argument is that Indians had no option except to try to dislodge the British nonviolently because they had been disarmed by the British after the Mutiny of 1857. So what we see as a Gandhian virtue was in fact a political necessity. Moreover, the argument goes, the outcome of the movement was governed by military (and not moral) considerations. The British introduced two key rules after the Mutiny of 1857–1858 in order to prevent a recurrence. In that mutiny almost all of the 139,000 sepoys of the Bengal Army—then the largest modern army in Asia—turned against their British masters. After the British suppressed it, the army was completely reorganized, with Europeans put in sole charge of artillery. The number of Europeans in the army was also increased so that Indian soldiers never outnumbered Europeans by more than five to two. This arrangement remained in place until 1914.[6]

The twist is in the tail: "until 1914." That is, the arrangement stood until the beginning of the First World War. That war, and the subsequent one, made it impossible for the British to uphold the two rules. The independence movement got going just when these safeguards crumbled. Finally, when the ratings of the Royal Indian Navy mutinied in February 1946, the maritime power that was Britain saw the handwriting on the wall (or on the waves) and soon quit.[7]

This militarily reductionist approach possesses one merit. It indicates the invisible changes that were occurring in the military balance of power, behind the visible mass movements, and takes some sheen off the nonviolent struggle by suggesting the possibility that its outcome may have been determined in the old-fashioned way—by a shift in the balance of power. It is a matter of serious conjecture whether India would have gained its independence when it did if Britain had not been exhausted, in all senses of the term, by the end of the Second World War. This idea once again suggests that Indian independence was not purely the outcome of a nonviolent struggle. Britain won the war but lost the empire. Hitler perhaps

Demythologizing and Analyzing Gandhi

also made his own dubious contribution toward Indian independence, even if saying so sticks in the craw.

But there is another elephant in the room that no one talks about. This is the role that the Indian National Army, or INA, may have played in the British decision to leave India. The INA was the brainchild of Netaji Subhas Chandra Bose, who, unlike Gandhi, had not disavowed violence in fighting the British and had clashed with Gandhi even within the congress, defeating Gandhi's candidate for the post of the president. About ninety thousand Indian soldiers of the British army had surrendered to the Japanese by 1942. Bose, having fled British detention in India, reached Germany and then traveled by submarine from Europe to Southeast Asia, where he forged an army out of these soldiers, who had surrendered *from* the British army, to fight *against* the British. This new army engaged the British army only briefly and unsuccessfully in Assam but created a sensation in India. What this demonstrated dramatically to all was that the British could no longer rely on the loyalty of their Indian soldiers, and the nightmare of the Mutiny once again began to stalk the dream of empire. Neither Indian nor British historians like to acknowledge the role that the formation of the INA might have played in advancing Indian independence. Indian historians like to depict the achievement of independence as the unalloyed outcome of the heroic nonviolent Gandhian struggle, while British historians like to depict it as an act of selfless British imperial magnanimity and to claim that "the fetters were never in fact broken by force, but began to be removed one by one as soon as they began to be rattled by the other."[8] Both fairy tales would like to banish the ghost of the INA.

Thus Indian independence was secured neither by the Gandhian movement nor exactly by nonviolent means. That the sometime Gandhian insistence on nonviolence becomes pathetic in the incongruity of its sublimity becomes apparent in Gandhi's advice to the Jews, to submit nonviolently and gallantly to Hitler—a position on which Martin Buber offers a noteworthy critique.[9] Gandhi urged the Jews to pray for Hitler, arguing that if even one Jew could set such a contagious example, the whole of Jewry could be saved.[10] If the Jews were wiped out in a nonviolent struggle, they would leave behind a noble example for the world to follow—a nonviolent Masada. Jews might well have wondered if they should allow themselves to be destroyed so that posterity might speak well of them.

Gandhi's policies toward the former untouchables and the Muslims have also been faulted. Former untouchables, many of whom now prefer to call themselves Dalit (downtrodden) accuse Gandhi of being patronizing by calling them Harijan and for not going all out to attack the caste system at the root. Dr. B. R. Ambedkar, the political leader of the people who now call themselves Dalits, felt quite bitter toward Gandhi and participated only partially in Gandhi's funeral. Some argue that Gandhi brought religion into politics and thus paved the way for Partition, although others point out that the British had already done so by granting separate electorates based on religion to the Muslims in 1909. Even Gandhi's death could not convince Jinnah of his sincerity. In any case, the "cold and immaculate Jinnah had triumphed over Gandhi." Pakistan, like Islam, was born in triumph; India was not.[11]

The Partition of India poses the most serious challenge to the mythos of Gandhi because it reveals the limits of many of his key ideas. Even while in South Africa, Gandhi had written that the true test would come on the question of Hindu-Muslim unity. It is worth recalling that the Indian National Congress, which he made into a political force, achieved virtually all of its major objectives except an undivided India. Anything one says on the issue of Partition is open to contestation, but the agitation leading to the formation of Pakistan does reveal some apparent limitations of two Gandhian claims:

Demythologizing and Analyzing Gandhi

that nonviolence can effectively combat violence and that voluntary suffering can transform the enemy. Gandhian non-violence could deal with the *organized* violence of the state in India, as represented by the British Raj, but it seems to have had no answer for the *random* violence unleashed by the Muslim League in the run-up to the Partition.[12] Nor could Gandhi's sacrifice, even after Partition, bring about a change in Jinnah's attitude. Although Gandhi had lost his life for backing Muslims and Pakistan, Jinnah, in his note of condolence, referred to him merely as a "Hindu leader" and disregarded his aide's interjection that this description might be reconsidered in the light of recent events culminating in Gandhi's martyrdom. Gandhi's response could well have been that not all nonviolent struggles succeed, no more than violent ones do, and that if one has not transformed an opponent's heart, it is because one has not suffered enough.

However, Partition, and not just the Independence of India, can be explained in terms of realpolitik. The Indian Civil Service officer Penderel Moon, in a note he prepared in December 1945, observed that the British might find it easier to obtain Hindu consent to Partition than Muslim consent to an undivided India. From the British perspective, keeping India united against Muslim wishes would certainly involve force, but dividing India against Hindu wishes might not involve force, and in any case, the force required was likely to be less. Although Hindus in the rest of India might have lamented the fate of their co-religionists in Bengal and the Punjab, they were unlikely to come to their aid.[13]

Gandhi's personal life has also been called into question. He prevented penicillin from being administered to his faithful dying wife, for he felt that the time for such treatment was past. Did Gandhi feel so close to God that he had begun to play God? His relations with his sons remained far from satisfactory. He wanted them to follow his lifestyle, but as his wife, Kasturbai, once put it colorfully: "You may be a *mahatma,* but I don't want my children to be *mahatmas!*"[14] Gandhi acknowledges that his sons "have some reason for a grievance against me. Indeed they have occasionally given expression to it, and I must plead guilty to a certain extent." He admits: "I did not prove an ideal father."[15] The back of a painting is not as alluring as the front.

For many, however, Gandhi stands on a pedestal despite seismic shocks and his feet of clay because much of that clay was gathered as he incessantly trudged the Indian country-side to secure India's independence, douse fires of religious hatred, and fight the sin of untouchability. The movements he launched touched one in every two hundred Indians. His movement for independence may not have been the sole fac-tor involved in the achievement of Indian independence, but it was certainly a key factor. His role was crucial, if only be-cause he left behind a nationwide Congress Party to which power could be transferred. The same historian who makes this sober assessment brings the same perspective to bear on other issues about which Gandhi was criticized when he writes: "Though he was an extraordinary mixture, we may conclude by asserting that his essential integrity is attested by two facts. He knowingly provoked Brahmin orthodoxy by his untouch-able or Harijan campaign, and he knowingly provoked Hindu fanaticism by his stand for the Muslims of Delhi after the post-Independence riots. Gandhi died for his faith, and in dying he created a nation."[16] He died, in fact, for the cause of Hindu-Muslim unity even after the formation of Pakistan. For him, the issue of Hindu-Muslim unity transcended geography.

II

Since Gandhi treated his life as an indivisible whole, perhaps it is not out of place to dwell on the political and social dimensions of his life. As we revert to the spiritual dimension, two issues confront us as we continue to demythologize his life, one more general than the other, although they are interconnected: (1) How did Gandhi rise above the various encumbering particularities found within Hinduism? and (2) How did Gandhi rise above the particularity of being a Hindu? In other words, how are we to understand the ethical dimensions of Gandhi's struggle in the context of doctrinal issues within Hinduism; and if Gandhi was born, lived, and died a Hindu, then how are we to harmonize the Hindu Gandhi with the universal Gandhi? The thrust of these questions should not be underestimated, for Gandhi self-consciously claimed to be an orthodox (*sanatani*) Hindu when his status as a Hindu was challenged, and as consciously insisted on not being *just* a Hindu when dubbed as such by the Muslim League and at times the British. More than one scholar has noted that he shared many ideas and ideals with orthodox Hindus, and some are even baffled by his advocacy of cow protection, on the one hand, and his indifference to Hindu idolatry, on the other.[17]

In what spirit did Gandhi support Hindu practices? According to Gandhi, cow protection put animal creation on the same level as human creation so far as the right to life is involved. It was an earnest of a future in which human beings will outgrow eating the meat of animals, just as they have evolved beyond eating the flesh of fellow human beings, or cannibalism. Although himself not given to worshipping idols, he wrote, "I value the spirit behind idol-worship. It plays an important part in the uplift of the human race." He also pointed out that real idolatry consisted in the refusal "to see any virtue in any other form of worshipping the Deity save one's own." So Gandhi connected the cow with humanitarianism, and idolatry with religious tolerance. So far as the various incarnations of God are concerned, Gandhi, like any

Hindu, accepted all the various names and forms attributed to God as connoting one formless God he called Rama.[18] This Rama was identical with God, who was identical with truth. Gandhi may be said to have thus monotheicized and ethicized Hinduism, but the point is that for Gandhi, these doctrines or dogmas were really moral or ethical practices.

In fact, given Gandhi's ethical bent, we might wish to ask another question here: What about Gandhi's own religious practices, as opposed to his attitude toward some of the general Hindu religious practices? Gandhi was actually twitted by some of his fellow Hindus for not visiting temples, or performing Hindu rituals, or celebrating Hindu festivals, although the charge never stuck given the plural nature of Hinduism. Two Hindu words help capture the spirit that pervaded Gandhi's practice of Hinduism: *svadhyaya* and *bhajan*. The former has an individualistic orientation and the latter a congregational one. The word *svadhyaya* stands for scriptural study and the prayer and meditation it entails. For Gandhi it included the study not only of the Bhagavad Gita and the Tulsi *Ramayana*, his favorite texts, but of the scriptures of all religions in the same spirit. The word *bhajan* stands for a hymn sung in unison by the faithful, which is often the composition of a famous poet-saint of the tradition, which, again, for Gandhi included hymns from other religions, such as "Lead Kindly Light" by Cardinal Newman, which confirmed Gandhi in his view that it was not necessary to see the whole staircase to heaven before taking the first step. Gandhi's prayer meetings combined these two elements. They usually commenced with readings from the world's scriptures, continued with Gandhi's sermon, such as it was, and concluded with the singing of bhajans. Gandhi's meetings could even be called a form of *satsang*, a word redolent with meaning in Hinduism; it evokes a gathering of God's devotees regardless of caste and creed. Thus Gandhi's credentials as a practicing Hindu are not in doubt. What requires further exploration is Gandhi's relationship to Hinduism and how that might be usefully understood within the framework of Gandhi's insistence that he was a sanatani, or orthodox Hindu. Although Gandhi challenged Hinduism in places, he did not contradict it as a whole; and although he transcended aspects of it, he did not supersede it.

III

Hinduism, from one point of view, may be identified as a religion whose distinguishing features consist of five doctrines: (1) dharma, or normative conduct, and what it might be based on; (2) the varnas, or the fourfold division of society; (3) the asramas, or the four stages of life; (4) the *purusarthas,* or the four goals of life, and (5) the *samanya dharmas,* or universal norms or duties, over and above the varna and asrama dharmas, or norms or duties specific to particular classes or stages of life.

The received Hindu tradition, of which Gandhi was a legatee, possessed certain regnant patterns with respect to each of these five points. With regard to dharma, the regnant view was that there are four sources or means of determining normative conduct: revelation (called *sruti*); tradition (called *smrti*); example or the emulation of the acts of the worthies (called *acara*); and what is most easily rendered in English by the term "conscience" (called *atmatusti*). This order had a certain hierarchical air about it. A devotee seeking to act correctly usually consults the sources in order—revelation; failing which, tradition; failing which, example; failing which, conscience—although Hinduism being what it is, different strands of opinion within it also claim the supremacy of each source. Gandhi respected all four sources but ultimately fell back on his "inner voice," or conscience. He expressed his veneration for the scriptures and respect for the spokespersons of the religion who rely on scriptures, but he declined "to be bound by any interpretation repugnant to reason or moral sense."[19]

Similarly, with respect to the doctrine of varnas, Gandhi accepted the fourfold division of society into (1) Brahmins, or priests and scholars; (2) Kshatriyas, or warriors and bureaucrats; (3) Vaishyas, or agriculturists and traders (the class to which he belonged); and (4) Shudras, or laborers, which were of two kinds, the not-excluded (*anirvasita*) and the excluded (*nirvasita*). The excluded Shudras were the untouchables. Varnas also have a hierarchy, but here also, although Gandhi accepted the classification, he rejected or even reversed the hierarchy, instead regarding the four divisions of society as complementary and dismissing the idea of one being higher or lower than the other.[20] We know that in practice he concentrated on the untouchables at the bottom.

The doctrine of the asramas, or the four stages of life, offers a template for life. One begins life as a celibate student (brahmacharya) and then leads the life of a householder (*garhasthya*). These two stages of living in the world broadly cover the first half of life. They are followed by residence in a forest while one is still a family person (*vanaprasthya*) until one renounces the world, becoming a *sannyasi,* and seeks liberation. Although the householders are the mainstay of society and acknowledged as such, the Hindu value system holds up the renunciant, the *sannyasi,* as its ideal type, at least spiritually. Those in this stage of life, into which one can leapfrog from the student stage if one is impatient for liberation, usually don saffron robes. The regnant view here attaches maximum value to sannyasa. But Gandhi, although he led an ascetic life, never took sannyasa and in fact made a conscious decision to live life in accordance with the *third* stage, a point alluded to in an earlier chapter.[21]

According to the doctrine of the purusarthas, human be-ings can pursue four legitimate goals in life. These are *kama* (the pursuit of pleasure), *artha* (the pursuit of wealth and power), dharma (the pursuit of virtue), and moksha (the pur-suit of liberation or salvation). They represent an ascending arc of values. The end to which the ultimate value is attached within received Hinduism is no doubt moksha, and while Gan-dhi openly states that his goal in life was moksha, he was all along most concerned with the pursuit of morality, or dharma, as a way of achieving it. As mentioned earlier, he had written as a teenager: "One thing took deep root in me—the convic-tion that morality is the basis of things, and that truth is the substance of all morality."[22]

Finally, Hindu scriptures, especially when they discuss the Hindu doctrines of varna and asrama, the doctrines of the classes of society and the stages of life, make a vital distinc-tion between those duties that are specific to one's class (e.g., warriors must protect) or one's stage in life (e.g., household-ers must beget children)—that is, *varnasrama dharmas*—and those duties that are incumbent on each person irrespective of class or stage in life. The latter, the samanya dharmas (gen-eral duties or duties in common), include truth, nonviolence, non-stealing, purity, self-control, and so on. The key question is: What is one to do if duties come into conflict? The classic case is of a warrior, whose varna dharma, or specific duty, is to fight, but whose samanya dharma, or general duty, is to practice nonviolence. Hindu ethics, in principle, tries to nego-tiate this gray area on a case by case basis, but in Hindu prac-tice, in Gandhi's time, the specific dharmas had come to pre-ponderate over the general or universal ones. Here Gandhi's intervention was decisively in favor of the universal duties of truth and nonviolence.

In relation to Hinduism, then, Gandhi valued the overall structure of the tradition but wrought cardinal changes within it by introducing ordinal changes into it, thus resolving the paradox of belonging to a tradition but also transforming it while following it. This is how the ethical dimension of Gandhi's struggle intersects with dogmatic Hindu positions. Gandhi achieved his outcomes by a shift in emphasis in principle and in praxis. That is why his programs, often moderate and even traditional in formulation, were often radical in their impact. And if we doubt whether a mere shift in emphasis can be revolutionary, we need only to remind ourselves that from one point of view, what Martin Luther did was to shift the relative emphasis from works to faith—thereby giving rise to the Protestant movement within Christianity. Every religious tradition seems to possess an elusive quality that exceeds its contents, a quality by which it is periodically reinvigorated.

This point can be illustrated by analyzing Gandhi's approach to untouchability. The classical justification of untouchability runs as follows: You are a Hindu; as a Hindu, you believe in karma—that your morality determines your destiny; birth (= rebirth) in a particular varna (class) or *jati* (caste) is based on karma; thus, if you are born an untouchable, that is the result of your karma. Here is a schematic depiction:

Hindu
  ↓
karma and rebirth
  ↓
the caste system based on birth
  ↓
untouchability

The Christian and Islamic answer to the problem of untouchability was to maintain that one must cease to be a Hindu to get rid of untouchability, because then the other dominoes of logic fall automatically. Dr. B. R. Ambedkar's

Demythologizing and Analyzing Gandhi

position was that one can stop being a Hindu and not stop believing in karma and rebirth—for the linkage between karma and caste is not accepted in Buddhism, Jainism, or Sikhism. So Dr. B. R. Ambedkar became a Buddhist. Most modern Hindu reformers retained their Hindu identity and belief in karma and rebirth, but they questioned birth as the basis for determining membership of a particular class or caste and instead emphasized worth or qualities as constituting the basis of the classification. Using this line of reasoning, no one can be an untouchable by birth; one becomes untouchable only by performing heinous actions. Where some attack the problem of untouchability at the level of Hinduism, others at the level of karma and rebirth, still others at the level of caste ascription by birth, Gandhi was almost unique in describing it as an excrescence on the caste system, to be attacked only and directly at its own level, without engaging the other levels. Holding to this most *conservative* doctrinal position among those available, he brought about a *radical* change in Hindu attitudes toward untouchability, exceeding the changes wrought by those who held more radical views, although the current generation of former untouchables might consider the changes insufficient. Many untouchables who criticize Gandhi do so from outside the pale of Hinduism, however. Unlike them, Gandhi was trying to address the issue from within the matrix of Hinduism. Gandhi, in other words, was for unraveling the Gordian knot, not cutting it.

And yet, just as a seam begins to unravel when a single thread is pulled, so Gandhi's views on untouchability had revolutionary implications for how the doctrines of Hinduism came to be interpreted. When Gandhi faced discrimination in South Africa, as when a white barber refused to cut his hair, he reflected: "We do not allow our barbers to serve our untouchable brethren. I got the reward of this in South Africa, not once, but many times and the conviction that it was the punishment for our own sins saved me from becoming angry."[23] The doctrine of karma has been used to justify discrimination against the untouchables in India. By using it to justify discrimination against him in South Africa, Gandhi upended the traditional explanation. Karma was used to blame the victim in the case of the untouchables; now Gandhi argued that Indians became the victims of racial discrimination as the karmic consequence of victimizing the untouchables. Those who discriminated against people on the basis of birth-ascription were discriminated against in the same way. Gandhi thus offered a moral rather than a caste-related take on the doctrine of karma.

This claustrophobically Hindu discussion of Gandhi's role in the modern formulation of Hinduism may now be followed by examining Gandhi's relationship with other religions, which he dealt with in broadly the same way: by placing the dogmatic elements in a larger ethical framework. Gandhi could not accept the dogma of salvation only through Christ, but he drew great moral inspiration from the figure of Jesus, whose painting he kept in his Johannesburg law office. He burst into tears on seeing Jesus's statue in St. Peter's Square in Rome. Similarly, after Partition, despite public objections, Gandhi had passages read from the Qur'an at his prayer meetings in Delhi. It was also in Delhi that he wept when shown a half-burnt copy of the Qur'an.[24] Gandhi could not be a Christian or a Muslim in the dogmatic sense, but he claimed to be both in accepting their moral teachings. Gandhi was always universalizing the particular and particularizing the universal.

IV

As we now perhaps see the universalizing principle operating in Gandhi's thought, a key question surfaces: Can Gandhi's own principles be universalized? His commitment to celibacy dramatizes the point at issue—did he, or can we, really expect the people of this world to be celibates, engaging in sex only for the sake of progeny, as an anguished Margaret Sanger wondered?

What was Gandhi's approach to this question?

He came at it from two opposite angles. With those who accepted his premises he would insist, without playing down the difficulty of the path and even comparing it to a razor's edge, that whatever was possible for him was also possible even for a child.[25] This take on the issue seemed to flow from his recognition of our common humanity; that is, whatever could be achieved by one could be achieved by anyone, by the mere fact of being a fellow human being. With those opposed to his premises, on the other hand, he urged opposition, as if truth would emerge from the churning of thought and action, just as nectar appeared when the gods and the demons churned the ocean in Hindu mythology. Gandhi then left the matter to the individual to decide about.

But is becoming celibate the only way to follow Gandhi?

An acolyte of Mahatma Gandhi's, Pyarelal, once advised his fellow Indians that "if they cannot follow Gandhi one hundred percent, then they might wish to follow him twenty percent or thirty percent." So if one cannot be a celibate like Gandhi, perhaps one can be faithful to one's spouse. The two are on the same continuum, namely, that of self-restraint. Seeing celibacy and faithfulness on a continuum helps us uncover a deeper link between two aspects of Gandhi's own life: his faithfulness to his wife and his subsequent vow of celibacy. We now see a logical progression. The two appear less apart, and as a result, Gandhi appears less apart from us. Whereas celibacy might be beyond our reach, chastity might not.

That Gandhi's ideas about truth and nonviolence were constantly evolving is in harmony with this approach. Such a calibration of his teachings is in accord with his teachings;

it is a part of his teachings. Gandhi's insistence that there is no such thing as Gandhism points in the same direction. After all, he called his autobiography the story of his *experiments* with truth. But if Gandhi experimented with truth, what was his laboratory? The laboratory was his life, and this is what makes his autobiography such a significant moral and spiritual document, as a record of his experiments.

Gandhi's concept of an experiment has a dynamic and a personal element that must not be lost sight of when considering how to apply Gandhi's principles personally. We have to carry out our own experiments as best as we can. Gandhi was well aware that such experiments involve risk.[26]

Once we realize this dynamic quality of our engagement with what we accept as our ideals, we also realize that progress down the pilgrim's path can be described in three apparently contradictory but reconcilable ways. If we choose to talk in terms of truth, then our progress may be described as (1) progress from error to error (for absolute truth may continue to elude us); or as (2) progress from error to truth (as we move forward to a position relatively closer to the truth than an earlier one); or as (3) progress from truth to truth (as we move from one relative truth to another higher but still relative truth). How we undertake this journey prompted by Gandhi is up to us, as is how we choose to describe it.

····

19

▄▄▄▄

Gandhi's Spiritual
Biography and
Contemporary History

The percentage of Americans who identify themselves as "spiritual" has been rising. According to a 2009 *Newsweek* poll, 30 percent of Americans call themselves "spiritual, not religious," up from 24 percent in 2005. However precisely measured the increase, the term "spiritual" is itself far from precise. To an extent, this is a function of the transition from "religious" to "spiritual" itself, for religion tends to be dogmatic and institutional, and hence definable, but spirituality is a more evocative concept, emphasizing individual freedom in the pursuit of truth. In a sense, then, people define their own spirituality. We have discovered that Gandhi's concept of spirituality contains two key elements: (1) goodness and (2) God. We might more formally refer to the latter as morality and theism. The preceding chapters dealt with his engagement with these elements. In this final chapter let us evaluate his spiritual biography in the light of contemporary history.

I. GANDHI'S TRUTH

Gandhi was always willing to stake his life, and others', in the pursuit of truth as he saw it. This commitment to truth is the golden thread that runs through the various events of his life. He staked his life when the occasion demanded it. He did not, for instance, fast to death to prevent the Partition of India. When he did stake his life, doing so naturally involved overcoming the *fear of death*. This is obvious. Less obvious is that he gave equal weight to both elements: fear and death. In ordinary parlance, death is the primary referent; we must overcome our fear of it. And this is clearly what some of Gandhi's moral actions involved. But for other actions he had to overcome not only his fear of death but also fear as such. What was he willing to die for? What is Gandhi's truth as revealed by his spiritual life?[1]

Gandhi is an iconic figure of the twentieth century. For the Indians, at any rate, he was Moses and Jesus rolled into one. He was a Moses because Indians were slaves in their own country, and he freed them with a mighty hand. He risked his life in doing so, ultimately sacrificing it in the process, like Jesus. He took on himself, as it were, the sins of Hindus, Muslims, and the British in one go. It would be difficult to diminish the magnitude of his achievement. Nevertheless, he is not the only towering giant of the twentieth century, which also produced a Churchill, a Mao, and a Stalin. And although we might not want to apply the word "spiritual" to them with the same enthusiasm that we do for Gandhi, their greatness matches Gandhi's in some ways. Sir Winston Churchill led a country, pushed to the brink of surrender, to victory over Nazi

Germany, despite the odds. His famous address, expressing England's determination to never surrender, delivered on June 4, 1940, is almost spiritual in the intensity of its determination.[2] Can anyone doubt that Churchill, too, staked his life on the truth as he saw it—even if it was an imperial truth?

Mao Zedong unified a China fragmented by imperial intervention and civil war.[3] And while the trust that he places in the barrel of a gun is diametrically opposed to the trust that Gandhi placed in the biblical ideal of turning the other cheek, can anyone doubt that he staked his life on the truth as he saw it—even if it was a brutal truth? As for Joseph Stalin, he turned the Soviet Union into a global power, fulfilling the promise of a revolution that had shaken it to the core early in that century. Can anyone doubt that he, too, staked his life on the truth as he saw it—even if it was a communist truth?

Some might object to lumping these three with Gandhi because Gandhi believed in God. And this was not really true of the others, at least to the same extent. Churchill was not an avowed atheist, but the British Empire was his real God. And although Mao joked about getting ready to meet God in his old age, God was hardly the driving force of his life. As for Stalin, he actively promoted atheism as a state ideology (although he was not above using the Russian Orthodox Church in the mortal struggle against Nazi Germany).[4] Gandhi attributed his outstanding achievements to his faith in God, but these three political leaders achieved as much by keeping God out of the picture. So does Gandhi's commitment to theism compromise this comparative analysis?

Perhaps not. During the late 1920s, Gandhi altered his definition of the virtuous life from one dedicated to the search for God to one dedicated to the search for *truth*. We examined this dialectical switch earlier.[5]

Gandhi sought the absolute truth but recognized that it

was beyond the grasp of a mere human being and, on account of its absoluteness, could never be fully grasped. But realizing that understanding would never be complete did not make him abandon the search. A passerby once asked in jest about Confucius, "Is he not the person who insists on pursuing a goal that he knows is impossible to achieve?" The same might well be asked about Gandhi. What the impossibility of attaining absolute truth meant for him was not that the search be abandoned, but that it needed to be conducted in a sophisticated way. This, in turn, meant two things: No one can be sure of being in the right. And no one can be sure that someone else is in the wrong. It follows that no one should be either dogmatic or intolerant. Nor should one be rigid, because views can change with the passage of time.

But doesn't this view throw the door wide open to random subjectivity? Not according to Gandhi, because he recognized at least two built-in checks. First, he insisted on the need to *act* on the truth as it appears in the *now*. To support that argument, he would cite Confucius: "To know what is right and not to do it is cowardice." It is very important to remember that for Gandhi, truth was not abstract but concrete. In other words, *truth* always implied *right*. It must always either yield or become the right thing to do, or at least what someone currently thinks is the right thing to do. What bothered Gandhi, unlike the philosophers, was not so much the contradiction between one thought and another as the contradiction between thought and action. Insisting on action was one way Gandhi kept at bay the dangers that are inherent in trying to keep an open mind. The purpose of education for him was to convert an empty mind into an open mind. The second way he kept flexibility from lapsing into opportunism was by insisting on a pure moral life. Living morally would foster a strong hold on truth. But Gandhi never confused truth with certainty.

II. GANDHI'S NONVIOLENCE

Let us now think again about Gandhi, Churchill, Mao, and Stalin in a spiritual context. It is clear that from a Gandhian perspective, theism does not pose an obstacle to the comparison. Like Gandhi, all three were seeking truth, even if it meant that Churchill asked the British viceroy in India in 1944 why Gandhi was not dead yet. Or that Mao regarded Indians with contempt for their apparent spinelessness in the face of British imperialism. Or that Stalin, like other communists, saw Gandhi as nothing more than a reactionary.

The comparison is not Gandhi's problem to resolve but ours. All three were searching for their own truths and endangering the lives of others by doing so. So was Gandhi, according to his own wife. Why, then, do most people believe that only he was a spiritual luminary? Perhaps the answer lies not in what they did but in *how* they did it—not so much in the end but in the means.

Mahatma Gandhi insisted on the use of nonviolent means even in a militant struggle. The key to his spiritual life in this sense is nonviolence (ahimsa). What we seek to achieve by nonviolent means can often be achieved by violent means as well. The aim of using nonviolent means is to transform the opponent, but violent means can sometimes do the same thing. One can argue that the only purpose in knocking a person down is to pick up the person in a more reasonable frame of mind. Both Germany and Japan were defeated by violent means, but both have long since abandoned violence. They have even embraced their former enemies, just as their former enemies have embraced them. But Mahatma Gandhi was interested in the use of nonviolence in principle, not merely out of expediency. This is the key point to consider in the context of Gandhi's spiritual trajectory. Although truthfulness came to him naturally, nonviolence came to him as the result of training (just as faithfulness came to him naturally but celibacy as the result of striving). At one stage in his life, Gandhi believed in adopting violent means to rid India of British rule. But he resigned from the Congress Party in 1934 after realizing that the party had accepted nonviolence out of expediency and not genuine conviction. This was a fateful step, as it meant that he could not officially make decisions for the party. The party usually followed his lead, but on the crucial matter of Partition, in 1947, it bypassed him and agreed to it. Although Gandhi could not have foreseen that result, he would have realized that he was taking a major step by resigning—and on a matter of principle.

Gandhi was tempted to rehearse his past in the light of his commitment to nonviolence. Consider the following incident in his early life, referred to but not elaborated on earlier. While in his teens, Gandhi took to what some people would now call substance abuse. He began smoking and, as many in our own time do, stole in order to pay for his addiction. At first he could not help himself. But then he decided to end the habit of stealing. He also decided to atone for it.

> I decided at last to write out the confession, to submit it to my father, and ask his forgiveness. I wrote it on a slip of paper and handed it to him myself. In this note not only did I confess my guilt, but I asked adequate punishment for it, and closed with a request to him not to punish himself for my offence. I also pledged myself never to steal in future.
>
> I was trembling as I handed the confession to my father. He was then suffering from a fistula and was confined to bed. His bed was a plain wooden plank. I handed him the note and sat opposite the plank.
>
> He read it through, and pearl-drops trickled down his cheeks, wetting the paper. For a moment he closed

his eyes in thought and then tore up the note. He had sat up to read it. He again lay down. I also cried. I could see my father's agony. If I were a painter I could draw a picture of the whole scene today. It is still so vivid in my mind.

Those pearl-drops of love cleansed my heart, and washed my sin away. Only he who has experienced such love can know what it is. As the hymn says: "Only he Who is smitten with the arrows of love, Knows its power."[6]

After narrating this incident, Gandhi concludes the chapter by telling the lesson he drew:

This was, for me, an object-lesson in *Ahimsa. Then I could read in it nothing more than a father's love, but today I know that it was pure Ahimsa.* When such *Ahimsa* becomes all-embracing, it transforms everything it touches. There is no limit to its power. This sort of sublime forgiveness was not natural to my father. I had thought that he would be angry, say hard things, and strike his forehead. But he was so wonderfully peaceful, and I believe this was due to my clean confession. A clean confession, combined with a promise never to commit the sin again, when offered before one who has the right to receive it, is the purest type of repentance. I know that my confession made my father feel absolutely safe about me, and increased his affection for me beyond measure.[7]

Note the transition in these lines from a filial to a moral interpretation of the event, as involving ahimsa. Without forcing a new interpretation on the incident, Gandhi the apostle of nonviolence assesses it differently from Gandhi the teenager "in recovery."

III. MEANS AND ENDS

Why was Mahatma Gandhi so concerned about the means?

When we normally talk about means and ends, we tend to make a clear distinction between the two and to assume that they are different. When I say, "I need to go to the market," I am stating the *end*. The vehicle in which I travel is my *means* of getting there. We can treat the two for all practical and even philosophical purposes as distinct. The axiom "The end justifies the means" makes sense only from such a perspective.

The distinction between means and ends is consistent with our experience of daily life, but they can be related so closely that one might affect the other. This might seem like a truism. After all, unless the two were related in some way, how could one conceivably produce the other? But the relation between them goes beyond that. The means we use has consequences for the end we seek. If our vehicle is not reliable, we might arrive late or not at all. This point might seem trivial, but sometimes means and ends differ too drastically for that implication. For instance, our car en route is a moving object, but our destination is a fixed point. The means, then, is radically *different* from the end in this respect. How could two elements so radically opposed influence each other? But consider another example, one in which the means clearly affect the end. A surgeon operates by means of a scalpel to secure a patient's good health, but an infected scalpel will produce the opposite effect.

The relation between means and ends operates at several levels. We have used ordinary illustrations so far. But the relation can vary a great deal in different spheres of life. The seed is the means and a crop is the end; wealth is the means and a luxurious life is the end; election is the means and a public office the end, and so on. And the distinction between means and ends holds in every case. Gandhi's main interest was human affairs, and he found that the relation between means and ends in this sphere was so close that the former implied something about the latter and therefore deserved special notice. We could amplify this point in terms of cause and effect rather than means or ends. We could then argue that the effect is latent in the cause, which would mean that the two exist on a continuum—or even as a single process, in which case the distinction would be analytically helpful but ultimately artificial. The same process has a cause from one perspective and is an effect from the other perspective. If gold is the cause and a bracelet is the effect, for instance, then a bracelet cannot be of silver; its cause is gold, after all, not silver. The effect cannot go beyond the cause.

In human relations, Gandhi believed that the means and the ends were so closely implicated in each other that the end could *not* justify the means. We usually invoke the saying "The end justifies the means" to excuse an action that goes against the grain of what we want to achieve. People usually say it to justify an immoral action done for ideological reasons, such as killing millions of people in a revolution. So even if the means seems inconsistent with the end, the end makes the means seem acceptable. We believe that the end justifies it. If we claim that going to war will achieve peace, we must claim that the end justifies the means. Gandhi did not think that this claim would hold true in the long run, because the means would inevitably be implicated in the end—and possibly tarnish it. For him, then, using violence as a means to put an end to violence would be self-defeating. Far from ending violence, it would generate yet more violence. If we want to achieve the end in its purity, therefore, he would argue, we must use means that are pure; otherwise, we would be like surgeons operating with infected knives. Churchill, Mao, and Stalin believed that their ends justified their means. And this belief might have led to their impressive achievements. But Gandhi did not believe in that justification. And this belief led to *his* achievements.

IV. WHY USE NONVIOLENT MEANS?

What did Gandhi hope to accomplish by emphasizing nonviolence as a mode of resolving conflicts between communities and nations? How might we answer this question, keeping the intimate connection between means and end in mind? Gandhi himself rarely frames the question explicitly this way. But an answer is implicit in his life and work. To find the answer, we must first gain a broad perspective.

If someone suddenly attacked me and my family while I was sitting at home, even killing some of them, what would I do? Most people in my position would call the police and hand over the attacker to the police.

And yet this unremarkable act on my part is the product of a revolution in human affairs, one that occurred centuries ago. To grasp this point we need to step back for a minute and think about it again from the following perspective. If I am sitting in my own house, and someone attacks me and my relatives and kills my next of kin, *then why should I hand the perpetrator over to the police and not kill him or her right there myself?* Would it not be the most natural thing in the world to do?

People learned the hard way, over the centuries, that they must *not* act in this way if they want communal life to thrive and civilization to flourish, for it leads to private revenge and blood feuds. If I kill the attacker who has killed my children, then his or her relatives will come after me, seeking revenge, and the violence will go on and on. People in most societies have by now learned the lesson so well that it has become second nature to call the police. But imagine the amount and depth of socialization involved in this cultural response that inhibits my natural reflex to kill an assailant on the spot and instead leads me to call the police. And even if a jury mistakenly finds the assailant innocent because of some legal loophole, I may still not take revenge on my own. And I would not want to do so, because I know that it is better to live in a society where the rule of law prevails, despite occasional miscarriages of justice, than in one given to private revenge or vigilantism. *I would have to forgive*—I would have to act *spiritually* even in such a situation, for the good of all.

To revert to Gandhi. People have learned this lesson at one level, but they still turn violent when nations or communities become involved in a conflict. The Gandhian project was (and is) to make people realize that they can achieve as much by rejecting *communal* revenge as they did by rejecting *private* revenge. According to Gandhi, we have become so used to using violence, and its extreme form, war, as a means of conflict resolution that we can no longer conceive of another way, just as people were so used to private policing for centuries that it seemed the only possible way to secure justice. Now we know better. We resort to a public justice system to achieve the same result with acceptable levels of collateral damage. The use of violence for large-scale conflicts seemed set in concrete until Gandhi blasted it with his project of nonviolent protest.

But the project does not end there. It is actually at this point that Gandhi's insistence on ahimsa gains traction. By this he meant not just nonviolence but love—even love of the enemy. Martin Buber has remarked that nothing becomes one more than to act toward others in the spirit of justice—*unless* it be to act in the spirit of love. For must justice be the only calculus in human affairs, even in the struggle against injustice? Gandhi offers us an innovative interpretation of love. Love overflows the narrower boundaries of justice, as anyone who has led family life knows. The basic sentiment binding the parties together within a family is not justice but love. This might be why appeals to human brotherhood (there we have it!) invoke the family as a metaphor in juxtaposition with justice. What brotherhood (and sisterhood) means is that our adversary in the struggle for justice should not be treated as an enemy but as a fellow human being, just as issues of justice within a family are resolved within an overarching framework of human affection, rather than through adversarial engagement, as they would be in a court of law. To regard enemies as family members does not mean an idealization of the family, or mere sentiment, but rather the realization that there is a difference between resolving problems of justice when the two parties do not care about each other beyond the issue at hand and resolving problems of justice when they do care about each other. The family is a metaphor for the latter context.

Let us examine a simple incident from Gandhi's life with this in mind. When fully veiled Muslim women crowded around him when he visited the shrine of a Sufi saint in Ajmer toward the end of his life, he said to them, "Do you observe *purdah* (veiled seclusion) with your next of kin?" All of them removed their veils. He was kin.[8]

That this anecdote encapsulates more than may be immediately obvious becomes clear when we place it in context of the modern controversy regarding *hijab,* or headscarf. Modern reformers approach hijab from the standpoint of human rights and justice, emphasizing that this custom is unjust to women. But Gandhi never said a word about rights or justice. He approached it not in terms of impersonal public discourse but in terms of personal familial discourse. To be sure, he was not on a crusade to get Muslim women to give up purdah. But Gandhi achieved the effect within his immediate circle, which French president Nicolas Sarkozy tried to secure punitively. Even if he had succeeded, it would not have been without generating considerable resentment. What did Gandhi do?

He changed the terms of reference of the relationship, the very parameters of the encounter, by invoking another model for it, and achieved the desired outcome sans resentment and, if anything, with mutual regard and even affection. This is how the same issue, when approached from a conventional angle and then a Gandhian one takes on a different hue. The resolution of the issue of veiling along family lines is not far-fetched. As Gandhi knew, when an Indian male encounters a woman in India whom he has not met earlier and does not know by name, the proper way to address her is as "mother" if she is senior in age, "sister" if she is his own age, and "daughter" if she is perceptibly younger.[9] So a Gandhian argument could be developed along the following lines: If Muslim women are willing to be so addressed and accept such a social matrix in interacting with men even outside the immediate family, and if their fathers, husbands, and brothers are likewise willing to accept it, then do they need to veil themselves?

The real world is, of course, characterized by injustice rather than love. Gandhi insisted that injustice is a form of untruth and that it must be opposed, but with nonviolence. This equation of truth and justice is a hoary Indic tradition. "Verily, that which is justice is truth," says the Bṛhadāraṇyaka Upaniṣad (I.4.14.). "Therefore they say of a man who speaks the truth, he speaks justice or of a man who speaks justice that he speaks the truth."[10] Gandhi's belief that truth implied justice comes within this tradition. In this sense, satya (truth) and ahimsa (nonviolence) went hand in hand for him, the latter being the way of realizing the former. The key Gandhian insight here cuts deep. It is the realization that using violence to resolve an injustice, *no matter how grave the injustice,* ultimately involves becoming unjust in the pursuit of justice.

Gandhi's insistence that the fight against injustice be nonviolent should not be seen as in any way compromising his position that one must fight against injustice. If it is important to know that Gandhi stood for nonviolence, it is equally important to know that Gandhi would not stand injustice. This becomes clear when we realize that although Gandhi preached nonviolence as opposed to violence, he preferred violence to cowardice. Thus, although he insisted on the need to fight injustice nonviolently, he also insisted on the need to fight injustice in any way possible if nonviolence was not possible for that person. This strand in Gandhi's life and thought enables us to view in a new light the baffling tendency on the part of some of his otherwise sober admirers to divinize him. Much of the elevation is sheer hagiography and mere euhemerism, but some of it is perhaps traceable to a feature of Hinduism: in Hinduism, God incarnates himself to fight against injustice in his world, over against the Abrahamic religions, in which God sends his prophets to do so. We can now see how the Hindu might be tempted to identify anyone who fights spectacularly against injustice as an emanation of divinity itself.

V. GANDHI'S CONTEMPORARY RELEVANCE

The events of September 11, 2001, provide a glowing point of intersection between Gandhi's spiritual biography and contemporary political history.

The Reverend Martin Luther King Jr., prominent among those who have inherited the Gandhian mantle, once described violence as the "voice of the unheard." Many commentators, especially liberals, have drawn attention to the grievances that Muslims have against the West, especially against the United States, and have tried to understand the attacks on the Twin Towers and the Pentagon and the other aborted attack not as acts of gratuitous violence but as a response to deep and possibly legitimate grievances. These commentators give Muslims the benefit of the doubt, but Gandhi's argument was that resorting to violence only compounds it. Injustice must be resisted, because it is a form of untruth, but it must be re-sisted nonviolently. So there is a double insistence in Gandhi: the need to oppose injustice and to oppose it nonviolently. It is easy to connect with the first moral proposition but not the second. And yet the latter may hold the key to Gandhi's mind.

Since, as Gandhi himself noted, "love" has many mean-ings in the English language, this might be as good a time as any to identify exactly what Gandhi meant when he some-times translated *ahimsa* (nonviolence) with the word "love." This sense comes out quite clearly when we juxtapose love with justice. When people seek justice in a state of alienation from each other, they are viewing it through the prism of re-venge and the hatred it implies. We need love because even justice, in this situation, is a refined form of revenge. When a murderer is executed, we say satisfiedly, "Justice is done," as happened in the case of Osama bin Laden. But another re-sponse is possible, one immortalized by the English reformer John Bradford: "There, but for the grace of God, go I." John Bradford's reaction came from the place Gandhi is trying to name by using such words as *ahimsa*, "nonviolence," and "civil disobedience" and through such expressions as "Love thine enemy" and "Hate the sin and not the sinner." Gandhi en-coded the word "love" with this meaning.

Gandhi's insight had gained in relevance since September 11, 2001. If we consider the attacks from the perspective of the perpetrators, they were merely reacting against American injustice. American injustice was their truth. And, up to this point, it was also Gandhi's truth. He would have urged them to fight injustice. But not the way they did.

They killed almost three thousand people. Maybe they were not all that innocent; maybe none of us is innocent in some pure unadulterated sense. But in this context, Gandhi would have said that those who perished in the attacks were innocent. They were not directly the agents of injustice. The perpetrators, however, insisted that the victims were part of the problem merely as occupants of the World Trade Center and the Pentagon, symbols of American domination. On this point the Gandhian (and Christian) insistence on hating the sin and not the sinner becomes important. An encounter between Indira Gandhi and Winston Churchill illustrates the significance of this distinction. They once met after India had been independent long enough for Churchill to have digested the fact. "How you must have hated us," he told her. She reputedly replied, "We never hated you. We hated the British Empire, against which we were fighting." Churchill is believed to have murmured: "But I did. But I did." Churchill was against Indian independence, and he hated the Indians for trying to achieve it; Gandhi's followers were against the British Empire but did *not* hate the British.

This anecdote encapsulates more than is immediately obvious. The Indians could have held the British of Churchill's generation guilty for all the horrors perpetrated on India throughout the two hundred years of the British Raj. They could have held the British collectively guilty for all the crimes of imperialism. But under the moral leadership of Gandhi the Indians did not take this route. Gandhi was not above denouncing imperial British rule over India as satanic, but he never accused an *individual* Briton of being the Devil or his child. The target was the system, which Gandhi saw as dehumanizing both Britishers and Indians. Both needed to get rid of it in order to once again relate to each other on the basis of a shared humanity.

The conversational exchange between Indira Gandhi and Winston Churchill affords greater proof of the spiritual impact of Gandhi's life than anything more sonorous that could be offered. This is what happens when injustice is resisted, and not only resisted but challenged, nonviolently. It brings about resolution without resentment, and it is resentment that ultimately takes the form of retaliation. In this context, ahimsa is non-retaliation par excellence. It is not the first but the second blow, delivered in return, that starts the fight. On this point, Christian and Hindu moral intuitions converge marvelously. Albiruni (973–1048), counted among the great scholars of the Islamic world, would have agreed.

> In this regard the manners and customs of the Hindus resemble those of the Christians, for they are, like those of the latter, based on the principles of virtue and abstinence from wickedness, such as never to kill under any circumstances whatsoever, to give to him who has stripped you of your coat also your shirt, to offer to him who has beaten your cheek the other cheek also, to bless your enemy and to pray for him. Upon my life, this is a noble philosophy; but the people of this world are not all philosophers. Most of them are ignorant and erring, who cannot be kept on the straight road save by the sword and the whip. And, indeed, ever since Constantine the Victorious became a Christian, both sword and whip have been employed, for without them it would be impossible to rule.[11]

This quotation, with its notion of turning the other cheek, brings us to the most difficult and delicate part of the Gandhian project. Gandhi insists that we protest and fight injustice; but he also insists that we not retaliate, that we not respond to violence with violence, that nonviolence is always an option. Given the harshness and injustice of the world, how long can we sustain nonviolent protest in the face of perverse or self-righteous hard-heartedness? What is turning the other cheek worth if it means getting slapped again, and again, and again? What if we don't succeed? At one level, Gandhi's answer was stark and simple: Do we win all the wars we fight? At another level, his answer was that we must voluntarily undergo the suffering it takes to change another person's heart. If one perishes in the attempt, one leaves behind an imperishable legacy. Gandhi knew that people who benefit from the status quo are not going to let it be altered without reacting, sometimes violently. So blood is bound to be shed in the course of nonviolent resistance. The real question is: Whose blood is it going to be? Once a young Muslim woman disciple of Gandhi's urged her fellow Muslims, in a Muslim-majority village, to restore to the Hindus the two decorative swords stolen from a Hindu temple. When they demurred, she immediately lay down on a cot and resolved not to drink or eat anything until they were restored. When the news reached Gandhi he sent her the following note: "Take water. Give God time to work his miracle." In other words, one must not be reckless even with one's own blood, even as one is ready to shed it.

A luminous and perhaps even numinous coincidence celebrates the relevance of Gandhi for our times. The Twin Towers were violently brought down on September 11, 2001. It was also on September 11, 1906, that Mahatma Gandhi launched his first satyagraha, his first nonviolent campaign, in South Africa.[12]

Is there a message for us in this startling coincidence?

notes

Introduction

1. Mohandas K. Gandhi, *An Autobiography: The Story of My Experiments with Truth* (Boston: Beacon Press, 1993), xxvi.
2. Ibid., xxvi–xxvii.
3. Cited in V. S. Naravane, *Modern Hindu Thought* (New York: Asia Publishing House, 1964), 168.
4. Cited in ibid.
5. Ibid., 169.
6. Louis Fischer, *A Week with Gandhi* (London: George Allen and Unwin, 1943), 96–97.
7. For a picture of these see Pyarelal, *Mahatma Gandhi: The Last Phase* (Ahmedabad: Navajivan Publishing House, 1958), vol. 2, p. 785.
8. Naravane, *Modern Hindu Thought,* 169–170.

Chapter 1. Birth and Adolescence

1. Mohandas K. Gandhi, *An Autobiography: The Story of My Experiments with Truth* (Boston: Beacon Press, 1993), 11.
2. Louis Fischer, *The Life of Mahatma Gandhi* (New York: Harper and Row, 1950), 14.

3. Robert Payne, *The Life and Death of Mahatma Gandhi* (New York: E. P. Dutton, 1969), 19. Almost next to the house is a temple dedicated to Krishna.
4. Payne, *Life and Death of Gandhi,* 20.
5. Gandhi, *Autobiography,* 4, 5 (quotation).
6. Ibid., 31. This passage is "perhaps the most celebrated passage in Gandhi's autobiography" (Ved Mehta, *Mahatma Gandhi and His Apostles* [Harmondsworth, UK: Penguin Books, 1977], 179).
7. Gandhi, *Autobiography,* 27–28.
8. Ibid., 6–7.
9. Ibid., 21.
10. Ibid.
11. Ibid.
12. Ibid., 23.

Chapter 2. Child Marriage

1. Mohandas K. Gandhi, *An Autobiography: The Story of My Experiments with Truth* (Boston: Beacon Press, 1993), 8.
2. Ibid., 8, 10.
3. Ibid., 8.
4. See Arvind Sharma, *Modern Hindu Thought: The Essential Texts* (New Delhi: Oxford University Press, 2002), 156, 169–174.
5. Gandhi, *Autobiography,* 31–32. Also see p. 205.
6. Ibid., 23–24 (quotation), 71, 104.
7. Ibid., 23–24, 71–72 (emphasis added), 105.
8. Ibid., 13, 10, 13 (quotation), 8 (quotation). Also see Louis Fischer, ed., *The Essential Gandhi* (New York: Random House, 1962), 245.
9. Reynold A. Nicholson, *The Mystics of Islam* (1914; London: Penguin Books, 1989), 31. The dialogue is adapted from Nicholson's recounting of the story about Rabia on the same page. The quotation is slightly modified.
10. See Mohandas K. Gandhi, *Hindu Dharma* (Ahmedabad: Navajivan Publishing House, 1958), 333.

Chapter 3. God Enters Gandhi's Life

1. Robert Payne, *The Life and Death of Mahatma Gandhi* (New York: E. P. Dutton, 1969), 26; Mohandas K. Gandhi, *An Autobiography: The Story of My Experiments with Truth* (Boston: Beacon Press, 1993), 32.
2. Gandhi, *Autobiography*, 20–21.
3. N. Ragunathan, trans., *Śrīmadbhāgavatam* (Madras: Vighneswara Publishing House, 1976), vol. 1, p. 579 (emphasis added).
4. See Paula Richman, ed., *Many Ramayanas: The Diversity of a Narrative Tradition in South Asia* (Berkeley: University of California Press, 1991); Ainslie T. Embree, ed., *The Hindu Tradition* (New York: Random House, 1972), 248–249.
5. Gandhi, *Autobiography*, 32.
6. Ibid., 32. For more on the recitation of the Ramayana see Philip Lutgendorf, *The Life of a Text: Performing the Rāmcaritamānas of Tulsidas* (Berkeley: University of California Press, 1991).
7. Payne, *Life and Death of Gandhi*, 590.
8. Mohandas K. Gandhi, *Hindu Dharma* (Ahmedabad: Navajivan Publishing House, 1958), 114, 120–121.
9. Gandhi, *Autobiography*, 46.
10. Payne, *Life and Death of Gandhi*, 620.

Chapter 4. Gandhi in London

1. Mohandas K. Gandhi, *An Autobiography: The Story of My Experiments with Truth* (Boston: Beacon Press, 1993), 80.
2. The Pulitzer Prize–winning author Joseph Lelyveld, for instance, in his *Great Soul: Mahatma Gandhi and His Struggle with India* (New York: Alfred A. Knopf, 2011), is quite economical in his coverage of Gandhi's London years.
3. Ved Mehta, *Mahatma Gandhi and His Apostles* (Harmondsworth, UK: Penguin Books, 1976), 85; Gandhi, *Autobiography*, 58. Louis Fischer, in his *Life of Mahatma Gandhi* (New York: Harper and Row, 1950), 28, acknowledges that "Gandhi's two years and eight months in England came at a formative phase of his life and must have shaped his personality," but he adds that

"their influence was probably less than normal." Moreover, although "his loyalty to the vow of no meat, no wine, no women" was already in evidence, his personality "burgeoned" only when "touched by the magic wand of action in South Africa." This view reflects a public perspective on Gandhi's life; the London years were arguably more influential in terms of his private life. He was, after all, encountering Western culture directly for the first time. Also see Robert Payne, *The Life and Death of Mahatma Gandhi* (New York: E. P. Dutton, 1969), 68.

4. Gandhi, *Autobiography*, 40.
5. Fischer, *Life of Gandhi*, 28; Payne, *Life and Death of Gandhi*, 56; Gandhi, *Autobiography*, 40.
6. Gandhi, *Autobiography*, 40.
7. Ibid.; Lelyveld, *Great Soul*, 34–35.
8. Mehta, *Gandhi and His Apostles*, 34.
9. Gandhi, *Autobiography*, 34.
10. Mehta, *Gandhi and His Apostles*, 88.
11. Gandhi, *Autobiography*, 50–51.
12. Ibid.; Fischer, *Life of Gandhi*, 28.
13. Gandhi, *Autobiography*, 52, 58; Benjamin Walker, *The Hindu World* (New York: Frederick A. Praeger, 1968), vol. 1, p. 376.
14. Gandhi, *Autobiography*, 56, 58 (quotation). This principle may also explain why, years later, Gandhi would insist that the monies pledged by India to Pakistan be released. Although the agreement between the two was mutual, Pakistan was the weaker party.
15. Ibid., 63; Mehta, *Gandhi and His Apostles*, 90 (quotation).
16. Gandhi, *Autobiography*, 63–66 (quotation p. 66).
17. Ibid., 71.
18. Ibid., 31–35, 135–138.
19. Ibid., 31, 67, 135.
20. Ibid., 33–34.
21. Ibid., 68.
22. Stephen Neill, "Mission: Christian Missions," in Lindsay Jones, ed., *Encyclopedia of Religion*, 2nd ed. (Farmington Hills, MI: Thomson Gale, 2005), vol. 9, p. 6084; Gandhi, *Autobiography*, 68.

23. Fischer, *Life of Gandhi,* 27. "He rarely went to the theater, but he went to church, sampling the various preachers of his time. He was impressed by Joseph Parker, the Congregationalist who presided over City Temple in Hoborn Viaduct, delivering sermons in down-to-earth speech, involving the congregation in the excitement of his own search for God" (Payne, *Life and Death of Gandhi,* 74).

24. Gandhi, *Autobiography,* 55, 57–58 (quotation p. 57). "What specially pleased him was Carlyle's description of Mohammad as a spiritual hero who fasted, mended his own shoes, patched his own cloak and received the gift of visions with equanimity" (Payne, *Life and Death of Gandhi,* 73).

25. Payne, *Life and Death of Gandhi,* 73; Gandhi, *Autobiography,* 69.

26. Gandhi, *Autobiography,* 68.

27. Payne, *Life and Death of Gandhi,* 72.

28. Lelyveld, *Great Soul,* 8.

29. Gandhi, *Autobiography,* 68.

30. Ibid., 67.

31. See Heinrich Zimmer, *Myths and Symbols in Indian Art and Civilization,* ed. Joseph Campbell (New York: Harper Torchbooks, 1962), 220–221.

32. Winthrop Sargeant, trans., *The Bhagavad Gītā,* rev. ed., ed. Christopher Chapple (Albany: State University of New York Press, 1984), 67.

33. Gandhi, *Autobiography,* 60, 94.

34. Ibid., 67. This verse, from Edwin Arnold's translation of the Bhagavad Gita, is quoted by Gandhi in his autobiography.

Chapter 5. Gandhi and Raychand

1. Robert Payne, *The Life and Death of Mahatma Gandhi* (New York: E. P. Dutton, 1969), 78.

2. Mohandas K. Gandhi, *An Autobiography: The Story of My Experiments with Truth* (Boston: Beacon Press, 1993), 87.

3. Ibid., 4. Gandhi's comment on the declaration is cited in Mary

Ann Glendon, *A World Made New: Eleanor Roosevelt and the Universal Declaration of Human Rights* (New York: Random House, 2001), 75.
4. Payne, *Life and Death of Gandhi*, 80.
5. Gandhi, *Autobiography*, 38.
6. Ibid., 88.
7. Ibid., 89; Payne, *Life and Death of Gandhi*, 80.
8. Payne, *Life and Death of Gandhi*, 88. The suffix *bhai* at the end of the name Raychand means "brother."
9. Ibid., 135–138.
10. Ibid., 137.
11. Cited in ibid., 80. The portrait that Payne presents of Raychand is worth citing here (ibid., 80): "Kierkegaard wrote about his encounter with a knight of the faith, finding him in the local tobacconist who sat behind his counter all week and went for a drive along the seashore with his wife and children every Sunday. The same idea had been celebrated by Gujarati poets, and Rajchandra was a perfect exemplar, although he sold diamonds and pearls rather than tobacco. Vast sums of money passed through his hands; he kept his account books in good order; he attended to the affairs of his business with the regularity of clockwork; and on his desk, beside the magnifying glasses and the jeweler's scales, he kept a small notebook in which he wrote down his thoughts day by day. He was happily married, rich, eloquent, and enviable, and what was most to be envied in him was his spiritual power."
12. Gandhi, *Autobiography*, 138 (quotation), 158–161.
13. Payne, *Life and Death of Gandhi*, 80.
14. *The Collected Works of Mahatma Gandhi* (New Delhi: Publications Division, Government of India, 1958), vol. 1, p. 90. They are listed below:

> What is the soul? Does it perform actions? Do past actions impede its progress or not?
> What is God? Is he the creator of the universe?
> What is *moksha* [salvation; freedom from rebirth]?

Is it possible for a person to know for certain, while he is still living, whether or not he will attain *moksha*?

It is said that after his death, a man may, according to his actions, be reborn as an animal, a tree, or even a stone. Is that so?

What is *Arya Dharma*? Do all Indian religions originate from the *Vedas*?

Who composed the *Vedas*? Are they *anadi* [without origin]? If so, what does *anadi* mean?

Who is the author of the *Gita*? Is God its author? Is there any evidence that He is?

Does any merit accrue from the sacrifice of animals and other things?

If a claim is put forward that a particular religion is the best, may we not ask the claimant for proof?

Do you know anything about Christianity? If so, what do you think of it?

The Christians hold that the Bible is divinely inspired and that Christ was an incarnation of God, being His Son. Was He?

Were all the Old Testament prophecies fulfilled in Christ?

Can any one remember his past lives or have an idea of his future lives?

If yes, who can?

You have given the names of some who have attained *moksha*. What is the authority for this statement?

What makes you say that even Buddha did not attain *moksha*?

What will finally happen to this world?

Will the world be morally better off in the future?

Is there anything like a total destruction of the world?

Can an illiterate person attain *moksha* by *bhakti* [devotion] alone?

Rama and Krishna are described as incarnations of

God. What does that mean? Were they God Himself or only a part of Him? Can we attain salvation through faith in them?

Who were Brahma, Vishnu and Shiva?

If a snake is about to bite me, should I allow myself to be bitten or should I kill it, supposing that is the only way in which I can save myself? (ibid., 90–91)

15. Payne, *Life and Death of Gandhi*, 98.
16. Ibid., 98. Gandhi enjoyed a curious relationship with snakes. He alludes to it in his autobiography (*Autobiography*, 429–430): "The rule of not killing venomous reptiles has been practised for the most part at Phoenix, Tolstoy Farm and Sabarmati. At each of these places we had to settle on waste lands. We have had, however, no loss of life occasioned by snakebite. . . . Even if it be a superstition to believe that complete immunity from harm for twenty-five years in spite of a fairly regular practice of non-killing is not a fortuitous accident but a grace of God, I should still hug that superstition."
17. Gandhi, *Autobiography*, 126. The pursuits are quoted in Louis Fischer, *The Life of Mahatma Gandhi* (New York: Harper and Row, 1950), 43.
18. Payne, *Life and Death of Gandhi*, 99.
19. Gandhi, *Autobiography*, 204–205. Gandhi goes on to say: "What then, I asked myself, should be my relation with my wife? Did my faithfulness consist in making my wife the instrument of my lust? So long as I was the slave of lust, my faithfulness was worth nothing. To be fair to my wife, I must say that she was never the temptress. It was therefore the easiest thing for me to take the vow of *brahmacharya*, if only I willed it. It was my weak will or lustful attachment that was the obstacle" (205).
20. See Jeffrey D. Long, *Jainism* (New York: I. B. Tauris, 2009), 165–170.
21. Padmanabh S. Jaini, *The Jaina Path of Purification* (Berkeley: University of California Press, 1979), 168; Payne, *Life and Death of Gandhi,* 374 (quoting Jaini).
22. Jaini, *Jaina Path of Purification*, 181.

23. Payne, *Life and Death of Gandhi*, 124, 194–195.

24. Ibid., 194–195, 125.

25. Ibid., 125, 80.

26. Payne, *Life and Death of Gandhi*, 80; Gandhi, *Autobiography*, 89. Payne has this to say about Raychand: "Rajchandra, whose full name was Rajchandra Ravjibhai Mehta, the poet and seeker after truth, had died in his early thirties. To the very end of his life, even when his body was reduced to a mere skeleton, he had devoted himself to contemplation, always hoping to see God face to face. Of all the men Gandhi encountered, he was the most lucid and intelligent, combining an intense moral fervor with an absolute conviction of the divine presence. He had read everything, remembered everything, pondered all problems, and appeared to be as much at home in heaven as on earth. To him Gandhi owed more than he could ever say" (*Life and Death of Gandhi*, 80).

27. Fischer, *Life of Gandhi*, 40. There is a suggestion in some accounts of Raychand's life that he may have achieved the final insight toward the end of his life; see Kristi L. Wiley, *Historical Dictionary of Jainism* (Lanham, MD: Scarecrow Press, 2004), 177.

Chapter 6. Gandhi's Conversion Experience

1. Mohandas K. Gandhi, *My Autobiography: The Story of My Experiments with Truth* (Boston: Beacon Press, 1993), 111–112.

2. Louis Fischer, *The Life of Mahatma Gandhi* (New York: Harper and Row, 1950), 42.

3. Ibid., 41.

4. Gandhi, *Autobiography*, 98; D. G. Tendulkar, *Mahatma: Life of Mohandas Karamchand Gandhi* (New Delhi: Publications Division, Government of India, 1960), vol. 1, p. 37; Fischer, *Life of Gandhi*, 41.

5. Gandhi, *Autobiography*, 112.

6. Fischer, *Life of Gandhi*, 42; Gandhi, *Autobiography*, 276. How morally catalytic the realization that "we are all tarred with the

same brush" can be is well illustrated by the following incident in the life of Jesus (*New English Bible,* John 7:35–38): "And they went each to his home, and Jesus to the Mount of Olives. At daybreak he appeared again in the temple, and all the people gathered round him. He had taken his seat and was engaged in teaching them when the doctors of the law and the Pharisees brought in a woman detected in adultery. Making her stand out in the middle they said to him, 'Master, this woman was caught in the very act of adultery. In the Law Moses has laid down that such women are to be stoned. What do you say about it?' They put the question as a test, hoping to frame a charge against him.

"Jesus bent down and wrote with his finger on the ground. When they continued to press their question he sat up straight and said, 'That one of you who is faultless shall throw the first stone.' Then once again he bent down and wrote on the ground.

"When they heard what he said, one by one they went away, the eldest first, and Jesus was left alone, with the woman still standing there. Jesus again sat up and said to the woman, 'Where are they? Has no one condemned you?'

"'No one, sir,' she said.

"Jesus replied, 'No more do I. You may go; do not sin again.'"

Chapter 7. Out of Africa

1. Mohandas K. Gandhi, *My Autobiography: The Story of My Experiments with Truth* (Boston: Beacon Press, 1993), 125; Louis Fischer, *The Life of Mahatma Gandhi* (New York: Harper and Row, 1950), 43.
2. Gandhi, *Autobiography,* 127–128.
3. Fischer, *Life of Gandhi,* 43–44.
4. Gandhi, *Autobiography,* 138.
5. Ibid., 139.
6. Ibid., 142.
7. Cited in Fischer, *Life of Gandhi,* 57.
8. Gandhi, *Autobiography,* 158.

9. Louis Fischer makes a significant observation at this point. After quoting an Oxford professor who said, "Gandhi *ought* to have hated every white face to the end of his life," Fischer notes that "Gandhi forgave the whites in Durban who assembled to lynch him and he forgave those who mauled and beat him. His soul kept no record of past sins against his body. Instead of prosecuting the guilty he pursued the more creative task of lightening his countrymen's lot" (*Life of Gandhi*, 53).

10. Ibid., 54.

11. Ibid., 56.

12. He established the Phoenix Settlement to implement the ideas he was developing as a result of being influenced by John Ruskin (1819–1880). Gandhi later translated Ruskin's book *Unto This Last* into Gujarati under the title *Sarvodaya*. Ruskin's book influenced Gandhi profoundly. He writes: "I believe that I discovered some of my deepest convictions reflected in this great book of Ruskin, and that is why it so captured me and made me transform my life. A poet is one who can call forth the good latent in the human breast. Poets do not influence all alike, for everyone is not evolved in an equal measure. The teachings of *Unto This Last* I understand to be: That the good of the individual is contained in the good of all. That a lawyer's work has the same value as the barber's inasmuch as all have the same right of earning their livelihood from their work. That a life of labour, *i.e.*, the life of the tiller of the soil and the handicraftsman is the life worth living. The first of these I knew. The second I had dimly realized. The third had never occurred to me. *Unto This Last* made it as clear as daylight for me that the second and the third were contained in the first. I arose with the dawn, ready to reduce these principles to practice" (*Autobiography*, 299).

13. Ibid., 299.

14. Ibid., 313, 314 (quotation).

15. Fischer, *Life of Gandhi*, 73–74.

16. Ibid., 76.

17. Gandhi, *Autobiography*, 318–319.

18. Fischer, *Life of Gandhi*, 77–78.

19. Ved Mehta, *Mahatma Gandhi and His Apostles* (Harmonds-worth, UK: Penguin Books, 1977), 121.
20. Fischer, *Life of Gandhi*, 82.
21. Ibid., 84.
22. Mehta, *Gandhi and His Apostles*, 126.
23. Fischer, *Life of Gandhi*, 112. "Trains carried them back to the mines, where they were forced into wire-enclosed stockades and placed under company employees who had been sworn in as special constables. Despite whips, sticks, and kicks, they refused to descend to the coal face" (Fischer, *Life of Gandhi*, 113).
24. Mehta, *Gandhi and His Apostles*, 128.
25. Fischer, *Life of Gandhi*, 115.
26. Ibid., 115.
27. Mehta, *Gandhi and His Apostles*, 129–130.
28. Fischer, *Life of Gandhi*, 116–117.
29. Mehta, *Gandhi and His Apostles*, 130.
30. Ibid., 129.

Chapter 8. Spiritual Warfare

1. Mohandas K. Gandhi, *An Autobiography: The Story of My Experiments with Truth* (Boston: Beacon Press, 1993), 412. A succinct account of Gandhi's transformation and of his work in Champaran is contained in a conversation Gandhi had with Louis Fischer in 1942, which runs as follows. It begins with Gandhi's statement about being a loyalist.

"'I was a loyalist in respect to the British, and then I became a rebel. I was a loyalist until 1896.'

"'Weren't you also a loyalist between 1914 and 1918?'

"'Yes, in a way,' he affirmed, 'but not really. By 1918 I had already said that British rule in India is an alien rule and must end.' He remained silent as we trudged along. Finally he said, 'I will tell you how it happened that I decided to urge the departure of the British. It was in 1916. I was in Lucknow working for Congress. A peasant came up to me looking like any other peasant of India, poor and emaciated. He said, "My name is Rajkumar Shukla. I am from Champaran, and I want you to come to my district." He described the misery of his fellow agriculturists and prayed me to let him take me to Champaran, which was hundreds of miles from Lucknow. He begged so insistently and persuasively that I promised. But he wanted me to fix the date. I could not do that. For weeks and weeks Rajkumar Shukla followed me wherever I went over the face of India. He stayed wherever I stayed. At length, early in 1917, I had to be in Calcutta. Rajkumar followed me and ultimately persuaded me to take the train with him from Calcutta to Champaran. Champaran is a district where indigo is planted. I decided that I would talk to thousands of peasants but, in order to get the other side of the question, I would also interview the British commissioner of the area. When I called on the commissioner he bullied me and advised me to leave immediately. I did not accept his advice and proceeded on the back of an elephant to one of the villages. A police messenger overtook us and served notice on me to leave Champaran. I allowed the police to escort me back to the house where I was staying and then I decided to offer civil resistance. I would not leave the district. Huge crowds gathered around the house. I cooperated with the police in regulating the crowds. A kind of friendly relationship sprang up between me and the police. That day in Champaran became a red-letter day in my life. I was put on trial. The government attorney pleaded with the magistrate to postpone the case but I asked him to go on with it. I wanted to announce publicly that I had disobeyed the order to leave Champaran. I told him that I had come to collect information about local conditions and that I therefore had to disobey the British law because I was acting in obedience with a higher law, with the voice of my conscience. This was my first act of civil disobedience against the British. My desire was to establish the principle that no Englishman had the right to tell me to leave any part of my country where I had gone for a peaceful pursuit. The government begged me repeatedly to drop my plea of guilty.

Finally the magistrate closed the case. Civil disobedience had won. It became the method by which India could be made free.'

"'This,' I said, 'is perhaps another clue to your position in India.'

"'What I did,' he interrupted, 'was a very ordinary thing. I declared that the British could not order me around in my own country.'

"'It was ordinary,' I commented, 'but you were the first to do it. It's like the story of Columbus and the egg.'

"'What's that?' he asked.

"'Have you never heard the story of Columbus and the egg?' I asked Gandhi.

"'No,' he confessed, 'tell me.'

"I told him. He laughed. 'That's right,' he said, 'it was an ordinary thing to say that I had the right to go peacefully anywhere in my own country. But no one had said it before'" (Louis Fischer, *A Week With Gandhi* [London: George Allen and Unwin, 1943], 97–99).

The story of Columbus and the egg may require a word of explanation. Once Columbus asked his associates at the dinner table if they could make an egg stand upright. When they expressed their inability to do so, Columbus gently flattened one end of an egg and placed it upright on the table using the flattened end as the base. His associates found it easy to follow the procedure once he had shown them how it could be done.

2. Louis Fischer, *The Life of Mahatma Gandhi* (New York: Harper and Row, 1950), 262.

3. Ibid., 262, 264.

4. Robert Payne, *The Life and Death of Mahatma Gandhi* (New York: E. P. Dutton, 1969), 389, 385 (quotation).

5. Fischer, *Life of Gandhi,* 268–269.

6. Payne, *Life and Death of Gandhi,* 392.

7. Ibid., 394–395.

8. Ibid., 400.

9. See R. C. Majumdar, ed., *Struggle for Freedom* (Bombay: Bharatiya Vidya Bhavan, 1969), 471–472.

10. Webb Miller, *I Found No Peace* (New York: Simon and Schuster, 1936), 190.

11. Ibid., 192–196.

Chapter 9. Touching the Untouchable

1. Cited in Louis Fischer, *The Life of Mahatma Gandhi* (New York: Harper and Row, 1950), 277.

2. Sugata Bose and Ayesha Jalal, *Modern South Asia: History, Culture, Political Economy* (New Delhi: Oxford University Press, 1998), 151.

3. Ibid., 151.

4. Robert Payne, *The Life of Mahatma Gandhi* (New York: E. P. Dutton, 1969), 34.

5. Mohandas K. Gandhi, *An Autobiography: The Story of My Experiments with Truth* (Boston: Beacon Press, 1993), 276–278.

6. Mohandas K. Gandhi, *Hindu Dharma* (Ahmedabad: Navajivan Publishing House, 1958), 280.

7. Ibid., 279.

8. Payne, *Life and Death of Gandhi*, 439.

9. Ved Mehta, *Mahatma Gandhi and His Apostles* (Harmondsworth, UK: Penguin Books, 1976), 216.

10. See Rajmohan Gandhi, *Revenge and Reconciliation: Understanding South Asian History* (New Delhi: Penguin Books, 1999), 254–255.

11. Gandhi, *Hindu Dharma*, 303, 455. Payne gives an account of a satyagraha by Harijans in *Life and Death of Gandhi*, 480–481: "It happened sometimes that Gandhi had to suffer the irony of being the victim of a Satyagraha campaign. In August 1938, when he was resting at Sevagram, a small army of Harijans marched on the village and announced that they would remain until their demands were satisfied. They would take no food. They would refuse to be removed. They would confront Gandhi with their haunting presence until he had submitted to their demand that he should appoint a Harijan to the Indian cabinet. It made no difference to them that Gandhi was in no position to

appoint anyone to the cabinet, for they argued that he had always been able to obtain what he wanted by fasting unto death. They, too, would fast, and they would expect to be treated with the same indulgence which Gandhi received in jail. Attendants must be supplied; rooms must be set aside; they had already chosen their living quarters and expected the present inhabitants to vacate them.

"Gandhi submitted to the severe ordeal with good grace. The room they wanted was occupied by Kasturbai, and he suggested that they might prefer another, but they rejected the offer. So they mocked him with their high-sounding speeches and insistent demands, and took what they wanted. The Harijans vanished a few days later, but Gandhi was deeply shaken by this confrontation with a Satyagraha campaign."

12. Bose and Jalal, *Modern South Asia*, 151.

13. Cited in Payne, *Life and Death of Gandhi*, 440. Part of the text of Gandhi's response is worth citing: "'Without arguing, I affirm that to me this matter is one of pure religion. The mere fact of the Depressed Classes having double votes does not protect them or Hindu society in general from being disrupted. You will please permit me to say that no matter how sympathetic you may be, you cannot come to a correct decision on a matter of vital and religious importance to the parties concerned.

"'I should not be against even over-representation of the Depressed Classes. What I am against is their statutory separation, even in a limited form, from the Hindu fold, so long as they choose to belong to it. Do you realize that if your decision stands and the constitution comes into being, you arrest the marvelous growth of the work of Hindu reformers who have dedicated themselves to their suppressed brethren in every walk of life?'

"Gandhi added that he was also opposed to the other separate electorates 'only I do not consider them to be any warrant for calling from me such self-immolation as my conscience has prompted me in the matter of the Depressed Classes'" (Fischer, *Life of Gandhi*, 307–308).

14. Fischer, *Life of Gandhi*, 308.
15. Payne, *Life and Death of Gandhi*, 443–444.
16. Fischer, *Life of Gandhi*, 314.
17. Payne, *Life and Death of Gandhi*, 446.
18. Fischer, *Life of Gandhi*, 312.

Chapter 10. Fighting Fire with Light

1. Sugata Bose and Ayesha Jalal, *Modern South Asia: History, Culture, Political Economy* (New Delhi: Oxford University Press, 2002), 153–154.
2. Robert Payne, *The Life and Death of Mahatma Gandhi* (New York: E. P. Dutton, 1969), 493–494 (quotation), 496; Bose and Jalal, *Modern South Asia*, 160.
3. D. G. Tendulkar, *Mahatma: Life of Mohandas Karamchand Gandhi* (New Delhi: Publications Division, Government of India, 1963), vol. 8, p. 80.
4. Louis Fischer, *The Life of Mahatma Gandhi* (New York: Harper and Row, 1950), 478.
5. Payne, *Life and Death of Gandhi*, 566.
6. Sheela Reddy and Ira Pande, "A Nice Man to Know," in *IIC Quarterly*, 33, no. 2 (Autumn 2006): 61.
7. Payne, *Life and Death of Gandhi*, 579. A recent biographer, however, claims that the statement was made a year earlier; see Joseph Lelyveld, *Great Soul: Mahatma Gandhi and His Struggle with India* (New York: Random House, 2011), 319.
8. Tendulkar, *Mahatma*, vol. 8, p. 288.

Chapter 11. Mahatma Gandhi and Ramana Maharshi

1. *Talks with Sri Ramana Maharshi* (Tiruvannamalai: Sri Ramasramam, 1984), 485. The idea here is that a saint is born or reborn to help people. Ramana Maharshi states that Ramakrishna (1836–1886) will come again after three hundred years and countenances the statement that "Bhagavan will be reborn many times not because he needs it but because we need it" (See

R. Narayan Iyer, "Years of Grace," in *Ramana Smṛti Souvenir* [Tiruvannamalai: Sri Ramanasramam, 1980], 1).

2. T. K. Sundaresa Iyer, "A Lifetime with Bhagavan," in *Ramana Smṛti Souvenir* (Tiruvannamalai: Sri Ramanasramam, 1980), 3.

3. D. G. Tendulkar, *Mahatma: Life of Mohandas Karamchand Gandhi* (New Delhi: Publications Division, Government of India, 1961), vol. 2, p. 58.

4. Mohandas K. Gandhi, *An Autobiography: The Story of My Experiments with Truth* (Boston: Beacon Pres, 1993), xxvi; B. K. Ahluwalia, "Maharshi Ramana and Mahatma Gandhi," in B. K. Ahluwalia and Shashi Ahluwalia, eds., *Maharshi Ramana: His Relevance Today* (Delhi: Vivek Publishing Company, 1980), 124–125. B. K. Ahluwalia also writes:

> Subsequently when Harindranath Chattopadhyaya showed a photo of Mahatma, and said, "It is a pity that there was never any meeting between Gandhi and Bhagavan," Bhagavan said: "Some time ago, he came to Tiruvannamalai. A meeting had been arranged for him to be held on the road around the hill, beyond the Asramam. People here thought that he would come to the Asramam on his way back, but owing to the pressure of the crowds it was impossible and he went away direct to the station. It seems that he very much regretted this afterwards. Shankarlal Banker was very keen on bringing him here, and in 1938, when Rajendra Prasad and Jamnalal Bajaj came here and saw Skandasramam, they wanted to induce the Mahatma to stay there for some time. But it did not happen. If at Sabarmati, or at Wardha anyone said that he was mentally depressed, the Mahatma used to say, 'Go to Ramanasramam and come back after a month's stay there.' When Ramaswami Reddiar went to see the Mahatma immediately after taking office as Chief Minister, Madras State, the Mahatma, it seems, asked him how long he had been going to the Ramanasramam. When he answered that he had been going there for over thirty years, the Mahatma said, 'Is that so? I have tried thrice,

but so far have not been able to go there,' What could he do? How could he come here when he was not left alone for one moment?" (128–129)

5. Ahluwalia, "Maharshi Ramana and Mahatma Gandhi," 126–127.
6. Talks with Sri Ramana Maharshi (Tiruvannamalai: Sri Ramanasramam, 1984), 484–485.
7. Ibid., 504–505.
8. Cited by Ahluwalia, "Maharshi Ramana and Mahatma Gandhi," 126.
9. Talks with Sri Ramana Maharshi, 605–606.
10. Ibid., 606–607.
11. Ahluwalia, "Maharshi Ramana and Mahatma Gandhi," 127–128.
12. Talks with Sri Ramana Maharshi, 241. This does not mean that Ramana Maharshi did not himself observe or promote equality. A Muslim professor, Dr. Mohammed Hafiz Syed, had this to say to him after they met on January 3, 1936: "I wondered if I would be permitted to approach you and converse with you. My doubts were soon set at rest. I find that all are equal here. You have established an equality among all. I dined with you and others. If I should say so to my people in U.P., they would not believe it. The Brahmins would not drink water with me, nor chew *pan* with me. But here you have taken me and others like me in your fold. Though Gandhi is striving hard he cannot bring about such a state of affairs in the country. I am very happy in your presence.

"I regard you as God. I consider Sri Krishna to be true God because He has said, 'Whomsoever one may worship, the worshipper worships me only and I save him.' Whereas all others have said, 'Salvation is through me (meaning himself) only,' Krishna alone is so broad-minded and has spoken like God. You observe the same kind of equality" (ibid., 112–113).
13. Also see ibid., 489–491.
14. Ved Mehta, *Mahatma Gandhi and His Apostles* (Harmondsworth, UK: Penguin Books, 1977), 124–125.

15. Robert Payne, *The Life and Death of Mahatma Gandhi* (New York: E. P. Dutton, 1969), 457, 448–452.
16. Ibid., 449.
17. G. V. Subbaramayya, *Sri Ramana Reminiscences,* 2nd ed. (Tiruvannamalai: Sri Ramanasramam, 1967), 111.

Chapter 12. Spiritual Temptations

1. "In 1912, he read that some Indian dairymen were in the habit of blowing hot liquid through a pipe into a cow's uterus, a process that somehow enabled them to extract the last drops of milk, and his compassion for the cow at last gave him the strength to take a vow that he would never drink milk again" (Ved Mehta, *Mahatma Gandhi and His Apostles* [Harmondsworth, UK: Penguin Books, 1977], 181).
2. Mohandas K. Gandhi, *An Autobiography: The Story of My Experiments with Truth* (Boston: Beacon Press, 1993), 455 (emphasis added).
3. Raynor C. Johnson, *A Religious Outlook for Modern Man* (London: Hodder and Stoughton, 1963), 206.
4. Cited by Raynor C. Johnson, *The Imprisoned Splendour* (New York: Harper and Brothers, 1953), 408–409. He observes elsewhere (*Religious Outlook,* 356): "A critical analysis of good works is called for. When the hungry are fed, when the sick are cared for, when slums are abolished, when ideal government is achieved—what have you done? You have increased the comfort and material well-being of people and set them free from anxiety in relation to the struggle for the necessaries of life. You believe you have done what you can to provide the setting in which their happiness is possible. You have provided, perhaps, a more favourable opportunity for happiness to follow; but happiness is a state of mind which you cannot command in another. You may have alleviated your neighbour's suffering, you may have increased his opportunity of enjoyment, and these are all good things to do, so far as *you* are concerned. The only certain goodness is in the *doing,* however. These things you have done

may lead the person for whom they are done to a little gratitude or greater kindliness, a step on the road of spiritual understanding; but it is equally possible they may not."

5. W. Y. Evans-Wentz, ed., *Tibet's Great Yogi Milarepa,* 2nd ed. (1928; New York: Oxford University Press, 1951), 271 (with slight modifications), cited in Edward Conze, "Buddhism: The Mahāyāna," in R. C. Zaehner, ed., *The Concise Encyclopedia of Living Faiths* (Boston: Beacon Press, 1967), 300–301.

6. Mother Teresa, *Mother Teresa: A Simple Path* (New York: Random House, 1995), 185.

7. V. S. Naravane, *Modern Indian Thought* (New York: Asia Publishing House, 1964), 72.

Chapter 13. Spiritual Serendipity

1. Mohandas K. Gandhi, *An Autobiography: The Story of My Experiments with Truth* (Boston: Beacon Press, 1993), 291. For a line with punch that is often cited, consider, for instance, the following statement: "It has always been a mystery to me how men can feel themselves honoured by the humiliation of their fellow-beings" (ibid., 155). See Louis Fischer, *The Life of Mahatma Gandhi* (New York: Harper and Row, 1950), 48.

2. Gandhi, *Autobiography,* 291–293.

3. Ibid., 292.

4. Ibid., 306–307 (emphasis added).

5. Ibid., 395.

6. Ibid., 397.

7. Ibid., 397–398.

8. Ibid., 398.

9. Ibid.; Robert Payne, *The Life and Death of Mahatma Gandhi* (New York: E. P. Dutton, 1969), 294.

Chapter 14. Beefing Up Vegetarianism

1. Mohandas K. Gandhi, *An Autobiography: The Story of My Experiments with Truth* (Boston: Beacon Press, 1993), 21.

2. Ibid., 23.

3. Ibid., 38–39.

4. Ibid., 42–43, 45 (emphasis added).

5. Ibid., 46, 48.

6. Ibid. Robert Payne notes in *The Life and Death of Mahatma Gandhi* (New York: E. P. Dutton, 1969), 65, that books promoting vegetarianism at the time claimed that "vegetables were supplied by God to fill one's needs and vegetarians are in some way in tune with God's infinite purposes" unlike non-vegetarians.

7. Gandhi, *Autobiography*, 60; Payne, *Life and Death of Gandhi*, 74.

8. Payne, *Life and Death of Gandhi*, 74.

9. Gandhi, *Autobiography*, 76, 78–79.

10. Ibid., 267–268.

11. Ibid., 247–248.

12. Ibid., 248.

13. Louis Fischer, *The Life of Mahatma Gandhi* (New York: Harper and Row, 1950), 25 (quotation), 26. On his articles see D. G. Tendulkar, *Mahatma: Life of Mohandas Karamchand Gandhi* (New Delhi: Publications Division, Government of India, 1960), vol. 1, pp. 306–314.

Chapter 15. The Sex Life of a Celibate

1. Mohandas K. Gandhi, *An Autobiography: The Story of My Experiments with Truth* (Boston: Beacon Press, 1993), 206, 208.

2. Ibid., 315–316.

3. Ibid.

4. Ibid., 208.

5. Louis Fischer, *The Life of Mahatma Gandhi* (New York: Harper and Row, 1950), 72.

6. Ibid., 206, 72–73; Gandhi, *Autobiography*, 206, 204.

7. Gandhi, *Autobiography*, 316; Fischer, *Life of Gandhi*, 72–73.

8. Gandhi, *Autobiography*, 316, 318.

9. Ibid., 208–209.

10. Ibid., 317, 208 (quotation).

11. Robert Payne, *The Life and Death of Mahatma Gandhi* (New York: E. P. Dutton, 1969), 462. Gandhi had a lot to say on this last point: "My wife I made the orbit of all women, and in her I studied all women. I came in contact with many European women in South Africa, and I knew practically every Indian woman there. I tried to show them they were not slaves either of their husbands or parents, not only in the political field but in the domestic as well. But the trouble was that some could not resist their husbands.

"The remedy is in the hands of women themselves. The struggle is difficult for them. I do not blame them. I blame the men. Men have legislated against them. Man has regarded woman as his tool. She has learned to be his tool and in the end found it easy and pleasurable to be such, because when one drags another to his fall the descent is easy. I have felt that during the years still left to me if I can drive home to women's minds the truth that they are free we will have no birth control problems in India. If they will only learn to say 'no' to their husbands when they approach them carnally, I do not suppose that all husbands are brutes and if women only know how to resist them all will be well. I have been able to teach women who have come in contact with me how to resist their husbands. The real problem is that many do not want to resist them" (cited in ibid., 462–463).

12. Ibid., 463.
13. Ibid., 464.
14. Ibid., 464–465.
15. Cited in ibid., 465.
16. Cited in ibid.
17. Ibid., 465.
18. Ibid., 466.
19. Ibid., 522–523. For more on this see Nirmal Kumar Bose, *My Days with Gandhi* (Bombay: Orient Longman, 1974), 101.
20. Ibid., 91.
21. Ved Mehta, *Mahatma Gandhi and His Apostles* (Harmondsworth, UK: Penguin Books, 1976), 195.

22. Ibid.
23. Ibid., 194.
24. Ibid., 194, 182.
25. Ibid., 190–192.
26. Gandhi, *Autobiography,* 209–210, 329.
27. Ibid., 208, 211 (quotation).
28. Cited in Payne, *Life and Death of Gandhi,* 383; Bose, *My Days with Gandhi,* 1–2.
29. Mehta, *Gandhi and His Apostles,* 182.
30. Ibid., 213.

Chapter 16. The Bhagavad Gita, Gandhi's Other Mother

1. Mohandas K. Gandhi, *Hindu Dharma* (Ahmedabad: Navajivan Publishing House, 1958), 146.
2. M. A. Mehendale, "Sanskrit Language and Literature," in R. C. Majumdar, ed., *The Age of Imperial Unity* (Bombay: Bharatiya Vidya Bhavan, 1951), 245.
3. In this sense, Louis Fischer is not *quite* right when he says, "The *Gita* is as sacred to Hinduism as the *Koran* is to Islam, the Old Testament to Judaism and the New Testament to Christianity" (*The Life of Mahatma Gandhi* [New York: Harper and Row, 1950]), 29.
4. Mohandas K. Gandhi, *An Autobiography: The Story of My Experiments with Truth* (Boston: Beacon Press, 1993), 4.
5. Bhagavad Gita II:54–72; XII:13–20; XIV:21–27; XVIII: 49–56. All quotations from the Bhagavad Gita are from W. Douglas P. Hill, trans., *Bhagavadgita,* 2nd ed. (1928; Madras: Oxford University Press, 1973).
6. Gandhi, *Autobiography,* 67.
7. Ibid., 153.
8. Ibid., 159.
9. Cited in Ved Mehta, *Gandhi and His Apostles* (Harmondsworth, UK: Penguin Books, 1976), 94–95.
10. Robert Payne, *The Life and Death of Mahatma Gandhi* (New York: E. P. Dutton and Co., 1969), 613, 642.

11. Ibid., 641.
12. Ibid., 639–640. According to the actual text of the Mahabharata, the warrior who decapitated Dronacharya was not Arjuna but Dhrsthadyumna. The Indian public imagination, however, often, if mistakenly, attributes the killing of Dronacharya to Arjuna, his favorite pupil.
13. Ibid.
14. Ibid., 638.
15. Ibid. Robert Payne writes: "Sixty years before, when Gandhi first came upon Sir Edwin Arnold's translation of the Bhagavad Gita in London, he concluded that it could only have been written about the struggles of the human heart in search of a savior. Indeed, such an opinion could scarcely be avoided by anyone reading the English translation alone, for the rhythms of the Victorian verse do not permit the reader to see the battle at close quarters. In the original, however, the Bhagavad Gita is written in taut, springy couplets, almost physical in their impact; the commands of Krishna have an urgency, a kind of paroxysmic fury, which powerfully suggest the utterance of a god in a mood of intense and visionary exaltation; and what he says, in the eyes of most Sanskrit scholars, relates to both heaven and earth, to the world of the spirit and to the battle fought on the plain of Kurukshetra. 'My interpretation of the *Gita* has been criticized by orthodox scholars as being unduly influenced by the Sermon on the Mount,' Gandhi wrote, and it was no more than the truth. Godse's interpretation was more direct and more uncompromising. Yet both of them insisted on their own exclusive interpretations, refusing to acknowledge that a poem of such vast scope and authority must necessarily have many interpretations" (ibid., 645).
16. Ibid., 641: "All the mythological characters mentioned by Nathuram Godse in his speech—Rama, Krishna, Bhishma, Kansa, Arjuna and Dronacharya—were warriors who took part in the great battle on the fields of Kurukshetra. It was as though mythology held him by the throat, and there was no escape from it. The interminable bloodletting which accompanied the partition of India had taken place on some mythological Kurukshetra of

the imagination, and he saw himself as Arjuna, the hero who must put an end to the war. He was not the only Indian who thought the battles of ancient times were being repeated. So great and terrible was the war between the Hindus and the Muslims that many thought they had escaped out of history altogether. India seemed to be entering an apocalyptic age: the earth shuddering, while the lightning played on the faces of the heroes and the armies marched in silence and despair across the shadowy plains."

Chapter 17. Gandhi, God, and Goodness

1. Cited in V. S. Naravane, *Modern Indian Thought: A Philosophical Survey* (New York: Asia Publishing House, 1964), 183.
2. Ibid., 170.
3. Mohandas K. Gandhi, *Hindu Dharma* (Ahmedabad: Navajivan Publishing House, 1950), 3: "There is no such thing as 'Gandhism,' and I do not want to leave any sect after me. I do not claim to have originated any new principle or doctrine. I have simply tried in my own way to apply the eternal truths to our daily life and problems. There is, therefore, no question of my leaving any code like the *Code of Manu*. There can be no comparison between that great lawgiver and me. The opinions I have formed and the conclusions I have arrived at are not final. I may change them tomorrow. I have nothing new to teach the world. Truth and non-violence are as old as the hills."
4. Ibid.: "Life and its problems have thus become to me so many experiments in the practice of truth and non-violence. By instinct I have been truthful, but not non-violent. As a Jain *muni* [sage] once rightly said I was not so much a votary of *ahimsa* as I was of truth, and I put the latter in the first place and the former in the second. For, as he put it, I was capable of sacrificing non-violence for the sake of truth. In fact it was in the course of my pursuit of truth that I discovered non-violence. Our scriptures have declared that there is no *dharma* (law) higher than Truth. But non-violence they say is the highest duty. The word *dharma*

in my opinion has different connotations as used in the two aphorisms."

5. Ibid., 59.
6. Ibid., 59–60.
7. Ibid., 120–121. This passage was cited earlier as part of a longer quotation.
8. Naravane, *Modern Indian Thought,* 170–172.
9. Ibid., 176.
10. Cited in ibid., 178; Mohandas K. Gandhi, *An Autobiography: The Story of My Experiments with Truth* (Boston: Beacon Press, 1993), xxvii–xxviii, 279.
11. Gandhi, *Autobiography,* 503–504. Gandhi here speaks of truth rather than God, confirming that "at a certain stage in his development" he "began to show a decided preference for the interpretation of reality in terms of truth rather than in terms of Providence or a personal God" (Naravane, *Modern Indian Thought,* 180). V. S. Naravane quotes N. K. Bose on this point: "With his changed creed Gandhi could accommodate as fellow seekers those who looked on Humanity or any object as their God, and for which they were prepared to sacrifice their all. By enthroning Truth on the highest pedestal Gandhi thus clearly became a catholic, and lost all trace of separateness from every other honest man who worshipped gods other than his own." Naravane elaborates: "If Truth is God, the Buddhist and the Marxist can become the partners of the most devout Hindu, Muslim or Christian in the search for absolute value. Indeed, paradoxical though it sounds, even he who denies God now ceases to be an atheist" (*Modern Indian Thought,* 181).
12. Gandhi, *Hindu Dharma,* 73.
13. He can be confusing, as when he claims that he is an Advaitin (Gandhi, *Hindu Dharma,* 55).
14. Cited in Naravane, *Modern Indian Thought,* 178–179.
15. Gandhi, *Hindu Dharma,* 93.
16. Gandhi, *Autobiography,* 504.
17. Naravane, *Modern Indian Thought,* 179; Gandhi, *Autobiography,* 504 (quotation).

18. Cited in D. G. Tendulkar, *Mahatma: Life of Mohandas Karamchand Gandhi* (New Delhi: Publications Division, Government of India, 1961), vol. 3, p. 246–247.
19. Cited in ibid., 248–249.
20. Ibid., 251.
21. Stephen Hay, ed., *Sources of Indian Tradition,* 2nd ed. (New York: Columbia University Press, 1988), 286; Robert Payne, *The Life and Death of Mahatma Gandhi* (New York: E. P. Dutton, 1969), 456; Tendulkar, *Mahatma,* vol. 3, p. 249 (quotation).
22. Tendulkar, *Mahatma,* vol. 3, p. 250–251.
23. Ibid.
24. Ibid., 251.
25. Naravane, *Modern Indian Thought,* 195.
26. Cited in ibid., 189, 185, 190.
27. Cited in Tendulkar, *Mahatma,* vol. 3, p. 250.
28. Gandhi, *Autobiography,* 248.

Chapter 18. Demythologizing and Analyzing Gandhi

1. For some critiques of Gandhi see Harold Coward, ed., *Indian Critiques of Gandhi* (Albany: State University of New York Press, 2003); Richard Grenier, "The Gandhi Nobody Knows," *Commentary* (March 1983): 59–73.
2. Ved Mehta, *Mahatma Gandhi and His Apostles* (Harmondsworth, UK: Penguin Books, 1977), 87; Louis Fischer, *The Life of Mahatma Gandhi* (New York: Harper and Row, 1950), 228.
3. Cited in Krister Stendahl, "From God's Perspective We Are All Minorities," *Journal of Religious Pluralism* 2 (1993): 3. For more on faith in the Hindu and Buddhist traditions see Arvind Sharma, *Ramana Maharshi: The Sage of Arunachala* (New Delhi: Penguin Books, 2006), 190.
4. Recent scholarship tends to place the blame on the shoulders of the British in this matter; see Stanley Wolpert, *Shameful Flight: The Last Days of the British Empire in India* (New York: Oxford University Press, 2006). The following account is telling: "When asked how he felt about his Indian viceroyalty eighteen

years after Partition, Mountbatten himself admitted to BBC's John Osman, when they sat next to one another at dinner shortly after the 1965 Indo-Pakistani War, that he had 'got things wrong.' Osman felt 'sympathy' for the remorseful sixty-five-year-old ex-viceroy and tried to cheer him, but to no avail. Thirty-nine years after that meeting he recalled: 'Mountbatten was not to be consoled. To this day his own judgment on how he had performed in India rings in my ears and in my memory. As one who dislikes the tasteless use in writing of . . . 'vulgar slang' . . . I shall permit myself an exception this time because it is the only honest way of reporting accurately what the last viceroy of India thought about the way he had done his job: 'I fucked it up'" (ibid., 2).

5. See L. K. Advani, *My Country, My Life* (New Delhi: Rupa and Company, 2008), 824–832.

6. William Dalrymple, *The Last Moghul* (London: Bloomsbury, 2006), 10; Beatrice Pitney Lamb, *India: A World in Transition*, 3rd ed., rev. (New York: Frederick A Praeger, 1968), 347.

7. Sugata Bose and Ayesha Jalal, *Modern South Asia: History, Culture, Political Economy* (New Delhi: Oxford University Press, 1998), 163.

8. Percival Spear, ed., *The Oxford History of India*, 4th ed. (New Delhi: Oxford University Press, 2002), 834.

9. See Arvind Sharma, *Modern Hindu Thought: The Essential Texts* (New Delhi: Oxford University Press, 2002), 286–311.

10. Cited in Robert Payne, *The Life and Death of Mahatma Gandhi* (New York: E. P. Dutton, 1969), 486. It would be a mistake, however, to write off the effectiveness of Gandhian methods in a Nazi regime. Gene Sharp has drawn attention to two cases in which such measures succeeded under the Nazis. While Norway was under Nazi domination, and the country was being run by Vidkun Quisling, an attempt was made to Nazify the education system. But "between eight thousand to ten thousand of the country's teachers wrote letters" in protest. "All signed their names and addresses to the wording prescribed by the underground for the letter." The government closed all schools for a

month and threatened dismissal. At this, "tens of thousands of letters of protest from parents poured into the government office. A thousand teachers were arrested and sent away to concentration camps, serenaded by the students. When the schools opened, the teachers still refused to join the new organization which was being forced on them. The teachers who had not been arrested stood firm amidst rumours of their immediate arrest and even death. Eight months after the arrests, Quisling ordered the release of teachers, once raging at the teachers in a school in Oslo to declare: 'You teachers have destroyed everything for me.'" Sharp cites the further example of nonviolent action in the heart of Berlin, even in 1943, by the non-Jewish wives of Berlin Jews who had been arrested as part of the Final Solution. The wives having discovered the improvised detention center, six thousand of them appeared at the gate in the early hours of the morning. They continued their protest as the workday routine set in, their "accusing cries" rising above the traffic noise "like passionate avowals of a love strengthened by the bitterness of life." The Gestapo headquarters were nearby, but the protest was allowed to continue. "Scared by an incident which has no equal in the history of the Third Reich, headquarters consented to negotiate. They spoke soothingly, gave assurances, and finally released the prisoners" (Sharp, *The Politics of Non-violent Action* [Boston: Porter Sargent Publisher, 1973], 88–90).

11. Donald Eugene Smith, *India as a Secular State* (Princeton, NJ: Princeton University Press, 1963), 85; Payne, *Life and Death of Gandhi,* 528 (quotation). Gandhi blamed the separate electorates for Partition. We now better understand his opposition to separate electorates for untouchables and it is anybody's guess if he might not have fasted to death when separate electorates for Muslims were introduced, had he been active in India at the time. Mahatma Gandhi's grandson Rajmohan Gandhi has documented that it was the former untouchables who proposed to Gandhi that the word Harijan be used for them, rather than the other way around, as is usually assumed; see Rajmohan Gandhi,

Revenge and Reconciliation: Understanding South Asian History (New Delhi: Penguin Books, 1999), 254. And see Amrik Singh, "The Struggle for Pakistan: Before and After," in Amrik Singh, ed., *The Partition in Retrospect* (New Delhi: Anamika Publishers and Distributors, 2000), 428.

12. J. B. Kripalani, president of the Congress Party and an eminent Gandhian, addressing his Congress Party colleagues after they had accepted Partition, observed: "Some members have accused us that we have taken this decision out of fear. I must admit the truth of this charge. . . . The fear is that if we go on . . . retaliating and heaping indignities on each other, we shall progressively reduce ourselves to a state of cannibalism. . . . I have been with Gandhiji for the last thirty years. . . . Why then am I not with him [now]? It is because I feel that he has as yet found no way of tackling the problem [of Hindu-Muslim violence] on a mass basis" (Mehta, *Gandhi and His Apostles*, 171).

13. Ramachandra Guha, *India after Gandhi* (New York: HarperCollins, 2007), 44.

14. Ibid., 505. The quotation is a paraphrase of her remarks; see Mohandas K. Gandhi, *An Autobiography: The Story of My Experiments with Truth* (Boston: Beacon Press, 1993), 221.

15. Gandhi, *Autobiography*, 311.

16. Percival Spear, *India: A Modern History* (Ann Arbor: University of Michigan Press, 1972), 363, 364 (quotation).

17. Benjamin Walker, *The Hindu World* (New York: Frederick A. Praeger, 1968), vol. I, p. 373.

18. Mohandas K. Gandhi, *Hindu Dharma* (Ahmedabad: Navajivan Publishing House, 1958), 270, 65 (quotations), 120.

19. Ibid., 7.

20. Gandhi, *Hindu Dharma*, 320. Sometimes the untouchables are called the fifth varna (*pancama* or *panchama*) in popular parlance, but this name is not strictly speaking correct. According to the well-known Hindu legal text the *Manusmrti*, there are only four varnas (X.4).

21. Gandhi, *Autobiography*, 206.

22. Ibid., 34.

23. Ibid., 214.

24. Joseph Lelyveld, *Great Soul: Mahatma Gandhi and His Struggle with India* (New York: Random House, 2011), 222; Payne, *Life and Death of Gandhi,* 550.

25. Gandhi, *Autobiography,* xxviii.

26. Ibid., 307.

Chapter 19. Gandhi's Spiritual Biography and Contemporary History

1. For an earlier attempt to answer this question see Erik H. Erikson, *Gandhi's Truth: On the Origins of Militant Nonviolence* (New York: W.W. Norton & Company, 1969).

2. Churchill's words are so often quoted that it may not be necessary to reproduce them here, but a reminder of the stirring lines might be in order:

    "We shall not flag or fail. We shall go on to the end. We shall fight in France and on the seas and oceans; we shall fight with growing confidence and growing strength in the air.

    "We shall defend our island whatever the cost may be; we shall fight on beaches, landing grounds, in fields, in streets and on the hills. We shall never surrender and even if, which I do not for the moment believe, this island or a large part of it were subjugated and starving, then our empire beyond the seas, armed and guarded by the British Fleet, will carry on the struggle until in God's good time the New World, with all its power and might, sets forth to the liberation and rescue of the Old" (Lewis Copeland, Lawrence W. Lamm, and Stephen J. McKenna, *The World's Great Speeches: 292 Speeches from Pericles to Nelson Mandela,* 4th ed. [Mineola, NY: Dover Publications, 1999], 439).

3. Martin Jacques, *When China Rules the World* (London: Penguin Books, 2009), 94.

4. See Roy Jenkins, *Churchill: A Biography* (New York: Farrar, Straus, and Giroux, 2001); Jung Chang and Jon Halliday, *Mao: The Unknown Story* (New York: Knopf, 2005); Robert Service, *Stalin: A Biography* (Cambridge, MA: Belknap Press, 2005).

5. See also Mohandas K. Gandhi, *Hindu Dharma* (Ahmedabad: Navajivan Press, 1958), 59–60.

6. Mohandas K. Gandhi, *An Autobiography: The Story of My Experiments with Truth* (Boston: Beacon Press, 1993), 26.

7. Ibid., 28 (emphasis added).

8. Also see D. G. Temdulkar, *Mahatma: Life of Mohandas Karamchand Gandhi* (New Delhi: Publications Division, Government of India, 1960), vol. 8, p. 271.

9. When Madeline Slade, daughter of Admiral Sir Edmond Slade, joined Gandhi's ashram, he addressed her as his daughter and gave her a name that had the word "sister" in it: "After corresponding with Gandhi and a period of disciplined preparation, she sailed for Bombay on 25 October 1925, arriving on 6 November. Colleagues of Gandhi were there to receive her. Without delay she boarded an overnight train to Ahmedabad and from there went by car to the Sabarmati Āśram, where her eyes finally came to rest upon the man whose ideals she had now made her own. . . . His first words to her were that she would be his daughter. He gave her the name Mira Behn, after Mīrā of Rajasthan, the renowned devotee of Kṛṣṇa; Behn meant sister" (George James, "Mira Behn: An Environmentalist in the Himalayas," in Arvind Sharma, ed., *Windows to World's Religions* [New Delhi: D. K. Printworld, 2009], 108–109).

10. S. Radhakrishnan, *The Principal Upaniṣads* (1953; Atlantic Highlands, NJ: Humanities Press, 1996), 170.

11. Ainslie T. Embree, ed., *Alberuni's India* (New York: W. W. Norton and Company, 1971), part II, p. 161.

12. Louis Fischer, *The Life of Mahatma Gandhi* (New York: Harper and Row, 1950), 73.

index

Advani, L. K., 173
adversaries, treatment of, 70
aesthetic consciousness, 166
ahimsa, 58, 159, 195, 199–200,
   201, 203, 205
Ahluwalia, B. K., 224–225n4
Alam, Mir, 66–67
Albiruni, 205
Alcibiades, 4
Ambedkar, B. R., 85, 90, 176,
   184–185
anasakti, 148
Anasaktiyoga, 148
anekantavada, 50
Arnold, Edwin, 39, 127, 147,
   231n15
Asiatic Registration Act, 66
asramas, 135, 181, 182, 183
Augustine, 118
Aurangzeb, 11
Aurobindo, 101
Azad, Maulana, 95

Bajaj, Jamnalal, 104, 105,
   224n4
Banias, 30
Banker, Shankarlal, 224n4
Bengal, 177: partition of, 94;
   rioting in, 94–95
Bentham, Jeremy, 127
Besant, Annie, 38–39
Bhagavad Gita, 39–41, 87, 127,
   145–147, 180; allegorical
   interpretation of, 149–150;
   describing ideal types, 147,
   152; Gandhi's favorite passage in, 147; influence of, on
   Gandhi, 41, 145; literal interpretation of, 149–152; message of, 148–149, 152–154;
   as mother to Gandhi, 145;
   writing style in, 231n15
Bhagavata Purana, 23
bhajan, 180
bhakti, 153

Bihar, earthquake in (1934), 162–165
bin Laden, Osama, 203
biography, intersecting with myth, 13
birth control, 135–136; movement, 137
black plague, 120–121
Blavatsky, Helena Petrovna, 38–39
Boer War, 63
Bose, Netaji Subhas Chandra, 175
Bose, Nirmal Kumar, 140–141, 142, 233n11
Botha, Louis, 63, 68
Bradford, John, 203
Bradlaugh, Charles, 38
brahmacharya, 134. *See also* celibacy
Brahman, personal and impersonal aspects of, 160
British Empire, 10
Buber, Martin, 176, 199
Buddha (Gautama), 2–3
Buddhism, 116, 185

Carlyle, Thomas, 38
celibacy, 21, 64, 108, 134, 187–188; faithfulness and, 187; Gandhi's practice of, 35, 136–137, 139–142, 143–144; Gandhi's vow of, 21, 35, 49–50, 64, 133, 134–135, 142; in a life devoted to God-realization, 142–143; linked to realization of Brahman, 136–137

charity, 47
chastity, 187
Chatrasal of Bundelkhand, 11
Chattopadhyaya, Harindranath, 224n4
child marriage, 18, 19–21
Christianity, 47; converting to, in India, 37; Gandhi overcoming dislike of, 36–38; manners and customs of, 205
chun tzu (junzi), 147
Churchill, Winston, 84, 190–191, 193, 197, 204
City of Sudama. *See* Porbandar
civil disobedience, 85
Communal Award, 89, 90, 92, 109
communal farms, 68
compromise, 66
confession, 13, 195
confidence, 66
Confucius, 147, 192
Congress Party, 178, 193
consciousness, universality of, 166
contradictions, 155–156
control, beginning in the mind, 142
conversion experience, 54–55
coolie locations, 119–120
Coorg Congress Committee, 106
cow protection, 179
creation, accessing God through, 161

Dada Abdulla and Company, 46, 54, 56, 61
Dalits, 176

Dandi, Gandhi's march to, 74–75
death, fear of, 190
Depressed Classes, representation of, 85, 222n13
detachment, good deeds and, 113–116
Dharasana, battle at, 76–83
dharma, 181–183, 232–233n4
Doke, Joseph J., 66–67
dualism, fundamental, 169

earth treatments, 120–122
eating, related to mating, 142
Emerson, Ralph Waldo, 51
ends, distinguishing from means, 196–198
enlightenment, 3
Enlightenment, the, 166–167
Esoteric Christian Union, 39
example, power of, 156
experiments, 157, 188; *bramacharya*, 139–142, 143–144; dietetic, 142; earth treatment, 120–122; God's protection for, 122; meat-eating, 14–15; risk involved in, 188; truth, 3

faith, 172
family, metaphor of, 200
farms, communal, 68
fasting, 50–51, 142. *See also* Gandhi: fasts of
Fischer, Louis, 5, 10, 30, 33, 53, 58, 64, 131, 135, 172
freedom, choice of, 154
Freud, Sigmund, 140, 141

Gandhi, Indira, 204
Gandhi, Karamchand, 10
Gandhi, Kasturbai. *See* Kasturbai
Gandhi, Maganlal, 65
Gandhi, Mahatma (Mohandas Karamchand): absent from celebration on India's independence, 94; action leading to conviction, 131, 137; adolescence of, 13; advice to Jews, 175–176; allowing for different explanations of events, 170; ambivalent attitude of, toward caste, 31; ancestors of, 10, 11; arrest of, 75; atoning for sins, 109, 194–195; attitude toward British rule, 73; attitude toward other religions, 36, 47, 186; autobiography of, 29–30; becoming an English gentleman, 33; Bhagavad Gita's influence on, 145, 147; believing in the life of the spirit, 5; biographies about, 1–2; birth of, 9–10; on birth control, 137–138; birthplace of, 10–11; blaming separate electorates for the Partition, 236–237n11; bookkeeping of, in London, 33–34; *brahmacharya* experiments of, 139–142, 143–144; brought to God by fear, 23; calling for Indian independence from Great Britain, 73–74; casting

Gandhi, Mahatma (*continued*)
his lot with the untouchables,
31; ceasing marital relations,
21; celibacy of, tested, 35;
childhood stories influencing,
12; on conjugal fidelity,
18–19; considering the spiritual dimension primary, 2,
169–170; contemporary relevance of, 202–206; on contradictions, 155–156; conversion experience of, 54–58;
criticism of, 185; cultivating
nonviolence, 157; dangers to
his life, awareness of, 96–97;
death of, 27–28, 97, 107,
150–151, 178; dedicated to
repairing damage from
India's partition, 94; demythologizing, 171–172; desiring to serve, 112–113; devising new form of warfare, 83;
devoted to truth, 14; devotion to his parents, 13;
dietetic experiments of, 142;
dislike of Christianity, overcoming, 36–38; distinguishing between physical and
spiritual realms, 168; distinguishing means from ends,
196–198; divinization of,
202; drawn into politics, 161;
dual emphasis of, on truth
and nonviolence, 165; earth
treatment experiments of,
120–122; emerging vision of
Rama, 25; encouraging four

pursuits, 49; establishing new
norms of human contact, 3;
ethical theism of, 19–20; evolution in thinking of, 157;
experimental strain of, 157;
experiments of, 188; fasts of,
50–51, 85, 89–91, 94–96,
109–110; father of, 30; fears
of, 22–23, 190; feminization
of, 143; finding new applications for karma, 32; first *satyagraha* of, 206; first speech of,
60; forgiving whites in South
Africa, 217n9; forming
Indian ambulance corps, 63,
133–134, 136; forswearing
milk, 113; founding the Satyagraha Ashram, 122–124; on
God protecting the honest
experimenter, 122; on God
and truth, 157, 159–161,
165–166, 233n11; on gurus,
52–54; hearing God, 160–161;
Hinduism and, 179–186; as
his own guru, 53; hydropathic treatments applied by,
130; as icon, 190–191; ideas
of, challenged by India's partition, 176–177; ideas on
God, development of, 25,
157–160; importance to, of
confession, 13; influence of,
cultural explanation for, 102;
interpretation of the Bhagavad Gita, 149–150, 231n15;
on interpreting pledges, 34;
learning more about Hindu-

ism, 39–40; leaving no code, 232n3; leaving the Indian National Congress, 92; legacy of, 178; as legal advisor for Indians in South Africa, 120; linking Bihar earthquake with untouchability, 162–167; London years of, 29, 32–41; on love, 199–200, 203; marriage of, 16–18; maternalism of, 143; meat-eating experiments of, 14–15; mother's death, 42; mother's influence on, 12, 42–43, 86, 89; negotiating with Great Britain, 84–85; nervous about public speaking, 40–41; never embracing philosophy, 169; nonviolence commitment of, 193–194, 201–202; opposed to untouchability, 85–88, 110; opposition to, 96; organizing the Pretorian Indians, 61; patronizing the untouchables, 176; personal life of, questioned, 177–178; power, source of, 4–6; practicing celibacy, 136–137; praxis of, giving rise to theory, 156–157; prayer meetings of, 180, 186; preferring violence to cowardice, 202; preparing for London, 30–31; principles of, universalizing, 186–188; pursuing truth, 190, 191–192; questioning his control, 139–140; *Ramacaritamanas*'s

influence on, 24–27; Ramana Maharshi's spirituality different from his, 108; Raychand and, 43–52; receptivity of, 156; reflecting on duties as a public worker, 64; relationship of, with his sons, 177–178; relationship with Ramana Maharshi, 103–104; relations with the Zulus, 64; religion and morality synonymous for, 3; in religious ferment, 46; religious pluralism of, 47; religious practices of, 180–186; responding to anti-Indian ordinances in South Africa, 64–71; returning to India, 44–45; Ruskin's influence on, 217n12; saintliness and religiosity of, 42; Sanger's interview of, 137–138; *satyagraha* campaign against, 221–222n11; seen as completely surrendering to God, 111; self-reliance of, on religious matters, 31; on sex, 137–138, 143–144, 229n11; sexual temptation of, 138–139; snakes and, 214n16; source of power, 4–6; as speaker, 88; spiritual concepts for, 189; spiritual life of, pillars of, 19; supporting fringe religious movements, 39; Theosophy's influence on, 38–39; on not thinking, 107; traveling to England, 126–127; treating

Gandhi, Mahatma (*continued*)
his own children, 49; treating
pneumonic plague patients,
120–121; truth experiments
of, 3; on truth and nonviolence, 232–233n4; under-
standing the dangers of an
open mind, 192; vegetarianism
of, 26, 125–127, 131–132;
visiting Champaran, 72–73,
218–220n1; and the vow of
celibacy, 21, 35, 49–50, 64,
133, 134–136, 142; worship-
ing Rama, 157–158
Gandhi, Manilal, 76, 82,
129–131, 170
Gandhi, Manubehn, 140, 144
Gandhi, Putlibai. *See* Putlibai
Gandhi, Rajmohan, 236–237n11
Gandhi family, 44–45
Germany, embracing former
enemies, 193
Gesar epic, 146
Gitanjali (Tagore), 90–91
Gladstone, Catherine, 49
God: access to, 160–161; as element of spirituality, 189;
Gandhi depending on the
miracles of, 124; Gandhi's
developing ideas on, 157–160;
incarnations of, 179–180; as
law and love, 161–162, 164;
personal, 160; personal and
impersonal aspects of, 160;
protecting the honest experimenter, 122; truth and, 157,
159–161, 165–166

Godse, Nathuram, 27–28, 97,
150–152, 153,
231–232nn15–16
Gokhale, Gopal Krishna (G. K.),
4, 68, 72, 148
goodness, as element of spirituality, 189
good works: analysis of,
226–227n4; detachment
and, 113–116
Government of India Act, 92–93
Great Britain, reduced military presence of, in India,
173–175
Great Rebellion (1857), 93
Gurkhas, 75
gurus, 52–54

hagiographies, 101, 111, 171,
172
Harijans, 236n11. *See untouchables entries*
Harishchandra, King, 12, 14
Hemchandra, Narayan, 38
Heroes and Hero-Worship
(Carlyle), 38
high mystical theory, 20
hijab, 200–201
Hind Swaraj (Gandhi), 150
Hinduism, 3; charity and, 47;
contemporary history of,
raised to mythic levels,
153–154; counting of age
in, 9; doctrines of, 181–185;
Gandhi's desire to learn more
about, 39–40; Gandhi's relation to, 179–186; God incar-

nating himself in, 202; manners and customs of, 205; marriage in, 17; on negative emotions, 23; revealed texts of, 146; reviled in England, 39; sacred texts of, mentioning teachers' mothers' names, 12; salvation in, 23; separate electorate's effect on, 89; untouchability in, 86–88

Hindu-Muslim unity, Gandhi dying for, 176, 178

Hindu society, division of, by separate electorate, 85, 88

Hitler, Adolf, 174–175, 176

How I Became a Theosophist (Besant), 39

humanity: evoking, 200; spirituality at core of, 5

human relations, means and ends in, 197

hydropathy, 130

idealism, 168–169

ideal types, 147, 152, 182

idol worship, 179

immaterial world, 168

impersonal-personal interplay, 161–162

INA. *See* Indian National Army

indenture system, 62

India: British rule over, 10; converting to Christianity in, 37; cultural ethos of, 102; hagiography in, 101; indenture system in, 62; independence of, spiritual aspect to, 101–102;

nonviolent independence of, demythologizing, 173–176; Partition of, 93–94, 173, 176–177; religions originating in, 126; selfless action in, and seeking independence, 148; social reform in, 18; warring with Pakistan over Kashmir, 95–96; World War II involvement of, 93

Indian ambulance corps, 63, 133–134, 136

Indian Legislative Assembly, 82

Indian National Army (INA), 175

Indian National Congress, 27, 92–93, 176

Indian Relief Bill, 70–71

Indic religious tradition, spirituality and morality in, 32

injustice: opposing with nonviolence, 201–202; resistance to, 202–205; specific acts of, responding to, 69

intention, notification of, 68, 69–70

Iyer, T. K. Sundaresa, 102

Jaini, Padmanabh S., 50

Jainism, 50–51, 126, 185

Japan, embracing former enemies, 193

Jesus Christ, 2–3, 186

Jinnah, Muhammad Ali, 93, 173, 176, 177

jnana, 153

Johnson, Raynor C., 113–114

Judaism, 47
justice, 199–200; truth and, 201

Kalelkar, Kaka, 143
kansar, 17
karma, 32: freedom from effects of, 118; Gandhi's moral take on, 185–186; shift in, as spiritual goal is approached, 118
Kasturbai, 16, 23, 69, 90, 135, 177–178
Key to Theosophy (Blavatsky), 39
Khan, Khan Abdul Ghaffar, 75
Kierkegaard, Søren, 212n11
King, Martin Luther, Jr., 202
Kripalani, J. B., 237n12
Krishnamurthy, Jiddu, 111
Kühne, Ludwig, 130
Kumar, Shravana, 12, 14

Labour Party (UK), 93
Lalanath, Pandit, 109
Leninism, 156
Linlithgow, Victor Hope (viceroy), 93
London Vegetarian Society, 128
love: for the enemy, 199–200; Gandhi's innovative interpretation of, 199–200
Luther, Martin, 118, 184

MacDonald, Ramsay, 89
Mahabharata epic, 146, 149. *See also* Bhagavad Gita
Maharaj, Ladha, 24–25
Maharaj, Nisargadatta, 111

Maharshi, Ramana (Sri Bhagavan), 101, 103–110, 223n1 (ch. 11), 224–225n4, 225n12
Mahatma, as title, 1–3. *See also* Gandhi, Mahatma
Mahendra societies, 102
Manning, Edward Henry, 38
Mao Zedong, 190, 191, 193, 197
marriage, third party in, 20–21
materialism, 168, 169
material world, 168
means, distinguished from ends, 196–198
meat, defining, 34–35
meat-eating, as response to British Empire, 15
Mehta, Rajchandra Ravjibhai. *See* Raychand
Mehta, Ved, 87, 140–141, 143
Milarepa, 116, 117–118
Miller, Webb, 76–83
mind, as root of all sensuality, 142
modernity, 167
Modh Banias, 30
moksha, 2, 183
Moon, Penderel, 177
moral consciousness, 166
mothers, role of, in spiritual development, 12
Mother Teresa, 117
Mott, John R., 56
Mountbatten, Louis, 93, 235n
Mountbatten Plan, 27, 93–94
Mughal Empire, 11
Muslim League, 27, 93, 94, 177

Mutiny (1857), 93, 173–174
myths, intersecting with biography, 13

Naidu, Sarojini, 74, 75–76,
   78–80, 82, 103
Naravane, V. S., 5–6, 233n11
narcissism, spiritual, 116–117
Natal Act (1897), 63
Natal Indian Congress, 62
Natal Legislative Assembly,
   61–62
natural events, as moral events,
   163–165
Nauroji, Dadabhai, 105
Nazism, Gandhian response to,
   235–236n10
negotiation, willingness to
   accept, 66
Nehru, Pandit Jawaharlal, 4–5,
   89, 90, 101
Newman, John Henry, 180
nishkama karma, 104, 153
non-rational, presence of, 167
nonviolence, 58, 59, 193–194;
   as conscious suffering, 167;
   Gandhi's cultivation of, 157;
   incongruity of, 175–176; justification for, 198; responding
   to random violence, 177
nonviolent battle, at Dharasana,
   76–83
Norway, Gandhian response to
   Nazism in, 235–236n10

Olcott, Colonel, 38
Oldfield, Josiah, 127–128

open-mindedness, dangers of, 192
Osman, John, 235n

Pakistan: creation of, 93,
   176–177; existence of,
   173; warring with India
   over Kashmir, 95–96
Parker, Joseph, 211n23
passive resistance, 65. See also
   satyagraha
Passive Resistance Association,
   66
Patel, V. J., 82
Payne, Robert, 30, 47–49,
   52–53, 124, 138–139
Phoenix Settlement, 68, 109,
   136, 214n16, 217n12
plague, 120–121
Plea for Vegetarianism (Salt),
   127
pledges, interpretations of, 34
pneumonic plague, 120–121
Porbandar (India), 10
Pranami sect, 11
Prannath, 11
Prasad, Rajendra, 104, 105,
   162, 224n4
progress, spiritual, 188
promise keeping, as aspect of
   truth, 32
Protestant movement, 184
Punjab, 94, 177
purdah, 200–201
Purna Swaraj, 73
purusarthas, 181, 183
Putlibai: Gandhi's vow to,
   30–32, 34, 126–127; influ-

Putlibai (continued)
ence on Gandhi, 10, 11–12,
86, 89; saintliness and religiosity of, 42–43
Pyarelal, 187

Quisling, Vidkun, 235–236n10
Quit India movement, 93

Rabia, 20
Rajchandra, Shrimad, 48–49
Rama, 18–19, 22, 24, 157–160,
180; Gandhi's reverence for,
25; hymn to, 75; potency
of name of, 25; Ramana
Maharshi comparing
Gandhi to, 107–108
Ramacaritamanas, 24–27
Ramachandran, G., 87–88
Ramakrishna (Ramakrishna
Paramahamsa), 117–118,
141, 143, 223n1 (ch. 11)
Ramana Maharshi. See
Maharshi, Ramana
Ramanuja, 153
Ramayana, 108, 180; of
Valmiki, 24. See also
Ramacaritamanas
Rambha, 22
Ranade, M. G., 18
Raychand (Rajchandra Ravjib-
hai Mehta), 43–52, 135,
212n11, 215n26
realpolitik, 173, 177
rebirth, 3–4, 9
redemption, 154
Red Shirts, 75

reincarnation. See rebirth
religious pluralism, 47; Gandhi
exposed to, 36
retaliation, 205
revenge, communal, 58, 198–199,
203
Round Table Conference (London, 1931), 84–85, 87, 92
Royal Indian Navy, 174
Ruskin, John, 217n12

Sabarmati, 214n16
sacred texts, interpretation of,
152
saguna Brahman, 160
saints, subjected to temptations,
112–113
Salt, Henry S., 127
Salt Law, resistance to, 74–84
salvation, 23, 186
samanya dharmas, 181, 183
Sanger, Margaret, 137
sannyasa, 182
saptapadi, 17
Sarkozy, Nicolas, 200
Sastri, T. Ganapati, 102
satsang, 180
satyagraha, 58–59; beginnings
of, 65; effectiveness of, 71;
first satyagraha against the
British, 73; against Gandhi,
88, 221–222n11; principles
of, 65–70; science of, 5–6;
significance of, 71
Satyagraha Ashram, 122–124
Satyagraha Association, 66
Savarkar, V. D., 150, 151

Schweitzer, Albert, 156
selfless action, 148–149, 153
self-realization, 2
separate electorates, 85, 90,
    88–89, 176, 222n13,
    236–237n11
September 11, 2001, events of,
    202, 203–204, 206
sex: eating related to, 142;
    Gandhi and, 21, 136–137,
    138–139; Gandhi's view of,
    137–138, 143–144, 229n11.
    See also *celibacy*
sex consciousness, 166
Shankara, 152–153
Sharp, Gene, 235–236n10
Shatadhvani, 44
Shukla, Rajkumar, 219n
Sikhism, 185
sin, hating, 204
Singh, Khuswant, 95–96
Slade, Madeline, 239n9
Smuts, Jan Christiaan, 63, 66,
    67, 68, 70
socialization, 198–199
social reform, substituting for
    spiritual effort, 117–118
Socrates, 4
Song Celestial, The (Arnold), 39
South Africa: anti-Indian ordi-
    nances in, 64–71; coolie loca-
    tions in, 119–120; Gandhi's
    activities in, 49, 61, 63, 120,
    133–134, 136; religious plu-
    ralism in, 36; Zulus, 64
spirit, impossibility of imprison-
    ment of, 6

spirituality: Gandhi's concept of,
    189; self-identification with,
    189
Sri Bhagavan. *See* Ramana
    Maharshi
Stalin, Joseph, 190, 191, 193,
    197
Stendahl, Krister, 172
strangers, revealing hidden trea-
    sures, 40
Subbaramayya, G. V., 110–111
subjectivity, 192
suffering, acceptance of, 167,
    205–206
Suhrawardy, Huseyn Shaheed,
    95
superstition, 165
svadhyaya, 180
Swaraj movement, 73, 82
Syed, Mohammed Hafiz,
    225n12

Tagore, Rabindranath, 73,
    90–91, 164–167
tantra, 166
Tendulkar, D. G., 57
Teresa of Calcutta, 117
theistic consciousness, 166
Theory of Utility (Bentham), 127
Theosophical Society, 38–39
Theosophy, 38–39
Tilak, B. G., 148–149, 153
Tolstoy, Leo, 51
Tolstoy Farm, 68, 109, 214n16
transcendence, 147
Transvaal government, Asiatic
    department, 63

trust, 67
truth, 14; God and, 157,
    159–161, 165–166, 233n11;
    justice and, 201; progress
    toward, 188; pursuit of,
    190, 191–192; unequivo-
    cal nature of, 157; uphold-
    ing, 27
Tulsidas, 24

Union of South Africa, forma-
    tion of, 68
Unto This Last (Ruskin),
    217n12
untouchability: Gandhi's
    opposition to, 85–88,
    110, 163–166, 184–186;
    related to actions rather
    than birth, 185–186
untouchables, 182; admitted to
    Satyagraha Ashram, 123–124;
    Gandhi and, 31, 162–167,
    176; in modern India, 91;
    well-being of, 85–89
Upanishads, 51
Uttara Ramayana, 108

Vaishnavas, 126
Vaishya class, 125
vanaprastha, 135
varnas, 125, 181, 182, 183
varnasrama dharmas, 183
Vedas, 146
Vegetarian, The, 128
Vegetarian Club, 127
vegetarianism: consequences of,
    for Gandhi, 32–34; in Gan-
    dhi's early life, 125–127,
    128; Gandhi's promotion of,
    127–129; Jainism and, 50
violence, coming from selfish
    attachments, 149
Vishnu, worship of, 125–126
Vivekananda, 117

White City. See Porbandar
World War I, 174
World War II, 93, 174–175

Yervada Pact, 90

Zulu Rebellion, 63
Zulus, 64

DATE DUE